THE EVOLVING EURASIAN GEOPOLITICS

Strategic Choices for International Security

Volume One

Heavyweights of Eurasia:
The Russian Federation & The People's Republic of China

THE EVOLVING EURASIAN GEOPOLITICS
Strategic Choices for International Security

Printed in 2022. 6. 23
Published in 2022. 6. 30

Author Cagri Erdem
Publisher Synn Ilhi
Published by Keimyung University Press
Room 105 Bosangwan, Keimyung University
1095 Dalgubeoldaero, Dalseo Gu, Daegu 42601
TEL. +82-53-580-6233 FAX. +82-53-580-6235
Homepage. www.kmupress.com
Registration 1970. 9. 1 (#347-1998-1)

ISBN 979-11-6516-147-7 93340 Price ₩20,000

THE EVOLVING EURASIAN GEOPOLITICS

Strategic Choices for International Security

Volume One

Heavyweights of Eurasia:
The Russian Federation & The People's Republic of China

Cagri Erdem

KEIMYUNG UNIVERSITY PRESS

Table of Contents

List of Figures

List of Tables

List of Abbreviations

A2/AD Anti-access/area denial
ADB Asian Development Bank
AIIB Asian Infrastructure Investment Bank
APEC Asia-Pacific Economic Cooperation
ASEAN Association of Southeast Asian Nations
BCE Before Common Era
bcm billion cubic meter
b/d barrels per day
BFA Boao Forum for Asia
BRI Belt and Road Initiative
BRIC Brazil-Russia-India-China
BTC Baku-Tbilisi-Ceyhan
BVO Basin Water Management Bodies—Bassejnovoe Vodnoje Ob'edinenie
C. Circa
CCP Chinese Communist Party
CE Common Era
CIS Commonwealth of Independent States
CMEC China-Myanmar Economic Corridor
CNOOC China National Offshore Oil Corporation
CNPC China National Petroleum Corporation
CPEC China-Pakistan Economic Corridor
CRC China Railway Corporation
CSTO Collective Security Treaty Organization
DPRK Democratic People's Republic of Korea
EAEU Eurasian Economic Union
EEZ Exclusive Economic Zone
EMU European Monetary Union
EU European Union
ETIM East Turkistan Islamic Movement
ETR Eastern Turkistan Republic (1944-1949
FSB Federal Border Service
FSR Former Soviet Republics
FSU Former Soviet Union
GCC Gulf Cooperation Countries
GDP Gross Domestic Product
GNP Gross National Product
ICAS Interstate Council for Aral Sea
ICBM Intercontinental ballistic missile
IMF International Monetary Fund
INSTC International North-South Transportation Corridor
IO International Organization
IMU Islamic Movement of Uzbekistan

K2 Karshi-Khananbad
KMT Chinese Nationalist Party
LNG Liquefied Natural Gas
MSR Maritime Silk Road
NAFTA North American Free Trade Area
NATO North Atlantic Treaty Organization
NDB New Development Bank
NEP Northeast Passage
NGO Non-governmental Organization
NSGT Non-self-governing territories
NSR Northern Sea Route
NWP Northwest Passage
OPEC Organization of Petroleum Exporting Countries
OSCE Organization for Security and Cooperation in Europe
PLA People's Liberation Army
PPP Purchasing Power Parity
PRC People's Republic of China
QSD Quadrilateral Security Dialogue/colloquially the QUAD
RFE Russian Far East
RF Russian Federation
ROK Republic of Korea
SAM Surface to air missile
SCO Shanghai Cooperation Organization
SEZ Special Economic Zone
SREB Silk Road Economic Belt
SSR Soviet Socialist Republics
TN Tengiz–Novorossiisk
THAAD Terminal High Altitude Area Defense
TIRET Turkish Islamic Republic of Eastern Turkistan (1933-1934)
TNC Transnational Corporation
UAE United Arab Emirates
UK United Kingdom
UN United Nations
UNCLCS United Nations Commission for Limits of the Continental Shelf
UNCLOS United Nations Convention on the Law of the Sea
UNSC United Nations Security Council
USA United States of America
USSR Union of the Soviet Socialist Republics
WTO World Trade Organization
WWI World War I
WWII World War II
XUAR Xinjiang Uyghur Autonomous Region

Preface

This book is about the evolving geopolitics in Eurasia. My interest in Eurasia and geopolitics dates to the late 1980s, when the end of the Cold War and the demise of the Soviet Union caused unprecedented challenges across Eurasia. My Eurasian intellectual journey started through my travel to Berlin in November 1989 with my friends from Université Paul Valery - Montpellier III to witness one of the most remarkable geopolitical events of the *fin de siècle* with the disappearance of the iron curtain[01]. In the early 1990s, the meeting with Soviet diaspora and Kyrgyz exchange students while being a student at San Francisco State University, CA, had also influenced my perception of the relevance of Eurasia as a geopolitical identity.

As a graduate student at Syracuse University, NY, purposefully, I opted for a dissertation topic related to Central Asia to deepen my knowledge base of the region. After intensive language training at Moscow Lomonosov State University, I spent two years in Central Asia from 2003 to 2005, conducting field research, mainly being located in Tashkent, Uzbekistan, with frequent travels across the vast Central Asian geography. In later years, as a social scientist at British Aerospace Engineering Systems (BAE)-Technologies Solutions and Services in the US, I had the opportunity to conduct analytical research on Afghanistan and Iraq.

Eurasia has always been at the center of academic and personal interest throughout my academic career. Teaching for five years in Istanbul, Turkey, along with periodic travels to Eastern Europe, the Caucasus, and the Balkans as an Erasmus Program visiting lecturer, allowed me to get familiar with geopolitical issues in West Asia and Eastern Europe. Moreover, my decision to accept an academic position in South Korea was also part of my attempt to get familiar with Northeast Asian geopolitics involving the Korean Peninsula, Japan, the PRC/ROC, Russia, and US strategic interests. Consequently, it would be fair to assert that this book is the culmination of several decades of studying, researching, and writing over different issues pertaining to different corners of the Eurasian continent and geopolitics. The focus and core arguments of the book were sketched out following a long period of intellectual gestation. To this end, some chapters in this volume were inspired by my already published articles and book chapters utilizing some modified and updated materials.

Moreover, as a political scientist, I have always been fascinated by history and geography; they have always been instrumental in my peculiar way of reading international relations. This fascination has also affected the way I conceive and teach my courses, utilizing extensively political, physical, historical, topographical, climatic, or economic/resource maps, just to name a few. I firmly believe that the effective use of history and geography enriches the subject.

The recent unfolding events across the Eurasian space are all indicative of the significance of this massive landmass which is home to almost three-quarters of the global population. The geopolitical fault lines along the Balkans, the Caucasus, Central Asia, and Eastern Europe are all hot spots prone to territorial chess games among the global/regional powers, as was always the case in previous centuries. Over the writing of this book, the impetus of geopolitics in Eurasia became even more accentuated due to the rapid development of events such as the American pullout from Afghanistan, the Kashmir conflict, the ascendance of the Indo-Pacific region, the changing energy security scenarios, the Ukrainian conflict(s), Northeast Asian arms race to name a few.

In recent decades a sizable literature has grown out of extensive research. Although the existing scholarly literature makes ample use of the concepts of geopolitics and Eurasia as a general theme, the book in question is part of a larger project. The first volume focuses on heavyweights of Eurasian geopolitical space, namely the Russian Federation and the People's Republic of China.

Eurasia's great diversity in physical geography, resource endowment, political economy, ethnicity, and religion require a multi-volume book to address the issues at stake adequately. Accordingly, the following volumes will delve into different geopolitically relevant corners of Eurasia. Volume two of the series will contain chapters on Northeast Asia and Southeast Asia. Volume three will focus on South and West Asia. All three volumes will utilize the same geopolitical methodology to understand the evolving geopolitical aspects.

May 2022

General Map of Central Eurasia

Figure 1. *Central Eurasia*

THE EVOLVING EURASIAN GEOPOLITICS

Strategic Choices for International Security

Introduction

A Framework for Understanding Eurasian Geopolitics

Introduction:

A Framework for Understanding Eurasian Geopolitics

Since the beginning of the 21st century, rivalries among the great powers and challenges originating from newly rising regional middle powers for global affairs have overruled the old hierarchical structures. As a result, there were many attempts at different levels to revise the international system set up after World War II (WWII). It seems that the American/Western European engineered international order is facing substantial and numerous challenges with demands to accommodate the changing global realities. Similarly, the evolving Eurasian geopolitics needs to be scrutinized from that perspective.

Throughout the 20th century, the world witnessed mind-boggling demographic pressures, resulting in increasing poverty, food shortages, freshwater depletion, conflict, and environmental degradation affecting different parts of the world at differing levels. Currently, the globe is experiencing the cohabitation of two-speed population dynamics. First, although at a decreasing level, developing countries in Africa or South Asia notice a rampant population increase. On the other hand, the 21st century may prove that the global population decline may be the real problem for certain parts of the world. Some of the wealthiest parts of the globe are witnessing that trend with fewer people every year, such as the case in Japan, South Korea, Spain, Italy, much of Eastern Europe.

Moreover, along with the global population on the rise and economic development (high Gross Domestic Product-GDP growth rates), the struggle for limited natural resources and accessibility to those resources have become remarkably intense. This stiff competition has echoed in the rapid growth of commodity prices and variations in geopolitical considerations, particularly energy security. In that aspect, different corners of Eurasia have been of particular interest to the great powers due to its vast natural resources and its multiple strategic choke points.

Eurasia is home to several vital geopolitical maritime and terrestrial choke points[02]. For example, the Suez Canal, Bab al-Mandeb, Strait of Hormuz, Turkish straits in Western Asia; Malacca, Sunda, Lombok, and Makassar straits in Southeast Asia; Taiwan, Korea, Soya (La Perouse), Tartary, and Bering straits in Northeast Asia are a few to name in terms of maritime choke points (see Figure 1). Mainly, maritime transport is an essential tool to enable international trade since a significant percentage of global merchandise uses high seas to reach its destination. Hence, the stability of those choke points located on the strategic trade routes for commercial shipping becomes even more valuable for those wishing to revise the international hierarchical order set after WWII.

On the other hand, Afghanistan, Caucasus, Kashmir, and the Balkans are some important illustrations of terrestrial choke points across Eurasia where the interests of diverse civilizations/powers encounter each other. Interestingly, those Eurasian terrestrial choke points are considered major geopolitical fault-lines with a potential target of unrelenting claims for territorial control, which may give birth to a military confrontation. Any shifting in those geopolitical tectonic plates would have dire consequences for the rest of the world.

Figure 2. *Global Key Maritime Choke Points*

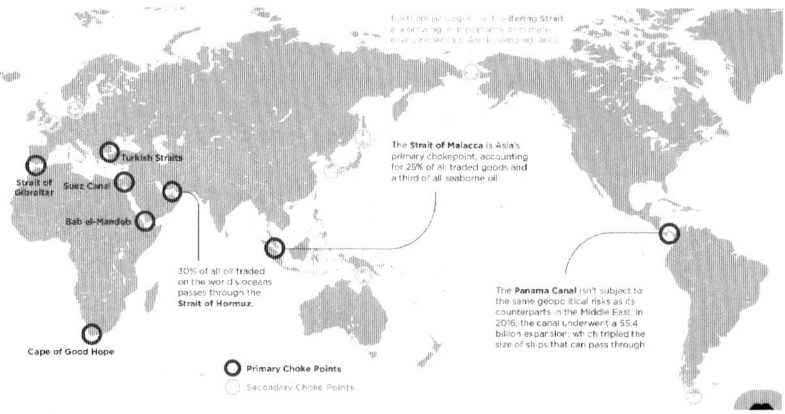

Note. GIS, visualcapitalist.com

The recent contemporary history is already a good indicator of that great power competition, illustrating conflicts resulting in major wars along geopolitical fault-lines. Since the famous Great Game[03] of the 19th century among Tsarist Russia, British Raj, and China's Qing

Dynasty in and around Afghanistan, the region has been continuously unstable. In the first half of the 20th century, the Balkans, where Tsarist Russia, Ottoman Turkey, and the Habsburgs dynasty clashed, gave birth to World War I (WWI). To this day, it is possible to see the remnants of that power competition through a geopolitical prism. Most vividly, the 2020 Nagorno-Karabakh conflict in the Caucasus region revealed Russian, Turkish, and Iranian conflictual approaches resulting in a 44-day war revolutionizing warfare with heavy use of drones. Finally, just next to Afghanistan, separated by the Wakhan corridor, the territorial conflict in the Kashmir region among Pakistan, India, and China pinpoints another geopolitical fault-line over the Himalayas. India and China, two sizeable Eurasian powers, quarrel against each other along their 3.440 km-long disputed Himalayan borders. The 2020 violent clashes in the Galwan Valley between Chinese administrated Aksai Chin and Indian administrated Ladakh of Kashmir region have noticeably transformed India-China bilateral relations. As evident from the above depictions, Russia and China, the heavyweights of Eurasian geopolitics, are the common denominators with a vested interest in most of those maritime or terrestrial choke points.

Moreover, the blockades or deliberate disruptions during political unrest may destabilize the area, possibly spillover to adjacent countries or regions. Consequently, it would be fair to argue that the vulnerabilities of those choke points can be used as a tool of forceful persuasion to inflict geopolitical changes. In that sense, at the center of the historical Silk Road, Afghanistan is an integral component of the Chinese initiated Belt and Road initiative (BRI)[04]. Although the BRI is usually seen as an economic development strategy with the aim of improving the infrastructure to intensify the Eurasian and global trade relations to gain access to new markets, address China's problem of industrial overcapacity, and avoid the middle-income gap[05], it also has a geopolitical rationale. The geopolitical leg of the BRI focus on exemplifying China's re-emergence as a global power by depicting it as a reliable regional and global partner and securing continuous access to energy sources in energy rich regions of Eurasia without being subjected to obstructions of the US Navy in the high seas (Chung, 2018; Wu, 2018; Yu, 2019).

Defining Eurasia

For the scope of this book, the concept of Eurasia is geographically defined as the vast landmass from the Okhotsk Sea to the Mediterranean/Atlantic Ocean, from the Arctic Ocean to the Indian Ocean. Over the last two decades, the great power competition resulted in many strategic maneuvers vis-à-vis natural resources, geopolitical fault-lines, and strategic choke points to enhance their position vis-à-vis others.

For instance, any strategic calculations and analysis concerning energy security/insecurity can no longer be reduced merely to a discussion of supply and demand in the global energy market. It must also take into consideration the parameters of international energy security from geopolitical and geoeconomic perspectives. In this milieu, natural resources 'Haves' and 'Have nots' are paying close attention to the developments in Eurasia. All key players (the new and old ones) are making every effort to retain influence over these strategic natural resources and geopolitical choke points to facilitate uninterrupted access for the sake of the well-being of their respective economies (Marketos, 2009).

In the 21st century, like in the previous historical periods, geography is still indispensable for analyzing some major geopolitical, environmental, and socio-economic conflicts of the contemporary world. Moreover, geographical reasoning can provide valuable hints about the challenges we currently face in international security. In that sense, Eurasia is host to many security-related competitions and witnesses severe tension along with small-scale violence (Lind, 2014). Therefore, it would be futile to reflect on geography just in static and descriptive terms. Most certainly, geography can improve our understanding of many malfeasances of our times, ranging from the global freshwater crisis to refugee/immigration matters to sustainable development.

Another piece of evidence implying the evolving Eurasian geopolitical shift is mapping the global economic center of gravity. Throughout the last two Millennium, the Earth's economic center of gravity based on calculations considering all the GDP produced in our planet indicates a firm shift towards the center of Eurasia (see Figure 2). Since the industrial revolution, the dynamics of the global economy were on the move to the West under the weight of Eurocentric transatlantic trade. However, China's spectacular economic growth rates obtained after the reforms initiated by Deng Xiaoping in the early 1980s, coupled with the rise of the rest of Asia, reversed the momentum and drifted the center of gravity incrementally to the East. Extrapolation of the data indicates that the world's economic center of gravity would settle by 2050 somewhere between India and China, which were the most significant economic powerhouses up to the 18th century. Subsequently, the major decisions and policies regarding the global economy and governance will command a more assertive foreign policy orientation from the rising regional powers.

The term "Eurasia" is rooted in classical theories and concepts of geopolitics, particularly the concepts of "pivot" and later "heartland." Although Eurasia is a highly debated, contested, and elusive term with different meanings and perceptions in time and space, this book will rely upon geopolitics and regionalism as a conceptual framework to understand the evolving Eurasian shifts in the balance of power[06] among the status quo great powers and rising middle powers.

Transformations within the international system can be foreseen by geopolitical analysis. Such analysis can focus the attention of policymakers on conditions that are likely to bring about geopolitical change. However, although geopolitical analysis does not and cannot predict the exact timing of events, unfolding crises, and critical moments, it would still provide important clues in deciphering the path of those radical changes forcing shifts in the geopolitical map.

Figure 3. Evolution of the earth's economic center of gravity

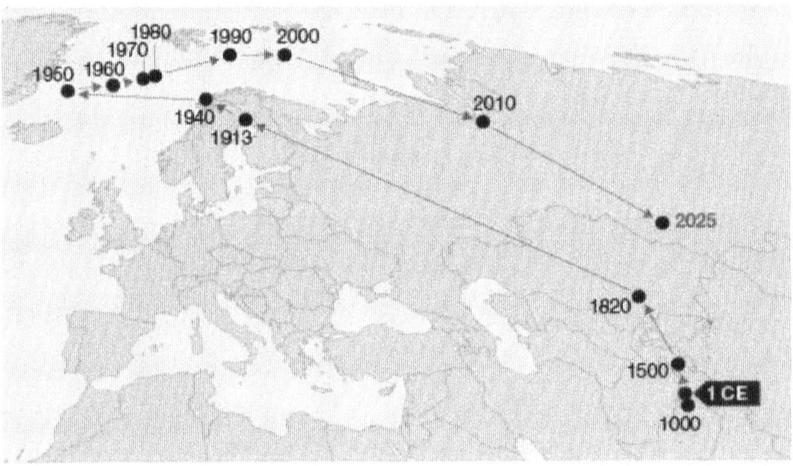

Note. McKinsey Global Institute (MGI) analysis using data from Angus Maddison, University of Groningen

It is noticeable that the Eurasian transport corridors have always captured and captivated Western and Eastern imaginations throughout history. All new initiatives and projects regarding Eurasian connectivity are indicative of those tendencies, inclinations, and fascinations. To a certain extent, all attempts initiated by the Eurasian geopolitical heavyweights Russia and China through regional intergovernmental organizations such as the Shanghai Cooperation Organization (SCO) or Eurasian Economic Union (EAEU) aim to rejuvenate the connectivity and historical links among the continent's nation-states. Consequently, the extension of railroads to distant parts of Eurasia, such as Yakutsk in the Sakha Republic of Russia and then to the Chukotka region, should be considered just as the natural continuity of the current "New Silk

Road" projects taking place at the heart of central Eurasia.

At this junction, it would be timely to provide a very brief intellectual review regarding the prominence of Eurasia in geopolitical thought (Auslin, 2020; Black, 2016; Bolt & Cross, 2018; Kelly, 2016; Lane & Samokhvalov, 2015; Markey, 2020; Sheng & Nascimento, 2021; Sussex & Kanet, 2015). However, as mentioned earlier, it is critical to recognize that Eurasia is a highly debated, contested and elusive term with different meanings and perceptions in time and space.

Geopolitics as a Conceptual Framework

This study utilizes a geopolitical method of analysis to elucidate the significance of evolving Eurasian power relations. In crude terms, the term "geopolitics" is defined as being the study of international relations "from a spatial or geocentric viewpoint, the understanding of the whole … being its ultimate object and justification" (Parker 2015, 2). The first use of the term "geopolitics" is associated with the Swedish political scientist Rudolf Kjellen in an 1899 article (Chapman, 2011).

Geopolitics is essential to the understanding of the behavior of human societies organized into complex, geographically well-defined systems. Evidently, in modern times, this approach has translated itself to the study of nation-states. While the methodology of geopolitics is inherently spatial, its subject matter draws heavily from other social sciences. Notably, three intertwined notions, namely, economics, war, and politics, are instrumental in understanding the behavior of nation-states. They are an indivisible entity together establishing the reality of the nation-state. Subsequently, the nation can be viewed as a wealth-producing and wealth-defending structure connected through a complex web of domestic and foreign relations performed by individuals governing the nation-state (Friedman, 2008).

Geopolitics offers an overarching approach by eliminating these distinct spheres of economics, military, and politics, which in turn provides a more coherent picture of the social reality of the nation-state. Political and military power continually influence economic life and vice versa. It is impossible to imagine war, peace, or development without taking into account politics and economics. Equally, it is inconceivable to think of domestic or foreign policy without weighing economic and military matters. In crude terms, the abovementioned three aspects are only conceived to organize human activities into manageable pieces. The reality is only seemingly made more manageable, and in fact, is falsified. The conventional classification of these aspects imagines distinctions that don't exist and complexities that hide rather than expose the nature of the problem at hand (Friedman, 2008).

This book's model of applied geopolitics starts with geography. It looks at how mountains, plains, rivers, and mineral resources constrain a nation's political, security and economic imperatives. Political geographers believe that power is firmly rooted in the physical nature of the world itself. There is no doubt that geopolitics is also an abstraction, but it has the virtue of not creating imaginary distinctions. Geopolitics by adding a forced simplification provides a more comprehensive view of reality. At this junction, it would be fair to assert that geopolitics is the quest for the center of gravity of reality. Most certainly, the factors and actors at play are never entirely political, military, or economic. However, they are neglected and deemed insufficient due to the fact that they are considered just too simple (Friedman, 2008).

Geopolitical thinking matured significantly at the fin de siècle with the intensification of imperialist map coloring. The unequivocal global dominance of the West translated itself to some political mottoes such as "*la mission civilisatrice*,"[07] "Manifest Destiny,"[08] "white man's burden,"[09] or "*ein Platz in der Sonne*."[10] Within the parameters of this sort of global political climate, Halford Mackinder (1861-1947) of the United Kingdom, Friedreich Ratzel (1844- 1904) of Germany and Alfred Mahan (1840-1914) of the United States started to emphasize the connection between history and geography (Mackinder, 1904; Mahan, 1987; Ratzel, 1987) .

Any discussion about Eurasian geopolitics must start with the seminal work of Sir Halford Mackinder 'The Geographical Pivot of History'. He referred to the Eurasian continent as the "world-island" containing two-thirds of the world's population and identifying the defining nature of certain geographic relationships, particularly the "Pivot" or "Heartland" area of Eurasia (Mackinder, 1904). Outside of the Pivot area is designated as the marginal or inner crescent. The parameter surrounding the heartland contains the "marginal regions", which he divided into four geographic areas. Asia is home to two of these regions that he called monsoon lands (China and India), separated from each other by Himalayan Mountain ranges. The remaining two areas surrounding the pivot are Europe and the "lands of the five seas" or the Middle East. Accordingly, these geographic regions coincide with the spheres of influence[11] of the four major religions with the most followers: two Abrahamic religions—Islam/Christianity—and Eastern religions—Hinduism/Buddhism (Erdem, 2016). For this early work on geopolitics, it is indisputable that the contemporary geopolitical hot spots in Eurasia seems to be just at the fringe to anything quintessential in international relations. His work stressed his concern that one power or alliance of powers could gain control of Eurasia and use that region's resources to dominate the world (Tuathail et al., 2016).

Figure 4. *Map of the Pivot Area*

Note. (Cohen, 2009)

Another eminent scholar of geopolitics, Nicholas J. Spykman, considered geography the preeminent factor in international relations because it was this subject's most enduring characteristic. The Geography of the Peace built upon Mackinder's work in a much more extensive and focused manner (Spykman, 1942, 1944). He asserts another layer of explanation so-called "*Rimland*," which is the intermediate region between the Pivot and the seas. He argues that there is a new mobility in the Eurasian landmass due to improvements in the infrastructure of rail, road, and airplanes, though the natural obstacles of transportation keep the central Eurasian region from realizing its potential in the immediate future. For instance, the containment policy[12] of the Cold War era had been developed upon the warnings of the renowned Sovietologist George Kennan about the likely Soviet expansion over Eurasia and onto its rimlands, underlining Mackinder's heartland thesis. Spykman's *Rimland* approach by tuning up Mackinder's *Inner Crescent* allocated a strategic function to Northeast Asia, and the RFE by firmly placing it on the geopolitical map (Erdem, 2016). Moreover, he highlighted two main geographical entities in international politics, namely the Old World and New World. The Old was composed of four geographical features. The heartland was Eurasia's core and followed Mackinder's heartland (Petersen, 2011). The Rimland was also similar to Mackinder's inner crescent. However, the third Old World feature included a circumferential maritime belt covering the Baltic, the North Sea, and the Mediterranean to the Sea of Okhotsk. The fourth and final feature was offshore islands such as England, Japan, Australia, and Africa (Cohen, 2009).

Moreover, in addition to the above mentioned two seminal works on the geopolitics, at the closing decade of the 20th century, Samuel P. Huntington introduced a transformative ideological piece of a geopolitical theory coined as "The Clash of Civilizations[13]." He presents his work as a theory of culture and civilization that utilizes a modernization theory of political violence (Huntington, 1993, 1997). In that sense, it is also very much a geopolitical theory, since civilizations are in part defined by a specific, generally fixed territory. He argues that the conflict in the post-Cold War era would take place between diverging cultures instead of ideologies. Indeed, Northeast Asia represents a cultural fault line separating Russian, American and Chinese/Japanese/Korean cultures from one another. Subsequently, it would be a zone prone to future conflicts.

Figure 5. *Evolving Eurasian Heartland Boundaries*

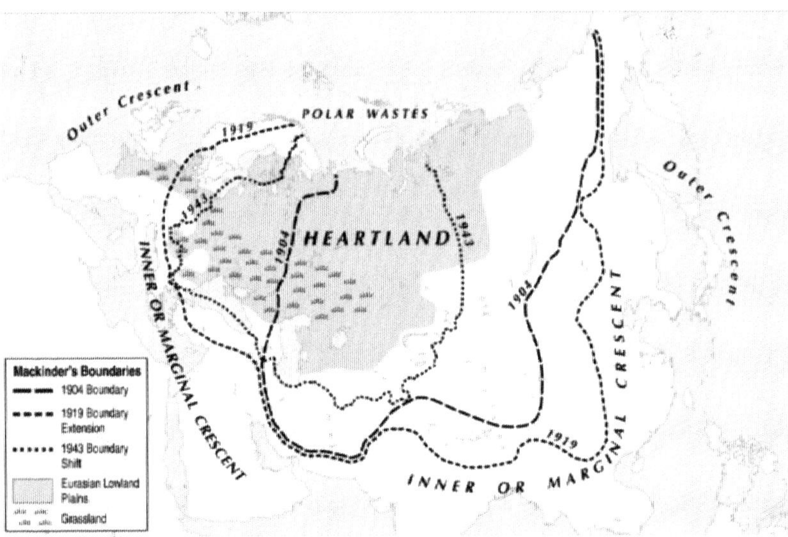

Note. (Cohen, 2009)

Eurasia as a Region

Eurasia as a region has achieved one of the most profound economic transformations in a considerably short period of recorded history, and it represents a wide range of diversity in terms of economic development, political governance, socio-cultural profile, socio-religious traditions (Dent, 2016). For instance, countries from Northeast Asia and to a lesser extend Southeast Asia are pivotal to understanding the overall rise of Asia in global politics. It would be valuable to discuss the relevant literature on regions and regionalism to design the cognitive map of the Eurasia as a region. The coming decades may notice the strengthening of the existing regional systems or the naissance of many loose and new regional systems (Erdem, 2015). This book conceptualizes the growth of regional systems as an important step within the process of globalization14. Moreover, a comprehensive study of Eurasia requires multidisciplinary approach to embrace different fields of research and offer valuable holistic perspectives on regionalism.

There are multiple definitions of the region, and each reflects the peculiarities of a specific historical period of the international system and adjusts itself to the changing environment. In the first half of the 20th century, certain definitions referred to geostrategic regions (Mackinder, 1919), to physiographic characteristics (Vance, 1951), or to homogeneity of economic and social structures within a national context (Odum, 1936; Odum & Moore, 1938). In the Cold War era, Bruce Russett illustrated the complex process of identifying a "region".

He emphasized a number of criteria such as cultural similarity, common political orientation, institutional membership, transaction flows, and proximity. A region is determined as such if it attained a certain minimum score when measured quantitatively against these criteria (Russett, 1967). Several scholars developed an approach of region as subsystems based mostly on geographic region such as either side of the North Atlantic (Hoffmann, 1963), Southeast Asia (Brecher, 1963; Modelski, 1963) or Africa (Zartman, 1973).

In the post-Cold War era, International Relations (IR) scholars started to redefine these concepts along with the concept of globalization. Holm and Sorensen provide four different definitions of the concept of region: geographical units with natural barriers (e.g., the Caucasus and Africa); social or cultural entities (e.g., Polynesia and Iberian Peninsula); organized political units (e.g., the European Union and the North American Free Trade Area); regions of identity (e.g., Central Asia and Latin America). Andrew Hurrell (Fawcett & Hurrell, 1995), with regard to regionalism identifies four categories. First, regionalization refers to the growth of societal integration within a region that takes in consideration an increasing flow of people and the intensification of market interaction. Second, regional identity is associated with an increase in its awareness, which in turn facilitates the regionalism. Third, regional interstate cooperation refers to the formation and intensification of intergovernmental and institutional relations. Finally, regional cohesion represents the ultimate manifestation of regionalism and incorporates the full development of the above-mentioned categories. Hurrell's definition also implies that regionalism is understood as an integral part of globalization. It is assumed that regionalism is a unifying process rather than fragmenting on international level. Bjorn Hettne after identifying three models of region—trading blocs, geopolitical division, and process of regionalization—claims that the "new regionalism" is the outcome of the process of regionalization and represents a version of "extended nationalism". Subsequently, he develops five levels of regionness or regional complexity with an evolutionary logic—geographical unit or ecological unit, social system organizes cooperation, regional civil society, and region as an acting subject. This new regionalism differs from the old one in three important ways. The new one is the product of a multipolar world order, created 'from within', and represents a multidimensional process. On the other hand, the old one was the product of the bipolar Cold War context, created 'form above', and specific in terms of objectives (Farrell et al., 2005; Hettne et al., 1999).

In addition, it is essential to address the mystery surrounding the question of regional/global dialectic or dichotomy. The growth of regional systems in the past decade does not constitute a threat to trends of globalization. Regional systems can be conceptualized as a component of globalization, challenge to globalization or as a parallel process of globalization (Kacowicz, 1998; Mittelman, 1996, 2000). However, in this essay, the growth of regional systems is assumed to be an important step within the process of globalization.

Regionalism in International Relations

Theories of regional integration find their origins in functionalism and neofunctionalism. David Mitrany the main proponent of functionalism, proposed the development of activities in the areas of agreement such as the growth of specialized technical organizations that cross national borders (Mitrany, 1946). According to this approach, technological and economic development lead to more supranational structures as states seek practical means to fulfill necessary functions (Deutsch, 1957; Mitrany, 1966, 1976). Due to the devastating effects of the WWII, Mitrany was concerned with the problem of war and saw the solution in the reordering of international relations along functional lines.

Neofunctionalism presented a refined and further elaborated version of functional theory to explain the development of more general and more political supranational bodies (Haas, 1961). The argument was that the major actors are situated at both the subnational level (e.g., labor unions and political parties) and at the supranational level. The governments' role is to be responsive to the demands from subnational or supranational actors. Neofunctionalism aims to reach a political community larger than a nation-state and looked for the conditions in which this new type of political community would evolve. The method of integration pursued by neofunctionalism is, indeed, taken from functionalism. Similar to functionalism, it proposed a step-by-step method starting from economic sectors and spreading through political fields for creating a supranational political community. Neo functionalists argued that economic integration generates a political dynamic that drives integration further. Closer economic ties require more political coordination in order to operate effectively and eventually would lead to political integration and this process was called "functional spillover" (Burley & Mattli, 1993; Mattli, 1999). This political integration is most likely if the countries in question maintain a high degree of economic and social transactions, possess a similar economic size and development level and have similar pluralist domestic institutions (Schmitter & Haas, 1964). However, due to the empirical developments in the European integration process, neofunctionalism has been discredited. Three major problems were recognized with the neo functionalist approach of integration by its critics: that a definable institutional pattern must mark the outcome of integration, that integration will move in one direction, and that incrementalism is the major form of decision-making (Haas & Whiting, 1975). However, several scholars argued that despite the empirical evidence from the European integration process, the framework was not wrong but just less relevant (Caporaso, 1998).

Neoliberal intergovernmentalism, on the other hand, like realism, puts states at the center of analysis but still take into consideration the impact of interest groups through domestic preference formation. Also, heads of the states are considered central players, which make it different from neofunctionalism. The process of interest aggregation, intergovernmental bargaining and enforcement of decisions are considered as essential elements of this approach of integration. Major advocate of this approach, Andrew Moravcsik developed a three step-process (Moravcsik, 1998). First, interests are recognized and mobilized to become active in politics (preference formation). Second step refers to political process of interests' aggregation at regional level through intergovernmental bargaining in order to reach favorable results for foreign counterparts and domestic constituencies. The last phase, after ratification, is institutional lock-in of the agreements. The liberal intergovernmental approach provides more sophisticated theory of preference formation than neofunctionalism (Choi & Caporaso, 2002). However, by focusing on intergovernmental bargaining neglect the ongoing social process. Paul Pierson calls this a "snapshot view of integration that is distorted in crucial respects." (Pierson, 1995).

Realism and regional integration may seem to be at odds at first glance. However, particularly after the end of the Cold War, realism has something to say about regional integration. The core of realist arguments is shaped by a number of assumptions (Grieco, 1993): states are the most important actors (Morgenthau, 1948; Waltz, 1979); international anarchy is the principal force shaping the motives, preferences and actions of states (Waltz, 1979), states are unitary rational agents, states facing the conditions of anarchy are preoccupied with power and security and often fail to cooperate even in the face of common interests (Waltz, 1979), international institutions affect the prospects for cooperation only marginally (Gilpin, 1986). The sub-national and supranational actors are not important in the preference formation in regional integration. Along the same line of logic, the realists' argument would be that the international institutions glorified by functionalist or neo functionalist approaches cannot diminish anarchy's constraining effects on interstate cooperation. The preferences of the states are formed by the position of the state in the international system. Under certain circumstances, realism can explain integration. For instance, Joanne Gowa's 1989 study shows that the stability of bipolarity after WWII facilitated the deep integration within Europe (Gowa, 1989). On the other hand, at the end of the Cold War along the realist thinking, Mearsheimer developed arguments about the absence of Soviet threat and the return of multipolar international system with mounting anxiety that would increase concerns about security and relative gains among the European partners (Mearsheimer, 1990). Grieco's extensive studies on the European integration and particularly on the Maastricht treaty indicate that weaker states used the European Monetary Union (EMU) to increase their influence by binding the strong states into an institutional framework. Relatively weak states would ensure that they have an effective "voice opportunity" while negotiating the nature of new international institutions (Grieco, 1995).

In the 1990s, the inability of rationalist theories—neoliberal and neorealist— to explain the change in the international system increased the eminence of reflectivist (Keohane & Martin, 1995) theories—critical theory, post-modernism, constructivism, and feminist theories. For instance, the constructivist framework of regional integration is mostly directed to the role of ideas, norms and identities in the integration process. The constructivist literature on regional integration noticeably is in the rise. For instance, Adler and Barnett updated and reinterpreted Deutsch's work on security communities (Deutsch, 1957) and the values behind it (Adler & Barnett, 1998). Jefferey Checkel offers various hypotheses on the preference changes and identities in the integration process (Checkel, 1999). On the other hand, Moravcsik admits that constructivists present an interesting and important set of questions about the effects of an integration process on individuals and states but they fail to make significant contributions to the empirical understanding of the integration process due to their unwillingness to take any risk of empirical disconfirmation (Moravcsik, 1999). But, constructivist approaches are mostly in the metatheoretical stage and have not yet developed recognized puzzles and common research strategies (Choi & Caporaso, 2002).

Most of the developments of the European integration process over the past decade have been asserted in the previous section through the studies of Mearsheimer, Grieco, Checkel, Moravcsik. The impressive journey throughout the 1990s consisting of the 1992 Maastricht Treaty, and the subsequent deepening of integration by the 1997 Amsterdam treaty and the 2001 Nice treaty can be considered as an indication of the reemerging importance of regional systems as a prominent form of governance after the end of the Cold War.

Yet, it is interesting to observe that all the theoretical frameworks outlined above—functionalism/neofunctionalism, liberal intergovernmentalism, realism, and constructivism— are limited mostly to the European system and the European integration process. However, the rise of regional governance over the past decade is not just restricted to Europe. Certainly, the unique nature of its integration process, its economic/ political influence in the international system and its cultural impact on global norm/value formation represents the rationale behind its appeal to scholars around the world. Consequently, the recent developments in Eurasia through the formation of the SCO and the EAEU indicate the evolving geopolitical understanding of Eurasia as a region.

This book primarily deals with Eurasian geopolitical heavyweights, namely the Russian Federation (RF) and the People's Republic of China (PRC). Rightfully, those two countries together constitute more than half of the Eurasian landmass. They have also been influential in shaping geopolitical outcomes across the continent throughout history. Moreover, the contemporary Belt and Road Initiatives (BRI) of China has the goal of replicating and rejuvenating the historical Silk Road through a wide range of infrastructure with the ultimate goal to increase the land connectivity across Eurasia. The envisaged land connectivity would offer China a geopolitical alternative to sealines-based connectivity.

The three chapters in Part One are dedicated to Russia's role in three distinctive geopolitical areas of Eurasia, namely Central Asia, the Arctic Region, the Russian Far East (RFE).

The first chapter examines the convoluted relationship between Russia and Central Eurasia region. Surely, Russia aspires to rejuvenate the old strong ties with the region. To that end, it utilizes all the available mechanisms of power ranging from energy to the doctrine of extraterritoriality to cultural/linguistic affinities. Indubitably, there are also several formidable challenges to realize those ambitions. For instance, the Taliban victory in Afghanistan, the prospect of potential domestic disturbances such as in Kazakhstan in 2021, or more assertive policies initiated by other Eurasian actors like China, Turkey, Iran, and India/Pakistan can all thwart Russian ambitions there. Moreover, Central Eurasian states can also choose to either resist Russia through regional alliance formation by confining Russia to regional structures or alternatively can form strategic alliances on a bilateral level with influential countries of the region to circumvent the soaring Russian intimidations or arm-twisting.

The second chapter addresses the Arctic from a geopolitical perspective as a region impacted the most visible way by global warming. The climatic changes gave birth to unprecedented engagement in the region through intricate geopolitical calculations by the traditional Arctic countries and diverse newly rising powers with polar ambitions. Russia is the dominant player in the Arctic due to its overwhelming geography. However, it is also possible to observe the growing uneasiness between Russia and the West, creating a bellicose scene vis-à-vis the issues at stake. The fragile ecological situation coupled with intensifying geopolitical confrontation opens the perilous possibility to reconfigure the region's political map as we know it.

The chapter on Bering Strait crossing focus on linking the entirety of Eurasia to the entirety of the Americas. Most certainly, there are some immense geopolitical benefits of such project. It would bring about a profound and lasting change to global economic and political outlook. Along with this line of logic, the Bering Strait crossing is much more than just a flamboyant infrastructure project (Murphy, 2015). The most valued function of the Bering Strait crossing and the extension of the associated railroad network would be to release the massive natural resources trapped underneath the tundra and permafrost for the benefit of Russia and the world. Moreover, the railroad project(s) would also build development corridors in those underdeveloped parts of the Russian Federation. The development of the resources and their rapid transportation to the global markets would contribute not only to the overall development of the region but also would be valuable for the resource- poor countries of Northeast Asia such as Japan, Korea, and China. This chapter will explore the possible impact(s) of the Bering Strait crossing as a formidable infrastructure project for the economic development of the RFE from the Russian perspective under the frame of geopolitics. Furthermore, it will equally scrutinize the implications for the adjacent countries to the region.

The three chapters in Part Two are dedicated to China's journey to a global identity by investigating Pax Sinica along the Silk Road, the Shanghai Cooperation Organization and the Uyghurs at Eurasian crossroads.

The chapter on Pax Sinica through the revitalization of the historical Silk Road examines the structural transformations taking place at the core of Eurasia. Pax Sinica, as a historiographical term, refers to a Chinese-provided peace reflecting a Sinocentric worldview along the historical Silk Road. Evidently, the BRI project initiated by Xi Jinping in 2013 has been influential in formulating new overarching policies to expand trade relations, improve security and enhance the overall well-being of the populace across Eurasia.

On the other hand, the chapter on the Shanghai Cooperation Organization (SCO) will reflect on the SCO in contrast to European system, while showing the shortcomings of the Eurocentric bias of these approaches. This multilateral association was established to provide security and maintain stability across the vast Eurasian region. The enhancement of trade relations, as well as cultural and humanitarian cooperation while counteracting emerging challenges and threats, have been the ultimate goals of the organization.

The final chapter will look at the tenuous situation of Uyghurs at the Eurasian crossroads. Xinjiang Province of China is the Gordian's knot in terms of geopolitical importance for the CCP's goals of establishing harmonious Eurasian connectivity through the revitalization of the historical Silk Road. However, the ethnic unrest in Xinjiang has historically been a source of tension for respective Chinese administrations, and the ethnic unrest has received wide global media coverage in recent times. This strategically important region is not only well-endowed in terms of natural resources but also acts as a buffer zone between Central Eurasia and the heartland of Han China while sharing borders with the post-Soviet Central Asian Republics, Russia, Afghanistan, India, and Pakistan.

Part I

Russia: Ambitions vs. Realities?

Part I

Russia: Ambitions vs. Realities?

Foreign policy is expressed in decisions of one state in relation to another, how others influence the given state, and how they shape its actions and behavior. In that sense, it is impossible to speak about one state's foreign policy freedom in its relations with others. For the same reason, inevitably, it is necessary to characterize and analyze Russia's relations with other states in those terms. At the turn of the 21st century, the foreign policy of Russia is best expressed by a system of relations among so-called great powers and rising regional powers. As the largest country, Russia has wide-ranging strategic interests in Eurasian geography.

The main puzzling aspect in Russian foreign and military policy is the desire to preserve its territorial integrity and eliminate perceived threats to its national security. Since the Tsarist and Soviet times, Russia extended its borders in an unprecedented way in historical terms by incorporating a large number of the new populace. But, on the other hand, its projected power did not always measure up to this task. In this overextended geography, surrounded by competing powers with historical grievances, the survival and continuity of the state have always been perceived to be in constant danger. Therefore, all foreign and military decisions were geared towards realizing that ultimate goal. Consequently, the Russian state's primary purpose is to create suitable conditions to minimize the risk factors for its security.

The rich history of Russian international relations give ample opportunities to determine Russia's place in the world. This history, in many respects, also provides commanding clues vis-à-vis Russia's current position in global politics. The rationale behind this line of thinking is, of course, that as the Russians turn to the past for guidance for the future, to fully understand and anticipate their policy steps, we should view the world through that same prism of history (Franklin, 2004; Widdis, 2004). Winston Churchill once famously observed that the key to understanding Russian "enigma" is its national interest. However, it is equally important to clarify what Russians themselves perceive to be their foreign policy interests and objectives. Therefore, it would be fair to say that there has been a great deal of transformation in Russia's perceptions of its national interest under President Putin. To this end, it is essential to find out the driving motive and rationale behind Russian foreign policy in recent times (Fawn, 2005; Kanet, 2010; Lo, 2002; J. Mankoff, 2009; Thorun, 2009).

Putin's Russia's single most important foreign policy feature is international recognition as a great power (Tsygankov, 2019). It is possible to notice this Russian foreign policy orientation in a wide range of geography from the West Asia to Eastern Europe to Central Asia. This desire and the need to be recognized and respected internationally is also supported by the domestic constituency. The annexation of Crimea and the Donbas region conflict in Ukraine are just some manifestations of Russia's geopolitical ambitions to be a great power again. The commentaries, speeches, or interviews given by President Putin, his Defense Minister Sergei Shoigu, and foreign minister Sergei Lavrov are all indicative of those foreign and security policy goals.

Moreover, Russian foreign policy circles believe that liberal democracies are in decline (also shared by Xi Jinping and several other governments around the world). The falling living standards, weak foreign policy initiatives formulated around appeasement, polarized societies due to ethnic, religious, and cultural cleavages of the West manufacture the idea that the American-led world order is in deep crisis. The firm conviction that the new multipolar order is taking shape reflects the shift in power to authoritarian regimes promoting traditional values. A resuscitated Russia under Vladimir Putin's navigation along with the other heavyweight of Eurasian geopolitics China gives an impetus to an avant-guard attempt to shape the upcoming new global order.

It would be valuable to focus on several important questions to decipher that rationale: What are the main conditions which influenced the foreign policy orientation? What are the significant events determining the course of international relations in contemporary times? What are the connections between foreign policy orientation and domestic situation, particularly the means and might of Russia?

The chapters in Part I will address several aspects of Russian foreign and military policy vis-à-vis evolving Eurasian geopolitics. The investigation of the three distinct regions of Eurasia, namely Central Asia, the Arctic region, and Northeast Asia. It will pay close attention to the conditions that influenced the current period's foreign and military policymaking processes and its geopolitical expression in Eurasia.

Chapter I

Russia in Central Asia: Evolving Balance of Power

Russia is, by and large, considered one of the great powers in the world. However, it would be fair to argue that this gargantuan power is struggling to rebuild its economic base in an era of transition after the collapse of the USSR. There are significant difficulties in guaranteeing a stable domestic order due to demographic shifts, democratic deficit, economic challenges, and institutional weaknesses. There is no denying that under President Vladimir Putin's leadership, Russia's foreign policy became more ambitious and assertive partly due to the increasing commodity prices and concentration of political power in the hands of few select. Consequently, the global economic and political conjuncture allowed President Putin to put several geopolitical objectives into practice in its near-abroad. The former Soviet Central Asian states have been closely watching the unfolding geopolitical chess game in the Caucasus and Eastern Europe. The 2008 de facto recognition of the independence of Abkhazia and South Ossetia in Georgia, the annexation of Crimea in 2014, and again the 2022 de facto recognition of the independence of Luhansk and Donetsk People's Republic in the Donbas region has been observed alarmingly by all constituent republics[15] of the former Soviet Union (FSU).

The concluding years of the Soviet system presented a puzzling paradox regarding Soviet Central Asia. Although many Sovietologists in the western world had long anticipated Central Asia as the starting point for the Soviet Union's eventual collapse based on cultural and religious premises, the Central Asian republics reluctantly left the USSR and were among the last ones to do so (d'Encausse, 1978).

This chapter will explore Russian foreign policy orientation in the Central Eurasian region[16], particularly vis-à-vis the former Soviet Central Asia. Furthermore, the analysis will investigate the degree of achievability of those geopolitical strategies put in place by Moscow and evaluate whether those strategies have been successful in the face of changing geopolitical conjecture in and around the region. Finally, the chapter will equally address the political/economic tools to attain those ambitions by delving into Russian policy regarding a wide range of issues such as energy security, military activities, Sino-Russian cooperation/competition, and Russian minorities abroad.

One conclusion is that Russian foreign policy strategies from a geopolitical point of view are relatively ambiguous. Although those strategies constantly aim to boost Russia's standing as a great power, there remains a considerable gap between those ambitions and the outcomes at hand.

Russian Conquest of Central Asia and the Soviet Period

The Russian conquest of Turkistan[17] started in 1865 by capturing Tashkent, the capital of Uzbekistan, and ended in 1884 by defeating the Turkmen tribes[18]. By the end of the 19th century, Central Asia was firmly under the control of Tsarist Russia, either directly or as protectorates. Various scholars have written about this period of Central Asian and Russian history extensively (Allworth, 1967; Becker, 2009; Brower, 1997; Campbell, 2022; d'Encausse, 1988; Khalid, 1994; Morrison, 2008; Rieber, 2007; Sabol, 2003; Sahadeo, 2007). Russian supremacy in Central Asia activated the colonial relationship that equally persisted under the Soviet Union.

One of the Russian colonial expansion objectives were to encourage cotton production to meet the growing needs of the textile industry in Russia. The American civil war and severe disruptions in the importations of cotton from the Confederate states played an essential role in the Russian decision to capture and use this climate-convenient area for cotton production. Russians believed that they could reach self-sufficiency in cotton production by using the newly conquered land in Central Asia[19]. However, the primary motivation was the British advances in Afghanistan, posing far-reaching concerns for Russian geopolitical interests in the region (Weinthal, 1998).

Figure 6. *Central Asia under Russian imperial administration*

Note. (Keller, 2020)

During this pre-Soviet period, Central Asia was politically delineated into Governorate-General of Turkistan and the Governorate-General of the Steppe[20]. After undergoing several changes, by the end of the 19th century, the Governorate-General of Turkistan grew to include five oblasts (regions): the Syr Darya, Fergana, Samarqand, Semirechie, and Transcaspia. Tashkent became the capital of the Governorate-General of Turkistan. Starting from this period, under Tsarist and Bolshevik administrations, Tashkent played a central role in implementing Russian policies in the region. Despite the creation of this new administrative organization, Russian intervention in local institutions in Turkistan was minimal. Until the Russian colonial expansion (LeDonne, 1997), the region and its people experienced a decentralized pattern of governance at the village level (mahalla)[21].

Central Asia in the Soviet era (1918-1991) witnessed some spectacular changes (Braker, 1989; Burg, 1986; Carlisle, 1994; Edgar, 2004; Gleason, 1986; Glenn, 1999; Hauner, 1989; Keller, 2001; Lorenz, 1994; Northrop, 2004; Ro'i, 2000; Rumer, 1989; Sabol, 1995; Shahrani, 1993). The Central Asian economy and the population's standard of living grew significantly by utilizing the principles of the command economy. However, at the same time, the Soviet command economy, along with its application in Central Asia, created a socio-economic environment conducive to unsustainable long-term economic patterns in the region.

Russia's Resurgence

The strategic dynamics in post-Soviet Eurasian space are in flux today. Nevertheless, several trends are underway that could have significant implications for the broader Eurasian security order that emerged after the Cold War. Perhaps the most consequential is the emergence of Russia as a more confident and assertive actor both globally and regionally.

The collapse of the Soviet Union was a shock with disastrous geopolitical outcomes creating a weak and frustrated Russia. Treated as a superpower for most of the 20th century, the Russian leadership had difficulties accepting the new realities on the ground. The declining influence in global affairs and inability to shape international outcomes had been identified with the economic decline, political chaos, and foreign policy weaknesses of the 1990s. To some extent, Putin's arrival to power echoes the resentment and irritation of the newly burgeoning Russian nomenklatura. Putin was determined to revamp the power of the Russian state and proclaim Russian power and influence abroad, particularly in the post-Soviet space. During his first decade in power, the rising energy prices gave Moscow sufficient momentum to initiate envisaged policies to rehabilitate the Russian power. As a result, the Russian economy significantly recovered, and Russia's influence abroad visibly increased.

Moreover, he rebuilt and solidified the state's power base on the domestic level by preventing further erosion from the center to the periphery. Putin's vision aimed to regain state control over the critical assets deemed strategic such as energy resources, for the recalibration of the Russian economy. The oligarchs resisting those new rules of the game had been either sent to exile or prison[22]. This autocratic-leaning picture had been complemented by wielding greater centralized control over the unruly media and making it a more docile tool to support any government policy. Putin's Russia became a revisionist power trying to overhaul the conditions imposed in the former Soviet geopolitical space blaming the West that it was imposed upon when Russia was weak. In crude terms, Russia resuscitated and reformulated its national interests without worrying about the West's perception, which dictated Russian foreign and security policy.

The Russian invasion of Georgia in 2008, Crimea in 2014, and the Donbas region in 2022 should also be evaluated within this context. Western policy to reinforce Kosovo's independence and the assurances given to Ukraine and Georgia for NATO membership has been instrumental in initiating such an outcome. From the Russian perspective, it was a genuinely defensive move that aspired to prevent further erosion of Moscow's decaying authority in its sphere of influence. The prevailing reverberation of those territorial quagmires was to force the West to reexamine the process of further enlargement of NATO into the Russian perceived traditional zone of influence. Moreover, the "Medvedev Doctrine" highlighting the protection of the rights and dignity of Russian citizens in the former Soviet geopolitical space as a priority of Russian foreign policy gave carte blanche to

Russian forces to intervene abroad in defense of Russian citizens. Once under firm Russian control, the Russians relied heavily on this existing local judicial and political institution of the village to govern the newly acquired region. For instance, village leaders (aksakals) were locally elected officials and commanded much respect among the populations[23]. These village leaders were able to function in their traditional role. Russians turned to these traditional village elders to regulate much of the economic and political life in Central Asia.

The Bolshevik Revolution brought about a widespread institutional change, altering both the political, social, and physical constitution of the region. The Bolshevik strategy to incorporate Turkistan into the Soviet Union was based upon the replacement of a united Turkistan with smaller national republics. This territorial engineering was begun in 1924 and did not correspond to any previous political boundaries. By 1936, five new Soviet republics were established on the territory of the old Turkistan.

9/11 and the US Interests in Central Asia

Following the game-changing event of 9/11, US strategic interests in Central Asia shifted significantly. The Taliban regime became the priority and a prime target for American foreign and security policy. The necessity to have partner countries in the region was a must from a logistical point of view for the successful conduct of operations on the ground. To this end, Operation Enduring Freedom required newly forged alliances in the region for overflight, landing, and basing rights in Central Asia. For instance, Manas International Airport near Bishkek and in the earlier phases of the US operation Karshi-Khanabad (K2) in Uzbekistan, not very far from the Afghan border, required the support of the respective Uzbek and Kyrgyz governments.

The possibility of stationing the US military in Kyrgyzstan and Uzbekistan after October 2001 changed in a dramatic way the essence of the Eurasian geopolitical chess game. Moreover, the US-led international engagement throughout the region opened paths for Central Asian countries to initiate new security arrangements at the core of Eurasia. The US military's engagement in the region prompted the interests of a large number of international organizations (IO) and non-governmental Organizations (NGOs) to expand their activities. Encouraged by the US presence, those organizations started tackling issues ranging from environmental deterioration to drug trafficking to gender inequalities.

From the Russian perspective, Putin's domestic counter-terrorism rhetoric was behind his decision to side with the US after 9/11. However, this major geopolitical reorganization in Central Asia had never been very popular among the Russian political elite to begin with and was considered just a temporarily useful tactical maneuvering. Moscow's unexpected agreement on US military deployments opened the gates of Central Asia to Americans until the full withdrawal of troops from Afghanistan in October 2021.

Although the common denominator forged through the American

Global War on Terror emphasizing the security threats originating from the Taliban and al-Qaeda gave a tactical upper hand momentarily to Russia, it debilitated Moscow's ability in the region by opening Central Asian Pandora's box to Americans. The preeminent Russian calculation was that the tactical advantage would turn into a significant strategic advantage over time by pushing Americans into an Afghan quagmire a la Vietnam without any meaningful outcome. Moscow was aware of the harsh Afghan reality from the lessons learned through its own disastrous and costly involvement in the 1980s. Although the earlier stages of the war were a swift and destructive victory for Americans, over the years, the US encountered experiences like Russians in the 1980s or the British in the late 19t century, a total stalemate without any noteworthy outcome. The financially unsustainable, costly war became America's longest foreign war lasting for two decades and spanning four presidencies. Since 1945, the US has very rarely achieved any meaningful victory[24], and the Afghan war's failure to defeat the Taliban was just another sign of this inability.

Russia's Policy toward Central Asia under Putin

Following the demise of the Soviet system, the 'young Russians' led by Yegor Gaydar were the chief influencers in the attempt to reform the system (Aslund, 2011). Gaydar and his entourage professed the need to 'cut out' the backward Soviet periphery to jumpstart the Russian state's modernization and its realignment with the West. During Boris Yeltsin's both terms at the head of the Russian Federation, many inept bureaucrats and politicians saw value in distancing Russia from the unreformable newly independent states of Central Asia (Baev, 2004).

During the first Yeltsin presidency, Central Asia saw only peripheral and marginal attention from Moscow. Only a few distinctive individuals, such as the Director of the Federal Border Service (FSB), Andrei Nikolaev, and to some extent the Kazakh president Nursultan Nazarbayev pushed for Russian intervention in Tajikistan due to his fears of the rise and spread of Islamic radicalism from Afghanistan to the rest of Central Asia (Karagiannis, 2006).

The second Yeltsin presidency witnessed the arrival of Yevgeny Primakov as minister of Foreign Affairs in 1996 and then as a prime minister in 1998. The notorious Primakov doctrine called for further expansion of Russian influence in the Middle East and the former Soviet geopolitical space through the formation of a close strategic relationship with China and India in Eurasia to overcome the American-sponsored color revolutions and entanglements.

Russia's withdrawal of its interest and engagement from Central Asia following the demise of the Soviet system was an agonizing experience for the Central Asian economies that had to involuntarily disengage themselves from a complex network of Soviet administrative planning and bureaucracy along with an inefficient subsidy system beset by corruption that was in place to support Central Asian SSRs. Nevertheless, strikingly, Russia, following the tumultuous years of the

1990s, has pursued much more assertive policies in the region after 2000.

Indeed, to this day, Russia is the most engaged and politically consequential external power in Central Asia as a former center of imperial control and Soviet rule. However, the Russian role in the region is vigorously contested and controversial. It is true that, on the one hand, it can be depicted as a pure colonial relationship bringing political repression, economic dependence, societal upheavals through the destruction of nomadic communities during Stalin's rule, and environmental catastrophe such as the Aral Sea disaster[25] through the cotton monoculture. However, on the other hand, the Russian/ Soviet rule was instrumental in the modernization of the region with big infrastructure development projects and, maybe most importantly, providing a highly successful universal education for Central Asians.

Of course, the well-established and institutionalized Soviet legacies were embedded effectively into the societal fabric of the region, persisting decades after the end of the Soviet system. Central Asian public opinion vis-à-vis Russia is reflected in consistently high favorability ratings and is still viewed as a place of economic opportunity or a prime migration destination for employment purposes. The proclivity toward Russia partly originates from Central Asian elites' shared similar educational and professional experiences under the Soviet system, bureaucratic norms and procedures inherited from Soviet practices, and the region's security and intelligence services have retained their extensive connections to Moscow.

The turning point for intense and devoted Russo-Central Asian relations was Vladimir Putin's ascension to the Russian presidency in 1999. The arrival of Yeltsin's hand-picked successor, as the new head of the state, reversed the foreign policy hesitations of the earlier administrations. The new roadmap elaborated by President Putin highlighted Moscow's priority attention to Central Asia.

Putin's main political motto was formulated under the rubric of counterterrorism with its origins in the Chechen conflict in the Caucasus (Trapsh, 2007; Trenin, 2009). This new political motto did also go well with the authoritative rulers of Central Asia. Putin did rehabilitate some degree of continuity and consistency in Russian foreign policy. Consequently, Moscow promoted newly revitalized Russian-led regional economic and security initiatives in Central Asia, such as the Collective Security Treaty Organization (CSTO), the successor to the Commonwealth of Independent States (CIS) Collective Security Treaty, the Russian-driven equivalent of North Atlantic Treaty Organization (NATO).

Moscow resurrected a range of bilateral leases that governed a network of Russian military installations in Kazakhstan, Kyrgyzstan, and Tajikistan. Russia by supporting the militaries of Central Asian states with activities ranging from Russian-made military hardware purchases to joint military exercises within the framework of CSTO frameworks to prevent the decoupling from the Russian privileged sphere of influence.

For instance, according to a 1996 agreement signed by Kazakhstan and Russia, the Sary Shagan anti-ballistic missile testing range near Lake Balkhash was leased by Russia. In addition, the Baikonur Cosmodrome, the world's first spaceport for orbital and human launches, is leased by the Kazakh Government to Russia until 2050. Kant Air Base near the capital city Bishkek of Kyrgyzstan is home to Russian Air Force units in agreement with a bilateral lease agreement signed between Russia and Kyrgyzstan in 2012 for the duration of fifteen years with the possibility to prolong automatically every five years. Russia's 201st military base, with a permanent base stationed in the cities of Dushanbe and Bokhtar of Tajikistan, is Russia's largest military facility outside its borders, conducting on a bilateral basis a number of joint military drills as part of the CSTO. The agreement signed between parties in October 2012 allows the Russian military base to remain in Tajikistan until 2042.

The economic dimension of Russian reassertion to Central Asia included new modalities of integration. With the sharp increase in commodity prices during the 2000s, the Russian macroeconomic indicators started to improve. However, the rapid economic growth along with gloomy demographic realities on the ground opened the door for a migrant exodus from Central Asia to Russia. Comparatively higher wages and an abundance of temporary/seasonal work seemed to be a win-win situation for both the Russian economy and the Central Asian labor force in search of employment. The remittances that were sent back to the region became a lifeline for the respective economies of Central Asian states[26].

For instance, Kyrgyzstan and Tajikistan are the two of the most migrant-dependent countries in the world. While the Russo-Ukrainian conflict, first in 2014 due to the Crimean invasion and later in 2022 in the Donbas region and the following impact of the western sanctions are taking a toll on the Russian economy, the Kyrgyz and Tajik economies will take the hardest hit due to the expected fall in remittances sent from Russia. Kyrgyz remittances amounted to the equivalent of 31.3 percent of GDP in 2020, with the vast majority of them originating from Russia. Tajikistan remittances displayed similar trends; the figure was 26.7 percent of GDP in 2020, more than half coming from Russia.

No doubt that a weakening of economic activity in Russia would curb the employment and incomes of Central Asian migrant workers and, subsequently, their prospects to send remittances. The most populous country in Central Asia, Uzbekistan, also sends millions of migrant workers abroad, and 55 percent of Uzbekistan's remittances come from Russia. But due to the more diversified structure and larger size of its economy, it is less dependent on remittances, which was still equivalent to 11.6 percent of GDP in 2020. The impact of remittances for the oil-rich Kazakhstan will be less significant than in the rest of the Central Asian countries. While 51 percent of remittances come from Russia, it was just 0.2 percent of GDP in 2020.

The Central Asian leadership has always been cautious with their remarks vis-à-vis criticizing Russia's military campaign in Georgia, Crimea, or the Donbas region, principally because their relations with Moscow are too consequential to jeopardize, such as the Russian labor market for employment and remittances, pivotal Russian pivotal role in the energy and energy-related sectors of Central Asia, and Russian security umbrella in the region.

Figure 7. *Members of Eurasian Economic Union (EAEU)*

Note. (Pieper, 2022)

Moreover, Putin was aware of the other economic tools available to him to increase Russian influence not only near-abroad but also in the international arena. The multilateral and supranational platforms such as CSTO and Eurasian Economic Union (EAEU) along other Russian-led regional bodies strive to institutionalize Russia's regional preeminence. The Central Asian states' participation in those platforms allows Russia to claim its lost self-esteem, which is essential to reckon Moscow's foreign policy identity as a great power in a multipolar global system. Additionally, the commodities, and particularly fossil fuels, were the forte for Russia's reintroduction to global politics as a trendsetter instead of being a trend follower. To this end, Russian energy giants such as Gazprom or Lukoil became major agents for policies to revendicate Russian national interests.

Under Putin's leadership, Russian policy toward Central Asia strikingly transformed from the rhetoric of the 1990s to a more tenacious and proactive approach affirming Central Asia's importance as another significant foreign policy priority.

Moscow, under the tutelage of Putin, similarly to the United States and around the same time, surprisingly got aware of the marvelous benefits of using the war on terrorism as a tool to unify the nation against internal and external challenges of the earlier period. The possibility of the spread of Islamic radicalism[27] from Taliban-managed Afghanistan through the loosely controlled bordering states, not only Tajikistan, Uzbekistan, Turkmenistan but also Xinjiang province of China, created an unusual temporary alliance between Russia, the Central Asian states, and China.

Energy and Pipeline Geopolitics

Although the geopolitics of energy were an element in relations between Russia and the rest of Eurasia during the 1990s, oil and gas became truly central during Vladimir Putin's presidency of Russia (Barylski, 1995; Bedeski & Swanstrom, 2012; Belyi, 2003; Goldthau, 2008; Heinrich, 2008; Ocelík & Osička, 2014; Poussenkova, 2010;

Rutland, 2008; Smith, 2006; Sussex & Kanet, 2015; Woehrel, 2009). In part, this development stems from changes under way not only within the Russian energy sector but also the changes taking place in global conjecture (Jeffrey Mankoff, 2009).

Central Asia is important for Russia's broader energy considerations for a number of reasons. This region constitutes an alternative to its own oil and natural gas resources for European and Asian markets. The interests of Western energy companies in the well-endowed Caspian basin started right after the demise of the Soviet Union. However, the land-locked status of the energy-rich countries of the region (Kazakhstan, Turkmenistan, Azerbaijan) and the double-land-locked status of Uzbekistan required the use of pipeline systems to bring the extracted resources to the global markets.

Bringing the oil or natural gas sector to a lucrative maturation required an intensive capital flow and the tacit approval of the US, which was the dominant force in capital markets. The global war on terror at the beginning of the century provided a new dynamism to regional development schemes and, subsequently, the plentiful availability of financial capital.

The basic premise was that the revenues generated from the resources would be utilized to develop the region to overcome the destabilizing factors. To this end, the Baku–Tbilisi–Ceyhan (BTC) pipeline is often characterized as the major Western inroad to the Caspian basin, with the possibility to extend to Kazakh and Turkmen natural gas and oil fields (Baizakova, 2010).

Yet Russia has successfully presented itself as an alternative oil supplier, thus denying similar opportunities to Kazakhstan and Azerbaijan. Through all these ups and downs, Moscow has played the oil game with a remarkable reserve and uncharacteristic precision. However, the existing pipeline grid was pointed toward the Russian Federation. For instance, the Tengiz–Novorossiysk[28] (TN) pipeline gives Russia a near-monopoly on the transportation of Caspian oil.

Putin has unfailingly pursued the rationale that hydrocarbons and counterterrorism are two distinct issues that should not be combined together in any strategic cocktail. Chechnya, where the oil infrastructure was completely destroyed while a pipeline was quickly laid through Dagestan to circumvent the troubled territory, was the first victim of that principle.

Moscow also moved rapidly to eliminate any further discussion and wild speculation about a trans-Afghan gas pipeline by reaching a series of agreements with Turkmenistan concerning the transportation of its gas northwards through Russian pipelines. Fundamentally, the Russian leadership took as the basis for its strategy the plain geographic fact (so often overlooked by experts intoxicated by the mixture of oil and terrorism) that Afghanistan, which would inevitably remain the center of the war against terror, was separated from the oil-rich Northern Caspian by thousands of miles and several state borders.

While Russia is engaged in extensive trading with Western Europe, recent events make it reasonable to raise the question whether there are scenarios under which Russia might act aggressively to challenge the existing global energy trading system. Russia possesses a high proportion of global energy resources and dominates sales to a major energy consuming region, namely Europe. It has already shown a proclivity to use its empowered energy position to either grab more resource rents from its immediate neighbors, or to wrest geopolitical or political benefits using energy as a lever (Jaffe & Soligo, 2009).

Although Russia holds the eighth largest oil reserves in the world, it surpassed OPEC member Saudi Arabia in terms of oil production in 2010. If we also add to this picture natural gas production and exports, Russia's status as a current and future energy producer is close to unrivaled. Consequently, Russia's position as a major energy supplier has a great significance not only for its foreign policy but for its relationships with major energy consuming countries (Jaffe & Soligo, 2009).

Energy trade is a key lever used by Moscow to achieve political acquiescence in Central Asia. The Soviet energy grid was a concrete manifestation of Soviet energy diplomacy with other Warsaw pact countries, which found its roots in the Brezhnev doctrine of restricted sovereignty. However, the same way, after the dissolution of the Soviet Union, Central Asian states found themselves highly dependent on that Russian energy grid—a legacy of Communist era—under the tight central control of Moscow, linking their hydrocarbon exports in a manner difficult to alter. Under the Presidency of Putin and Medvedev, the Kremlin began to reconstitute its old Brezhnevian strategies, utilizing energy as a lever to regain its status as a superpower and extend its influence in the Former Soviet Union (Jaffe & Soligo, 2009). There are already two concrete examples in the former Soviet space where Russia has used this energy leverage in what many believe were politically motivated attempts to alter the behavior of its neighbors: Ukraine[29] and Georgia[30].

Kazakhstan is the largest oil producer in Central Asia and second only to Russia among CIS countries with output of 1.9 million bbl/d in 2021. The country's economy depends heavily on the sale of its oil abroad. It also produces a substantial amount of natural gas. The United States has long sought to recruit Kazakhstan as a supplier for the BTC oil pipeline and continues to discuss ways of bringing Kazakhstan into the Trans-Caspian Pipeline (TCP) project, though Nursultan remains noncommittal. In addition, the energy grid of northern regions of Kazakhstan and southwestern Russian Siberia (along the Trans-Siberian railroad) are connected as a legacy of the Soviet times, which in turn plays a significant role in establishing energy security when and if there are technical problems with Kazakh power plants in that part of the country by importing additional electricity.

Russian energy giants, Lukoil and Gazprom, are Uzbekistan's significant partners in exploring and developing gas and oil fields in Uzbek territory. Due to the rapid population increase and corresponding economic growth in recent decades, domestic consumption has outpaced production, and Uzbekistan has become a net gas importer. As a result, Uzbek export of gas to Russia and China has been halted, and they have begun buying gas from Russia's Gazprom to meet domestic demand. Although the country may be home to sizable additional oil and natural gas resources, the costly exploration and development phases and the missing technological know-how still require substantial Russian support.

The main catalyst event for the Russian penetration into the Uzbek energy sector was the Andijan massacre of May 2005. The United States, the EU, and the OSCE were overtly critical of the Karimov government for human rights abuses accusing it of heavy-handed policies that pushed for an independent international investigation of the violence. On the other hand, Russia and China were very unequivocally supportive of the Uzbek government and categorized the events as a legitimate action against extremism. The Uzbek government responded by shutting down the Western organizations and companies active in the country. Correspondingly, the deals in the critical energy sectors were disadvantageous for Uzbekistan but on favorable terms for Russian and Chinese companies.

Russian and Chinese unfettered support for the Uzbek government was spotlighted at the SCO summit in Astana, Kazakhstan, on July 5-6. With the support of both Eurasian geopolitical heavyweights, the Uzbek government asked the United States to withdraw its forces from the Karshi-Khanabad (K2) base in southern Uzbekistan not far from the Afghan border, where they had been using since 2002 to support operations in Afghanistan.

On logistical grounds, no other oil-exporting country is in a position to fill Russia's role in provisioning petroleum products to Uzbekistan. The long-term serving President Islam Karimov's death and the arrival of Shavkat Mirziyoyev in 2017 did not reverse the course of Russo-Uzbek energy relations. The already existing Soviet pipeline infrastructure was repaired and updated to facilitate an uninterrupted Russian oil flow.

In Kyrgyzstan, Gazprom, a majority state-owned Russian multinational energy corporation, obtained the country's natural gas distribution network in 2014. Since then, Russia has become an active and significant player in Kyrgyzstan's energy sector as a reliable partner. The energy-poor Kyrgyzstan depended heavily on hydropower generation for its electricity needs. However, global climate change, the retreat of mountain glaciers, and periodic drought had a heavy toll on reservoir water levels, negatively impacting electricity production. As a result, Gazprom utilized its gas fields in neighboring Uzbekistan to supply the Kyrgyz network, and, by any standards, the reliability of gas distribution in Kyrgyzstan became more efficient. Considering the urgent need for gas and oil, Russian energy companies are indispensable for providing steady energy security for Kyrgyzstan (also Tajikistan), where most energy-related imports originate from Russia.

Turkmenistan is very well-endowed in hydrocarbon resources. The proven gas reserves are amounted to 19.5 trillion cubic meter (tcm). The total production amounted to 83.7 bcm in 2021. Respective Turkmen governments had no choice but use the Russian controlled pipelines. Thanks to the control of export routes out of Turkmenistan, Russia was long able to buy Turkmen gas at a discount, which it could then sell abroad for a substantial profit. Turkmen economy's excessive dependence on gas exports and its continued reliance on Soviet-era infrastructure has been weaponized and effectively used by Russia against Turkmenistan. The Russian decision to stop buying gas in 2016 had a pulverizing effect on the Turkmen economy. Up until 2010, Russia was the main market for Turkmen gas. However, following the opening of the Central Asia-China pipeline, Turkmenistan began exporting gas to China. While the share of Russia gradually declined (from a high of 40 bcm in 2008 to just four bcm in 2015), China's share of Turkmen gas exports grew in a steady way. In 2019, after a three-year hiatus, Turkmenistan resumed gas deliveries to Russia wrapped around 5.5 bcm per year, volumes remaining low compared to previous delivery levels. However, currently, China has superseded Russia as the top export destination for the Turkmen gas supplying 40 bcm of gas every year via the Central Asia-China pipeline that runs from Turkmenistan through Uzbekistan and Kazakhstan (which both also export smaller volumes through the pipeline) to Xinjiang province of China.

Although Turkmenistan has less oil but more natural gas, it still amounted to 600 million barrels of proven oil reserves with almost quarter of a million-bpd oil production in 2019. Mostly, the country transports its oil by tanker to the other side of the Caspian Sea, the Russian port of Makhachkala, Dagestan, and then to the Black Sea port of Novorossiysk. However, it seems that new Turkmen President Serdar Berdimuhamedov may opt to utilize further, as leverage against Russia, shipping the oil to Azerbaijan for export through the BTC pipeline. Both Kazakh and Turkmen governments show a genuine interest in building a trans-Caspian pipeline to connect to the existing BTC pipeline. The primary rationale behind such an attempt is the diversification of energy routes and to decrease the dependency on Chinese and Russian pipelines. However, Russia remains firmly in opposition to such an initiative fearing that it would diminish its energy grip and influence in Central Asia.

Russian and Chinese Entanglements in Central Asia

Eurasian strategic thinking, a la Mackinder, would consider Central Asia a testing ground for geopolitical competition between China and Russia. China's economic dynamism and rising status in the international arena present some perceived threats to Russian interests in its Central Asian backyard, regarded by Russia as its zone of influence. The critical aspect is to know if and how the evolving Eurasian geopolitics due to China's rise as a Eurasian power would affect its relations with Russia. Certainly, China could restrain excessive Russian influence in Central Asia by presenting alternative options to Central Asia, which in turn would also not get much objection from the US in terms of its geopolitical imperatives (Brzezinski, 1998, 2004).

The dynamics of stalwart Sino-Russian interactions work more nuancedly while the shifting of power in Eurasia gradually occurs. Russia and Central Asia are bound together on many different levels. Russia's long-standing cultural relations with Central Asian states, a shared Soviet history, and the use of the Russian language as a lingua franca, along with its significant military presence, still give Russia enduring leverage over China in the region (Pieper, 2022). China's dealings with Central Asian governments have not been based on a comparable level of cultural familiarity.

Until 9/11, the main Chinese engagement in Central Asia was contingent on securing political stability and, most importantly, preventing separatist spillover to Xinjiang province. The humble origins of the 'Shanghai Five' grouping in 1996 created a policy platform where Russia and China could work together to address strategic issues pertaining to Central Asia. Moreover, Russia and China's reciprocal resistance to the long-term American presence in the region after 9/11 also contributed to the creation of common ground between parties to build a strategic relationship. The alignment of Russian and Chinese geopolitical interests in Central Asia created a moment of a Faustian bargain for both countries. However, the changing priorities of the US through the pivot to Asia doctrine took the American component out of the Sino-Russian geopolitical calculations in Central Asia, which in turn opened, at least in principle, the path for potential strategic competition between Moscow and Beijing.

Energy security has been an outmost importance to China after becoming first time oil importer in 1993 (Cheng, 2008; Hu & Chen, 2008; Lanteign, 2007; Lei & Xuejun, 2007; Yi-chong, 2006). In the mid-2000s, China started to develop a more substantial interest in investing in the regional energy exploration and distribution industry, in which

Russia was the dominant force since Soviet times. While China got engaged more intensively in the Central Asian oil and natural gas businesses, it became a direct competitor with Russia as far as control over distribution networks was concerned. Chinese investments in Central Asia have created a new energy infrastructure directly impacting Russia's preponderance in this sector (Kassenova, 2022). As a result, Russia's previously overwhelming economic clout over the region started to vanish. By the time President Xi Jinping initiated the revival of the historical Silk Road through 'One Belt, One Road,' Russian trade volumes had seen a sharp decrease already. It was evident that Russia did not have a competitive economic edge or power to resist Chinese inroads into the region. The five Central Asian republics constituted the natural gateway for China's economic connectivity to the rest of western Eurasia. This gargantuan and ambitious project envisaged linking China with distant corners of Eurasia, ranging from the Indian Ocean to the Mediterranean to the Baltic Sea.

Chapter II

Challenging Perspectives on Security in the Arctic Region

After an initial period of détente following the Cold War, the Arctic Ocean became one of the last frontiers in the global arena where regional powers race to make territorial claims about this intimidating natural environment. As a result, rivalries among the great powers over untapped potential natural resources have become strikingly intense. On the one hand, this competition has reaffirmed itself through the rapid growth of commodity prices in general and energy prices in particular. But, on the other hand, it also required some adjustments in geopolitical considerations involving energy security. In that aspect, the Arctic Region has been of particular interest to the great powers due to its possibly vast energy resources and previously overlooked strategic location.

Generally speaking, the Arctic region is comprised of eight states: Canada, Denmark, Finland, Iceland, Norway, Russia, Sweden, and the United States. In a more restrictive way, of those eight states, only five border the Arctic Ocean: Canada, Denmark through Gronland, Norway through Svalbard, Russia and the United States. Essentially, the Arctic Ocean is the world's smallest and shallowest ocean. It covers an area of approximately 14 million square kilometers (Allain, 2011).

For instance, Antarctica, the fifth-largest continent, managed since 1959 by the Antarctic Treaty. The Southern polar region is designated as a zone exclusively for scientific research without any military activity. However, the Arctic region depicts an entirely different reality. Not only do the eight Arctic states try to maximize their gains in the region, but also other nations without direct access to the Arctic zone, such as China, endeavor to expand their leverage vis-à-vis the future lucrative shipping lanes and become an essential player by increasing their Arctic capabilities (Bennett, 2015; Brady, 2017; Jakobson & Peng, 2012; Sorensen & Klimenko, 2017; Y. Zhang et al., 2016). To this end, in 2013, China became a permanent observer in the Arctic Council, describing itself as a "near-Arctic" nation and designing a new heavy-duty icebreaker, possibly operational by 2025 to navigate through the Arctic Ocean (Buitrago, 2020).

Over the last two decades, there have been considerable interests vis-à-vis the region in western academic circles (Allain, 2011; Anderson, 2009; Byers, 2009; Emmerson, 2010; Gerhardt et al., 2010; Grant, 2010; Gupta, 2009; Howard, 2009; Sale & Potapov, 2010; Wilder, 2010; Young, 2011; Zellen, 2009) or in Russian academia (Bogoyavlenskiy, 2010; Bogoyavlenskiy & Laverov, 2012; Kolodkin & Shinkaretskaya, 2009; Konyshev & Sergunin, 2011; Kozmenko et al., 2012; Mazur, 2010; Pyzh & Kononvich, 2007; Selin & Nikolaeva, 2010; Selin & Tsukertan, 2008; Tamitskiy, 2012; Vasilev et al., 2009). In fact, any sort of analysis on energy can no longer be reduced merely to a discussion of supply and demand in the energy world market but must also focus on global energy security from geopolitical and geo-economic perspectives. In this milieu, major oil, and gas importers such as Europe, China, South Korea, Japan, and India are paying close attention to the developments in the Arctic region. To this end, Russia is making every effort to retain influence over the territory to have uninterrupted access to these strategic resources (Howard, 2009).

Figure 8. *Map of the Artic Region*

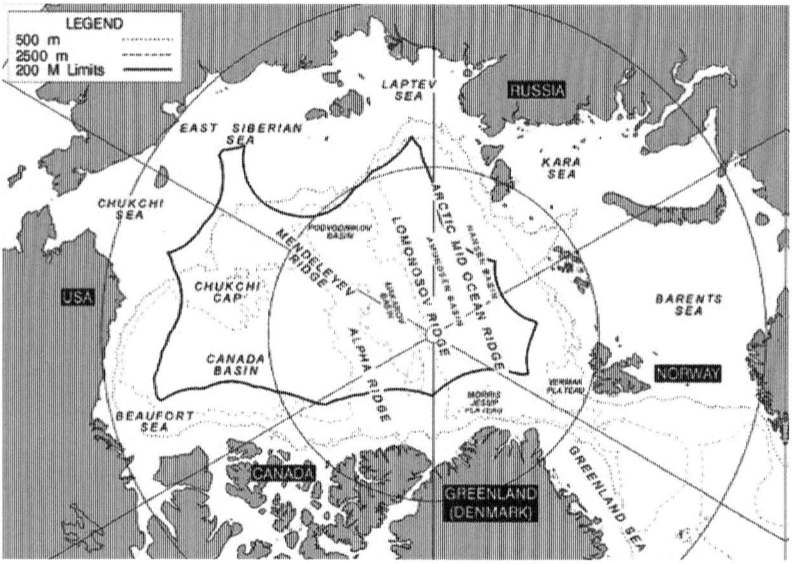

Note. (Weber, 2020)

Moreover, this book takes seriously the idea that the world is under the threat of global warming with the rapid degradation of natural habitats. The current environmental situation affects the world's physical and biological balance, severely impacting the Arctic Ocean, the mountain glaciers, Antarctica. The Arctic is opening up at an astonishing rate and is fast becoming the subject of increasing political and economic interest, not only to the Eight Arctic States, but also to the global community. This interest stems from the need for new sources of oil, natural gas and minerals, faster shipping routes, new fish stocks. (Gerhardt et al., 2010).

It is critical to understand that Arctic Ocean is one of the richest regions in the world in terms of its petroleum, natural gas, coal and several minerals and it has immense geopolitical importance. On the one hand, with the advancement in science and technology particularly over the last decades, it is possible to measure and quantify more accurately the economic potentiality of those resources. On the other hand, the same technological advancements help to assess and determine the rising global temperatures. Because of global warming, glaciers in the Arctic have started to melt, which in turn created an easier access to the natural resources of the region. Consequently, it would be fair to argue that this changing situation made the region more attractive for big powers surrounding it. Russia, with extensive coastline in the Arctic zone increased its strategic operations and started to sign some international economic agreements over the region (Byers, 2009; Dalby, 2003; Emmerson, 2010; Fairhall, 2010; Gerhardt et al., 2010; Grant, 2010).

In accordance with this line of logic, this chapter evaluates the Russia's new role in the Arctic region by the impact of global warming under the frame of other states' claims and international law (Burke, 2020; Byers, 2013; Powell & Dodds, 2014). Consequently, it attempts to analyze the new role of Russia in the Arctic region.

Geopolitics: Scramble for the Arctic

The race to partition this last frontier in the Arctic shows some similarities to the Scramble for Africa from Berlin Conference in 1884 to the WWI by European colonial powers, namely Belgium, the United Kingdom (UK), France, newly unified Germany and Italy, Portugal and Spain (Spohr, 2018). There are currently comparable attempts in the Arctic region to make territorial or maritime claims for energy resources, fish stocks, and the control of emerging shipping lines from Northeast Asia to Western Europe.

In the earlier times of the "Age of Discovery," many maritime explorers, from Willem Barentsz to Semyon Dezhnyov to Vitus Bering, attempted to uncover one of this planet's most remote geographic areas of Arctic Eurasia. Since the late 19th century Arctic expedition days of the Norwegian explorer Fridtjof Nansen, the region gradually gained more prominence. At the pinnacle of the Cold War, the Arctic zone witnessed a rapid militarization initiated as an outcome of superpower competition between the USSR and the USA. The deployment of missiles, radar stations, weapon-testing[31] centers has been instrumental in the development of infrastructure projects. Moreover, Murmansk (the largest city in the Arctic circle) on the Kola Peninsula became a substantial naval base through the deployment of nuclear-powered submarines. Murmansk, along with several bases along the coast of the Kola Peninsula, is home to the Russian Northern Fleet in the European part of the Russian Arctic. From a geopolitical perspective, the Barents

Sea, which connects the White Sea to the Atlantic Ocean, is particularly important to Russia. The Gulf Stream assures that the ports in and around the Kola Peninsula, including Murmansk, are accessible all year round. Unlike the Baltic Sea fleet in St. Petersburg or the Black Sea fleet in Sevastopol or the Pacific fleet in Vladivostok, the Northern Fleet can access the high seas much more freely.

However, climate change and global warming are transforming the facade of the Arctic at an unparalleled speed. Sea ice is receding in most places, permafrost soils are thawing, and the possibility of shipping along the Northern Sea Route, most of the year, has become a widely ordinary reality. Inevitably, there are serious geopolitical fallouts to all that Arctic meltdown at startling pace. Moreover, the prospect of decreasing seasonal ice gives birth to the possibility that once impenetrable; the Arctic Ocean can be used to move not only commercial merchandise but also military forces and equipment from the Pacific to the Atlantic Ocean or the other way around, which is not less revolutionary than the construction of Trans-Siberian railroad at the turn of the Great century in terms of its impact and consequences (Staun, 2020).

For instance, the Arctic is considered the "fourth wall" in Russian geopolitical thinking. Up until recent times, the Russian/Eurasian northern flank was inaccessible to foreign forces; consequently, there was no reason to allocate valuable and limited resources for defensive purposes to the region. However, the rising temperatures and melting sea ice give a different impetus to the evolving Eurasian geopolitics concerning the northern flank (Blunden, 2012; Dodds & Nuttall, 2016; Gresh, 2018; Nuttall et al., 2020; Powell & Dodds, 2014; Tamnes & Offerdal, 2016; Weber, 2020). In the future, there would be geopolitical vulnerability to aggressions from surface and subsurface ships against critical infrastructure.

On the one hand, the ecological balance in the region will change with the thinning of the ice. There will be implications for the global climate too. The waters of the Arctic Ocean will absorb more heat from the sun, thus introducing more energy into the ocean. On the other hand, there are serious geopolitical implications of the Arctic's melting. This will make the Arctic Ocean navigable throughout the year. The sea route linking the North American continent with Europe and Asia will shorten the shipping distance between Europe and Asia by over 4,000 kilometers and will lead to changes in the pattern of global trade and shipping. Maybe more importantly, the countries in the Arctic zone are now engaged in laying sovereignty claims on the new territories as well as the continental shelf of the Arctic Ocean for the possible hidden resources (Gupta, 2009).

The Arctic region also is witnessing a significant change in terms of conflict and cooperation (Borgerson, 2008; Dodds & Nuttall, 2016; Emmerson, 2010; Rowe, 2018; Spohr et al., 2020; Young, 1992; Young & Osherenko, 1993). In the recent past, militarization was in greater demand than cooperation. However, with the Cold War over and the Arctic's return to peace, the international community and international law are demanding greater cooperation and much less militarization.

The current issues facing the Arctic Region have been developed around the concept of sovereignty. There is no doubt that the Arctic States may eventually resolve their disputes in accordance with international law (Allain, 2011; Rowe, 2018).

The difference between these Arctic States is the degree to which they are cooperating and militarizing, thus making the future of the New Arctic uncertain and fragmented, to say the least. If the New Arctic is indeed based on cooperation, Arctic States must enter into it with a common goal and a common understanding of how real cooperation is to be achieved. Russia's approach in the Arctic has been to create a win-win situation, that is, "gain early military and commercial regional supremacy and hope to win equally at the United Nations and other multilateral tables. Uncertainty remains as to how Russia will attempt to maintain this win-win strategy as the other Arctic States are now approaching the Arctic differently. Canada, Denmark, and the United States, in varying degrees, have placed more emphasis on cooperation and bilateral governance structures. They are nevertheless feeling the pressure of Russia's militarization and ever increasing commercial capabilities (Allain, 2011).

The emerging change in Arctic politics has led many Arctic experts to question Russia's role in the New Arctic. Currently, the Arctic States are preoccupied with their respective Arctic possessions and focus on how to secure those possessions. As a result, Arctic States are unfamiliar to a pan-Arctic view of the region to shape the conditions in which sovereignty is exercised.

Russia is currently increasing its military activity in the Arctic by developing its fleet of ice breakers and its naval force, thus making its military the Arctic's strongest. Its impressive military build-up suggests that Russia has the potential to be a very unpredictable and aggressive player in the Arctic. On the other hand, since the summer of 2007, the Russian Duma has repeatedly reassured the international community of its good intentions in the Arctic region and its respect of its obligations under the Convention and the rules of international law. Russia participated in the Arctic Council and respected its obligations under the Ilulissat Declaration[32]. Russia and other Arctic States are all in process of increasing their military presence and developing their infrastructure for the anticipated increase in population that will be associated with the increased exploration and exploitation of the Arctic's natural resources (Allain, 2011).

Global Energy Security and Eurasian Arctic

World population is projected to increase by some 2 billion people from its current level of 8 billion by the middle of the 21st century. Almost all of that increase will originate from developing countries. Consequently, energy demand will grow even faster. It is important to acknowledge that modern economies are vitally dependent on reliable and affordable energy supplies. Taking in consideration the fact that approximately 2 billion people currently do not have access to electricity in daily living, the developing world is not likely to accept restrictions on either the form or the quantity of energy it uses before reaching some adequate standard of living matching other developed countries. In basic terms, this means that the international demand for reliable energy supplies will increase over the foreseeable future. Along this line of logic, global energy consumption is expected to jump 53% by 2035, largely driven by strong demand from places like India, China and Indonesia.

On the one hand, energy resources are a source of potential international cooperation. The shared interest of energy producers and consumers in energy trade can be the source for harmonious relations among states. International cooperation is needed to bring resources from remote reserves to consumer centers. To this end, energy development projects can be structured in a way that all the participants benefit (Moran & Russell, 2009; Ross, 2004; Russett, 1979; Stulberg, 2007; Victor & Victor, 2003; Winchester; Winrow, 2007; Yergin, 1988).

On the other hand, energy can be a source of potential conflict among states. Energy resources are regarded as a source of zero-sum or mixed-sum competition because the amount of hydrocarbons in the world is limited. (Billon, 2005; Broache, 2010; Chun, 2008; Ebel, 2009). To a great extent, politics determines economics and reflects the concern for war. The view that force and the threat to use force are salient features of the international system means that states must prepare for the possibility of conflict. Heavy reliance on foreign suppliers for strategic resources such as oil, natural gas and coal can be a threat to national security. Consequently, in a situation of crisis or war, access to those vital resources can be denied. Given the importance of energy to a state's ability to wage war, supply disruptions could put at risk national security and independence.

Environmental Changes and the Arctic Region

Global warming is the 21st century's phenomenon with serious effects on the world. Recently observed changes in the Arctic region and sea ice cover may be an indication of global climate changes. The region is going through some serious climatic changes and it is very straightforward to observe that most of the Arctic ice cap melting took place over the last decade.

Transportation through the Arctic seems enticing by its own. A sea journey from Western Europe to China requires a road through the Suez Canal and it takes 15 days. However, along the Siberian Coast—free of ice during summer time—ships can do this journey in 10 days; it is an important saving in terms of time, fuel and carbon emissions.

Global warming increased the importance of geopolitics in the Arctic region. Natural resources are the main rationale behind this pivotal geopolitical importance of the region. As a result of this global warming phenomenon, a sort of power struggle is taking place among the bordering states of the Arctic—Russia, USA, Canada, Norway and Denmark. Without thick ice cover, the region's rich oil, gas, mineral deposits and shipping lanes begin to exploitation.

Opening up the Arctic to development—shipping or natural resources—will undoubtedly bring benefits, however, unfortunately ecological damage, too. At this point, a recent report by the Finish government warned the states for combating oil spills in case of an accident. Even with the use of current high technology, it would be impossible to deal with such environmental catastrophe in icy waters. The Arctic is probably the most environmentally sensitive region on the planet, yet few treaties exist to protect it. (Keskitalo, 2007; Rosamond, 2011; Sale & Potapov, 2010; Sawhill, 2000; Titley, 2010; Wilder, 2010; Young, 2011; Zellen, 2009).

It is argued that Russia has operated in the Arctic since 1960s, however, with the impact of global warming and technological advancement, it is much easier to operate and exploit the region's valuable resources. Russia had the world's longest Arctic border which is more than 10.000 miles. In fact, Russia has some islands in the Arctic Ocean; the country's northern border effectively ends where the Arctic Ocean begins. Yet, the Russian government makes the argument that its territorial perimeter should spread to the northward. The government claims that there is a mountain range—Lomonosov Ridge—which goes to the North Pole. This is shown as a proof by Russian government in order to make claims to a much bigger piece of the Arctic region. To this end, Russia has sent teams of scientists to the Arctic Ocean in order to collect evidence for their claim.

Russia's Arctic Policy

There is a growing interest in the Arctic on the part of the Russian government. Indeed, Russia is the most determined and assertive player in the Arctic. In May 2007, Vladimir Putin, then President of Russia, proposed the creation of the National Arctic Council, which would be charged with the role of coordinating Russian national policy and strengthening Russian interests in the Arctic. The country obtains a big chunk of its gas, oil, nickel, cobalt, copper and platinum from her Arctic regions. Needless to say that Russia's wealth in natural resources is at the center of its new Arctic policy and development strategy. Indeed, from Moscow's perspective, Russia's wealth of energy reserves strengthens its position and influence on the international stage and thus forms the foundation of Russia's security strategy in the Arctic (Honneland, 2020; Lagutina, 2021; Laruelle, 2014).

In 2001, Russia formally presented to the UN Commission for Limits of the Continental Shelf (UNCLCS) its claim to the approximately 1.19 million square km of the maritime region of the Arctic. Its reasoning was that the 2,000-kilometer long Lomonosov Ridge, an underwater mountain range in the Arctic, is connected to Russia's Siberian continental shelf and hence, under the UN Convention on the Law of the Sea (UNCLOS) rules, belongs to Russia. The Russian claim was rejected. Undeterred, a Russian expedition planted a Russian flag, made of titanium, on the ocean floor under the North Pole in 2007, to buttress its claim. The Russian move was considered highly provocative and was strongly criticized by other countries that in turn intensified their own efforts in claiming the Arctic Ocean (Gupta, 2009).

In September 2008, the Russian Security Council considered an ambitious plan for the development of its Northern regions adjoining the Arctic shoreline. Its strategic bombers have started flying over the North Pole. Russia's renewed interest in the Arctic coincides with its assertive foreign policy and worsening relations with the West. The Russian President has declared that Russia would like to convert the Arctic region as a resource base for Russia in the twenty-first century (Gupta, 2009).

In September of 2008, the Russian Security Council also approved a new policy on the Arctic. This new policy, entitled *Fundamentals of the State Policy of Russia in the Arctic in the Period until 2020 and Beyond*, and signed by Russia's President, Dmitry Medvedev, created a significant amount of discussion as it set out an ambitious plan to develop an economic and military infrastructure in the Arctic. It offers a good overview of the policy and states that its main goal is to ensure that provisions of the country's national security strategy are fully realized throughout Russia's Arctic zone. It is important to note that the Russian policy focuses not only on increasing its military presence in the Arctic, but also on developing and preparing the Arctic Region for exploiting its resources[33].

Russian capabilities for research in the Arctic are much stronger than the other Arctic states.[34] Moreover, Russian private companies are well equipped to function in the Arctic as well. Indeed, some major

Russian mining companies maintains complete independence from Russian military nuclear-powered icebreakers thanks to their brand new Arctic vessels.

Therefore, it would be fair to assert that Russia is the world's leading oil and natural gas producer. However, it needs to find and develop new fields in order to keep that leading position in global energy markets. The Arctic region seems to be a natural and expected match for those Russian policy goals.

Chapter III

Connecting Eurasia and the Americas

Geopolitical confrontation over raw materials has become distinctiveness since the early stages of colonialism which in brief terms was the practice of controlling another area and exploiting its people and resources. The access to wealth, markets, and raw materials, along with national prestige, has been the main inspiration and rationale behind those endeavors. Although the classical definition of colonialism disappeared gradually after WW II, and colonialism is generally considered to be a relic of the past (with still a few exceptions[35] remaining), the 21st century still witnesses a similar stiff rivalry. This competition has reaffirmed itself in the rapid growth of commodity prices and some adjustments in geopolitical considerations. For the most part, Russia has been benefiting from this situation due to its abundant natural resources on its vast territory.

The rich history of Russian political and economic relations gives ample of leadership examples. The avant-garde pushes the boundaries of what is accepted as the norm or the status quo in various issue areas. That Russian peculiarity creates many opportunities to determine Russia's place in the world. This history, in many respects, provides also commanding clues vis-à-vis Russia's current position in the global political economy. First and foremost, the Bering Strait[36] crossing project, although it seems for many as a misapprehension, reflects that Russian avant-garde drive and spirit.

The Bering Strait rail system by letting free those vast natural resources trapped underneath the tundra and permafrost would facilitate the development of those resources in question and their rapid transportation to the global markets can contribute to overall development of those regions. There is no doubt that those rail connections in the Russian Far East[37] (RFE) would also generate development corridors within which new urban centers would flourish, and existing ones would gain further dynamism—having an impact similar to the construction of Trans-Siberian Railroad[38] in the early 20th century.

Right now, most of the Siberian population is concentrated around Trans-Siberian railroad, and the RFE is practically empty. As new cities erupt or the existing ones enlarge, they will magnify the erection of brand-new manufacturing businesses/assembly lines, and necessitate the construction of school systems, electricity grids, water systems, health/hospital systems; this will indubitably entail an expansion of the labor force and overall population, which in turn would increase the population density in those thinly populated areas. Equally, it would be fair to assume that, on a geopolitical level, the movement of goods between Eurasia and the Americas, at previously unheard-of speeds, would revolutionize global productive connections (Deniston, 2013; Douglas, 2007; Nikishenkov, 2011; Panin, 2013).

The Northeast Asia is also home to four biggest economies in the world—namely, Japan, Korea, China, and Russia. The member countries of this strategic quadrangle, all together, represent slightly more than one-fourth of the Global Domestic product (GDP)[39]. Moreover, if we include in that picture the United States and Canada, then that figure would reach a level more than the half of the global GDP. Consequently, the Bering Strait crossing would connect all those economies in a very efficient way.

The main questions in this chapter are centered on the contemporary characteristics of the Northeast Asia; thus, inherently exploratory and attempt to understand the possible impact(s) of connecting Eurasia and the Americas by investigating through a geopolitical prism. Hence, the chapter is to contribute to a better perception of what/how different factors constrain/shape the future trajectories in the Northeast Asian strategic quadrangle. In that aspect, among others, the RFE plays a centripetal role to instigate the cooperation in the region.

Table 1. Northeast Asia GDP in PPP

Current Rank Asia	Current Rank World	Country	2021 GDP (PPP)
1	1	China	26.5 trillion USD
2	4	Japan	5.5 trillion USD
3	6	Russia	4.3 trillion USD
4	14	South Korea	2.4 trillion USD
5	19	Taiwan	1.4 trillion USD
6	124	Mongolia	0.42 trillion USD
7	160	North Korea	0.12 trillion USD

Note. Author's own calculations based on primary data

To this end, this chapter will delve into the RFE after providing a comprehensive overview of the relevant literature on geopolitics and regionalism. The subsequent sections will highlight the rationale behind connecting Eurasia and the Americas by focusing not only on the significance of natural resources of the region for the global economic development but also the importance of economic growth for this sparsely populated part of the Russian Federation. The remaining sections will address the relationships taking place in the Northeast Asian strategic quadrangle between Russia and Japan/China/Korea by bringing attention to the significant benefits for all parties through connecting Eurasia and the Americas through the Bering Strait.

Although the Russian Far East/Siberia and Bering Strait crossing may seem inconsequential as the periphery at the edge of Eurasia, the intensification of the globalization, the revolutionary transformations in telecommunications/transportations technologies, the global climate change, and global demographic trends indicate otherwise. Northern Sea Route[40] (NSR) and the Bering Strait witness significant geopolitical changes. For instance, it is possible to observe attempts to militarize the region.

Russia is currently increasing its military activity in the Arctic by developing its fleet of ice breakers and its naval force, thus making its military the Arctic's strongest. Russia's seven newest icebreakers have multi-mission capabilities and are fueled by nuclear reactors capable of breaking through ice twice as thick as its diesel competitors. Russia has 18 icebreakers in its military fleet, including the largest and most powerful icebreaker in the world (Woody, 2020). On the other hand, the Bering Strait crossing and accompanied infrastructure projects by creating a mutually propitious milieu would be instrumental in establishing that cooperative behavior for all nation-states involved.

The Russian Far East in Historical Context

For centuries, the territories of the Russian empire located to the east of the Ural Mountains were considered as places of promise and natural resource wealth (Kangas, 2007). Over the last three centuries, imperial Russia expanded both northward and southward across Siberia. After the Treaty of Peking was signed in 1689, Russia directed its energy toward the Sea of Okhotsk, Kamchatka, Chukotka, the Kuril Islands, and Alaska. Russia entered the Amur region in the mid-nineteenth century. In 1856 and 1857, Russia seized Chinese territory north of the Amur River. In 1860, all land east of the Ussuri River was ceded to Russia, thus extending the Russian empire from the Baltic to the Pacific (Troyakova, 2007).

After the disastrous Crimean War of 1854–56, Russia's priorities shifted away from the Northeast Pacific. Alaska was sold to the United States in 1867. The central and northern Kurils were handed over to Japan in exchange for Sakhalin in 1875. Soon a combination of external and internal developments forced the Russian government to upgrade the Far East to accommodate imperial priorities. In 1884, the Transbaikal, Amur, Primorye, and Sakhalin districts were merged to create the new Priamurskii governorship. This new territorial entity established an institutional framework for the regional identity of the Far East (Troyakova, 2007).

As the Trans-Siberian Railroad extended steadily eastward, it brought European and Asian Russia together. Not only ethnic Russians but also other imperial subjects such as Ukrainians and Tatars moved to the Far East, where they discovered Chinese, Koreans, and Japanese populace residing within the Priamurskii governorship. This unusual ethnic mix of its times shaped regional development and added a cosmopolitan shade to Russian life.

Figure 9. Russian Empire circa 1914

Note. (Znamenski, 2007)

From the end of the nineteenth century through the years leading up to World War I, the region played an important economic role in East Asia. It attracted loans and investments that supported its industrialization process. Although the economic interaction between the region and the rest of Russia was limited, the Far East was the gateway for Moscow to initiate relations with Asian countries. Labor resources were satisfied by migration not only from the European part of Russia but also from China, Korea, and Japan. In general, the region was seen as a place for agriculture, political exile, and military base for the Russian Pacific Fleet at Vladivostok (Bliakher & Vasil'Eva, 2010).

During the early Soviet period, the region, now known as the Far Eastern Republic, developed as a relatively autonomous economic area. However, in the 1930s, Moscow adopted a model of centralized state control and support. The Soviet system imposed a centrally planned economy, limiting the region's economic ties with the outside world. The central government provided substantial economic support because of the geostrategic significance of the region, but it paid little attention to the long-term economic viability of the Far Eastern economy. Moscow stressed the development of mining and defense industries, eventually turning the region into a fortress (Kuhrt, 2012).

During the apex of the Cold War years, the massive Soviet arms buildup in the Far East and the Northeast Asia was a constant source of considerable concern for all neighboring countries—China, Japan, and South Korea. By the early 1960s, as a result of the deteriorating relations, the Sino-Soviet border was closed. Mao Zedong[41], the ultimate leader of China, openly spoke of his countries' legitimate claim to the southern part of the Russian Far East[42] which is referred sometimes as outer Manchuria. Seemingly, this hostile environment was not conducive to economic contacts.

Moscow later eased its grip and the Far East became one of the few regions in the Soviet Union where the central authorities encouraged an export-based development strategy. In the 1970s and 1980s the region was supposed to benefit from expanded trade with Asian countries, particularly through a number of compensation agreements between the Soviet Union and Japan. The region's natural resources were offered in order to finance purchases of machinery and equipment for further resource development. As a result of these agreements, several projects were implemented, including the Vostochnyi port near Nakhodka, and the South Yakutia coal complex. Initial work to develop the oil and gas deposits offshore of Sakhalin Island also began. The region also has considerable reserves of iron, lead, zinc, silver, gold, lumber, farmland, and fish (Sullivan & Renz, 2010; Zausaev, 2012).

By the mid-1980s the Far East began to reorient from a military outpost to an economic player. The successful development of China's growing economy improved the chances for greater trade and joint projects between the two countries. Indeed, over the past twenty years, Russia and China have sought new points of agreement for broader and more institutionalized cooperation.

During the last years of the USSR, in 1986 and again in 1988, the Soviet leader Mikhail Gorbachev called for the integration of the Soviet Union into the Asia-Pacific region. He stressed that the Cold War era was coming to an end and the Soviet government would like to open the Far East by adopting a more diversified economic profile for the region.

Up to recent times, Russia did not develop strategy and implement large-scale economic programs for the development of port facilities in the waters of the Chukchi Sea, Bering Sea, the Sea of Okhotsk, and the East Sea. After the tormented first decades following the collapse of the USSR, the REF became one of the most strategically important regions of Russia, and its development carries national and global significance. The further development of the manufacturing capacity of the region would determine Russia's role in a significant economic zone of the world, namely the Asia-Pacific region. The degree to which the transportation, telecommunications, and social infrastructure of the RFE are developed will strategically predetermine the export potential of the country (Rozman et al., 2006).

Significance of Natural Resources for Global Economic Development

It is central to emphasize the relevance of natural resources regarding the Bering Strait crossing project. Natural resources, certainly, are a source of potential international cooperation. The shared interest of producers and consumers in commodity trade can be the source of harmonious relations among states. International cooperation is needed to bring those resources from remote reserves to consumer centers. To this end, development projects such as the Bering Strait crossing can be structured in such a way that all the participants would benefit from them (Moran & Russell, 2009; Ross, 2004; Russett, 1979; Stulberg, 2007; Victor & Victor, 2003; Winchester; Winrow, 2007; Yergin, 2006).

On the other hand, a competition for natural resources—necessary for any economic development—can also be a source of potential conflict between states. For instance, energy resources are regarded as a source of zero-sum or mixed-sum competition because the amount of hydrocarbons in the world is limited (Chun, 2008; Ebel, 2009). To a great extent, politics determines economics and reflects the concern for war. The view that force and the threat to use force are the salient features of the international system means that states must prepare for future conflicts. Heavy reliance on foreign suppliers for strategic resources, such as oil, natural gas, and coal, can be a threat to national security. Consequently, in a situation of a crisis or a war, access to those vital resources can be denied. Given the importance of energy to a state's ability to wage war, disruptions in supply could put national security and independence at risk.

In that aspect, the Siberia and Russian Arctic Region have been of particular interest to the great powers due to its possibly vast natural resources and strategic location. In fact, any analysis of energy issues can no longer be reduced merely to a discussion of supply and demand in the world market, but must also focus on global energy security, from geopolitical and geoeconomic perspectives (Vahn, 2017). In this strategic milieu, major oil and gas consumers such as the United States, European Union, China, Japan, South Korea, and India are paying close attention to the developments in that particular region. To this end, Russia is making every effort to retain influence over its strategic resources (Howard, 2009).

It is critical to understand that Siberia (Akaha, 1997; Davis, 2003; Forsyth, 1992; Gentes, 2008; Groisman & Gutman, 2013; Hill & Gaddy, 2003; Hudgins, 2003; Jordan & Jordan-Bychkov; Naumov, 2006; Wood, 2011) and Russian Arctic are one of the richest regions in the world in terms of its petroleum, natural gas, coal and mineral resources. It also has immense geopolitical importance.

Challenges and Opportunities of the Bering Strait Crossing for the RFE

Since the beginning of the 20th century, Russia and the United States have been holding talks on probable collaboration on this issue and gave some important indications of joint efforts to construct a railway tunnel under the Bering Strait to link Siberia with Alaska. During the Asia-Pacific Economic Cooperation (APEC) Forum in 2012 at Russian Pacific port city of Vladivostok, Russian Railways President asserted the fact that the project to extend a railway line to Kamchatka and then to build a tunnel across the Bering Strait could be actualized in not a very distant future. (Douglas, 2007) The technical and financial aspects of the project are not that much related to the tunnel itself (somewhere around 100 kilometers), but in building links to the tunnel from existing rail lines in Russia, the United States and Canada. On the one hand, from the Russian perspective, the Bering tunnel is meant to connect to the Trans-Siberian and Baikal-Amur Mainline subsequently—*Baikalo-Amurskaya magistral*—and would require about 4,000 kilometers of rail lines to be built from Yakutsk (Sakha Republic/Yakutia). On the other hand, in the United States and Canada, approximately 2,000 kilometers of track would need to be made ready from the tunnel's landing point to the existing rail connection in Canada. It's hard to come up with exact figures on the total cost of the project. However, estimates range from $35 billion to as much as $100 billion (Panin, 2013).

Moreover, Russia plans to build also a railroad that links Eurasia with Sakhalin Island—extremely well endowed regarding natural gas fields—and eventually reaching Japan's northern island of Hokkaido. The Ministry for Development of Russian Far East said that construction would start in 2017 on the 580-kilometer railroad that will connect the Khabarovsk region and Sakhalin Island. A bridge is envisioned over the narrowest part of the Tartary Strait[43]. The total cost of the project is estimated to be at around $10 billion (Nishimura, 2013).

In recent years, the RFE has also been a point of interest in academic circles (Alexeeva, 2008; Arsenov et al., 2005; Barkovsky, 2006; Blank, 2011; Bliakher & Vasil'Eva, 2010; Kangas, 2007; Kuhrt, 2012; Nemchaninova & Buldygerova, 2012; Rozman, 2008; Sullivan & Renz, 2010; Troyakova, 2007; Vishinevskii & Demyanenko, 2010; Zausaev, 2012). It is considered as a region in crisis due to troubled economic conditions, corrupt governance, and problem-ridden cross-border relations with China, Japan, and both Koreas (Rozman, 2008). Due to some fears that the Russian Far East might disengage itself from the center and other regional/global powers may end up having a major grip in the region, Moscow started to show some genuine interest in those eastern border provinces (Kangas, 2007).

The region in question covers a broad geographical area from Siberia to Russia's Pacific coast, forming the northeastern corner of

Asia. Although the Far East constitutes one-third of Russia's total landmass, it has only 6.6 million residents—4.7 percent of the total population. The low population density, just over one person per square kilometer, makes the region one of the most sparsely populated places in the world. The scarcity of residents exists alongside a wealth of natural resources that have attracted the interest of the Russian central government as well as foreign investors. The current situation is deemed so critical that President Putin approved a law offering land plots of 2.5 acres to any Russian citizen willing to migrate to the RFE with the aim of boosting the economy in the region. Furthermore, the foreign entrepreneurs investing $10 million or more in the economy of the RFE could receive Russian citizenship without going through required five-year legal legal stay on Russian territory (Kovalev, 2017). Evidently, Russian politicians, bureaucrats/technocrats are all concerned about the level of socioeconomic development in that region (Troyakova, 2007).

However, it would be fair to assert that the developmental troubles of the RFE partly related to the region's history and location. The USSR did also neglect socio-economically the region until its collapse in 1991. After the disintegration of the Union, the RFE, like many other regions, was to a great extent abandoned by the financially struggling central government in Moscow. The extended negligence towards the region has left the RFE provinces economically vulnerable, demographically challenged, and geographically isolated. The Russian government has recently begun to focus unequivocally on rejuvenating the RFE. The decades-long dynamic economic growth and surging global trade in neighboring China have drawn the international community's attention to the potentiality of further developments in the Pacific region. The geopolitical center-of-gravity moving to the East through the transformation of the global political and economic state of affairs gave birth to a reassessment of Moscow's policy in the RFE. Notably, given the region's exorbitant amount of natural resources and its strategic location, Russia initiated an overhauling process of its policy guidelines vis-à-vis the region (Alexeeva, 2008; Blank, 2011).

Russian leadership considers the development of transportation infrastructure as a fundamental element for uplifting those large underdeveloped regions of Siberia and the RFE. According to some experts the planned road, rail, and pipeline system would handle 3% of total global trade. Moreover, it will make possible to connect more of eastern Russia's hydroelectric potentiality—Russian leadership envisions a 4,000-km rail line from the Lena River to the Bering Strait, as a high-priority task and very consequential in terms of economic development. The Lena is the easternmost of Siberia's three great river systems—others being Yenisei and Ob Rivers—and is the tenth longest river in the world. Consequently, it will allow development of previously inaccessible mineral resource deposits. The connection of the power systems of Siberia, the RFE, and North America would generate significant economies in electricity supply (Douglas, 2007).

There is no doubt that a spectacular economic growth is taking place in Asia and the world's economic center swings towards the Pacific region. The prevalence of transatlantic trade is losing momentum to the benefit of transpacific trade. Industrial regions of China, South

Korea, and Japan can be linked up to Russian railroad system with the ultimate goal of connecting them to the manufacturing centers of the Midwestern United States and the critical Pacific ports in California, Washington State and British Columbia. The Bering Strait crossing can be an essential raison d'être to trigger such project. Consequently, it is possible to observe a significant geopolitical shift towards the Pacific region. Due to global warming, the melting of Arctic ice is opening up northern shipping routes and the Arctic development is increasingly becoming an area of significance with major untapped resource deposits. The extensive resources available in the Arctic can be developed, and raw/semi-processed/processed goods can be rapidly delivered to the industrial centers in question at each end of Asia and North America, radiating the effects of a higher level of productivity throughout the global economy (Deniston, 2013).

Strategic Quadrangle in Northeast Asia: Russia, China, Japan and Korea

Northeast Asia is home not only to two members of United Nations Security Council (UNSC)—China and Russia—but also three countries with nuclear weapon capabilities—Russia, China, and North Korea—and the world's two largest economies—Japan and China. All those aspects converge around the unstable pivot of the Korean peninsula. Probably, it ranks today among the most dangerous areas of the planet, tormented by security problems of nuclear and missile proliferation (Rozman et al., 2008). However, despite all those unfavorable facets, the Bering Strait crossing can present an opportunity to strengthen the evolution of social, economic, and political ties among Japan, Russia, China and both Koreas. Currently, Northeast Asia, regarding the political uncertainties, along the Middle East holds a dangerous potential to transform the global outlook. However, an economic interdependence facilitated by transport corridors of the Bering Strait crossing would be a significant catalyst in that direction.

The Third Eastern Economic Forum that was held in Vladivostok in September 2017 affirmed again the efforts of Moscow to attract the much-needed foreign investment and expand international cooperation for the economic development of the RFE. Those resolutions are good indications showing the vulnerabilities of the RFE such as the process of depopulation since the collapse of the Soviet Union. The primary rationale behind those Eastern Economic Forums in Vladivostok since 2015 is to make the foreign investment/economic collaboration attractive and beneficial to all parties in Northeast Asia. President Putin highlighted, at numerous occasions, the country's Far East region should become an absolute priority for the entire 21st century. Some radical reformists even argued about the so-called "Doctrine of De-Moscovication" of the Russian Federation by shifting the political and economic center of gravity from European Russia to the East of the Ural Mountains (Velanskaya, 2017).

Russo-Japanese Relations

Two new extensions of the iconic Trans-Siberian railroad network are good indications showing the Russian strategic thinking for the region. The first bridge would connect Vladivostok with Sakhalin Island through the Tartary Strait while another bridge would connect the southern tip of Sakhalin with Japan's north most island of Hokkaido. Consequently, Japan, for the first time in its history, would be joined directly and uninterrupted way with the Eurasian continent.

The Third Eastern Economic forum in Vladivostok was again instrumental in drafting the Muscovite plans of this direct rail connection to strengthen relations between the two countries. Historically speaking, the proposed bridge and tunnel would be as revolutionary as the Channel Tunnel joining Britain with the rest of Europe. There is no doubt that the materialization of this project will be a breakthrough in global politics. The envisaged rail connection would boost Japan's trade with Eurasia and the Americas by lowering the transportation cost/time and increasing the dependability. That would give the much-needed stimulus to an already stagnant Japanese economy.

The strategy of Russia's Japan diplomacy aims to create an atmosphere of mutual trust and long-desired stability in bilateral relations—like Moscow's initiatives vis-à-vis the Korean Peninsula—with the hope that there would be some spillover impact and positive ramifications in other issue areas. To this end, during President Putin's 2016 visit to Japan, the leaders declared a joint initiative on economic ventures in the South Kuril Islands and still being truthful to their respective positions regarding the Northern Territories. That was a win-win situation for both sides. For Japan, it was a step towards securing an economic presence in the region to further its territorial claims over the islands. For Russia, it is a great convenience to attract much-needed foreign investment to this undeveloped corner of the RFE.

Consequently, the long-disputed Kuril Islands issue between Russia and Japan may finally come to a halt, and the process of diplomatic normalization process can be initiated through the signing a comprehensive peace treaty.

Russo-Chinese Relations

Historically speaking, Sino-Russian relations probably are going through their golden years since the end of the Cold War. Both countries are working closely in a number regional or international organizations such as Shanghai Cooperation Organization (SCO) and BRIC[44] or Chinese initiated projects such as One Belt-One Road[45] (OBOR). This last project involves the Silk Road Economic Belt (SREB) project, covering land routes and the Maritime Silk Road (MSR) Project, covering sea routes (Toksoz, 2017). On many levels, those are manifestations of China's rapid rise to global power status and unquestionably, changed the parameters of the strategic chess game in global politics. Consequently, its relationship with Russia is also frequently renegotiated because Russia is an important neighbor and a crucial natural resource base in a time of ever-growing Chinese energy hunger. Overall, it would be fair to describe the flourishing Sino-Russian relations as a game changer in international relations.

However, Chinese investment and China's growing presence in the RFE is viewed with suspicion by some Russian policymakers and administrators or simply locals. The arrival of Chinese migrants through Chinese investment is often perceived by locals as an expression of China's de facto territorial expansion. Russian public sensitivity over the issue originates from the ever-expanding Chinese economic and demographic realities (Zeihan, 2017).

Russia is almost twice the size of China regarding the territory, but China's population is about ten times that of Russia. Remarkably, as mentioned earlier in the article, the population of the RFE, comprising seven provinces, is only a little more than 6 million—an average density of less than one person per square km. Furthermore, the region is going through a depopulation process with low birth rates and migration to the other areas of the country deemed having better living and working conditions. Since the establishment of the Russian Federation in 1991, the RFE has lost almost a quarter of its population (Tselichtchev, 2017). That depopulation trend is notably affecting the agricultural sector. For instance, China and Russia have a long border of over 3000 km mostly along the RFE. The southernmost areas bordering China contain the majority of the RFE's arable land, and one-fifth is already owned or leased by Chinese entrepreneurs to produce vegetables, grains, and livestock.

Economic interests for both sides are complementary, not contradictory. The RFE needs Chinese labor resources, investment, and technologies. On the other hand, China needs the RFE's land and natural resources. In 2014, Russian government enacted a bill establishing the Territories of Accelerated Development (TAD) law for the RFE creating special economic zones providing significant tax and other benefits to attract the foreign investors. However, Russia's desirability as an employment destination is fading away fast because the earnings in China are catching up very fast with Russian level.

Russo-Korean Relations

After the establishment of the Korea Arctic Scientific Committee in 2011, Korea opened its first research station in Svalbard-Northernmost island of Norway in the Arctic Ocean. In 2009, for the first time, Korea used the NSR by sending two cargo ships from Ulsan and to Rotterdam via the Bering Strait. Throughout the last decade, there was an increased awareness about the Arctic region among the Korean public. In October 2013, The Korean shipping liner, Hyundai Glovis completed Korea's first cargo transportation through the NSR after a 35-day navigation (Tonami, 2016).

South Korea enjoys a unique, stable and mutually beneficial relationship with one of the most critical Arctic coastal states, namely

Russia. Unlike the remaining Northeastern countries, there are no unsolved issues between those two countries. The relationships between Russia and South Korea are dependent on strategic triangular relations between South Korea, Russia, and North Korea. Russia borders North Korea just south of Vladivostok, and from the USSR times did provide full support as a staunch ally of North Korea.

Although South Korea and Russia virtually had no contact for four decades after the end of the Korean War, the 1980s saw a change in not just in Soviet behavior vis-à-vis South Korea but also South Korean behavior regarding the USSR. The rationale behind that strategic move from the Soviet point of view, it was very challenging to ignore the rising economic power of South Korea. On the other hand, from increasingly prosperous South Korea Korean point of view, the communism was not anymore something to be feared. After the normalization of the relations in the 1990s, Russia considers South Korea as an influential player in the Northeast Asia and a key partner for its economic revitalization policies in the RFE. On the other hand, Russia views North Korea as a decisive factor in its diplomatic and geopolitical renaissance (Tonami, 2016).

Most recently, the Russo-South Korean relations look very promising after South Korean President's speech at the Third Eastern Economic Forum in September 2017 highlighting the desire to expand financial, economic and trade links in Northeast Asia. The South Korea's new northern policy was constructed around the strategy of "nine bridges" in the region, to open the era of the Pacific Ring. The approach involves projects ranging from the natural gas pipelines to railroads to the Northern Sea Route. Evidently, President Moon's principal concern revolves around the current insecurity on the Korean peninsula. South Korean authorities' attempts to create better ties with Russia are related to finding possible new diplomatic overtures to resolve the North Korean nuclear crisis. Moon Presidency by promoting trilateral projects involving both Koreas and Russia is aiming to connect the Korean Peninsula and the Russian Far East, and subsequently bringing the peninsula to a peaceful cohabitation.

At the same venue, along with the same line of logic, President Putin also indicated Russian enthusiasm to put together infrastructure projects with the participation of North Korea would facilitate the delivery of Russian energy resources to both Koreas. The integration of the power lines and railroad networks by connecting Russia, South Korea, and North Korea would also create an uninterrupted transport corridor from Pusan to London. Most importantly maybe, those initiatives would form a great platform to build up the much-needed atmosphere of mutual trust and stability on the Korean Peninsula. In crude terms, we can call those attempts as the revival of the Sunshine Policy.

Consolidating the Korean Peninsula with the RFE would open a direct connection not only with Russia but also with the members of Eurasian Economic Union[46] (EAEU). The Russian grand strategy to create Russia-Korean economic corridor would require inherently the interaction all three countries, which in turn would be the preferable approach to the alternative proposals presented by the Americans—economic sanctions or military solutions. It seems that carrot-and-stick model is more suitable than tit-for-tat as a foreign policy orientation. The anticipation of material gain may push North Korea into a position of de-escalation regarding the nuclear issues.

The recent developments vis-à-vis the REF in particular have a great potential to create a window of opportunity for further improvements of bilateral relations in the region. The construction of a major transport route by including infrastructure projects such as high-speed electric trains, a highway, power lines, oil and gas pipelines, and fiber optics would most certainly create an environment of trust and stability. Opposing arguments, mainly from some economists, indicate serious concerns and doubts about the economic feasibility of the project. It would be important to remember that at the Turn of the Century, on a macroeconomic level, some economists/experts claimed that the Trans-Siberian Railroad—built between 1891and 1916—would also not pay for itself, but it did so in only six years. More importantly, this visionary project, politically and militarily made the Tsarist Russia a powerful player in any Eurasian geostrategic calculations. Equally, the current project would also take some years to complete but would pay for itself considerably fast. It could contribute tremendously to Russian political/economic power in Eurasia.

Moreover, the Bering Strait crossing has a wider significance for global politics, security, and economics because of the adjacent states with almost 30 million km^2 forms one-fifth of earth's landmass and half of global GDP. The Russian Federation and the United States are two of the most prominent states of the international system as permanent members of the UN Security Council.

There is no doubt that the REF has many barriers to economic development. It is imperative for Northeast Asian countries to establish a friendly and mutually beneficial relationship by following their converging interests. While discussing long-term prospects of cooperation, it is possible to envisage some scenarios of economic development that may be useful to policymakers. Active involvement of Korea and Japan in the economic development of the Russian Far East seems to be the best way to accelerate not only the economic development of the region but also give a long due stimulus to their slowing economies. Consequently, it is possible to generate powerful arguments for such a policy regarding the region (Arsenov et al., 2005).

On the other hand, the very dynamic Chinese economy shows remarkable strength in the region and all over the world. Moreover, the length of the territorial border between Russia and China in the RFE makes possible the development of joint production facilities by creating "frontier zones" of economic interaction. This desired economic interaction could make the region more attractive for Chinese labor, promoting stable/friendly interstate and inter-regional Russian-Chinese relations.

Moreover, the relationship in this Northeast Asian strategic quadrangle can be characterized by mutual security, cooperation and mutual economic development. There is no doubt that the countries in question have different political/economic systems and social structures and, more importantly, different national interests. Consequently, there are often misapprehensions regarding a number of issues. Nevertheless, through a regional cooperation scheme, all sides would get familiar with these situations and may circumvent misreading each other. The strategic partnership between Japan, Korea, China, and Russia should be forged based on interests, rationality, and the rule of law by avoiding the sentiments of fantasizing or idealizing each other. The REF can present a good opportunity and inductive to create an environment where the mutual interests of all sides would come together.

Although much remains to be done, this chapter mainly focused on the RFE and the strategic quadrangle countries in Northeast Asia. It was not in the scope of this chapter to provide an extended discussion on the possible impacts on the Americas. However, the chapter would benefit substantially by extending the analysis to the US and Canadian sides of the Strait. The investigation of the possible benefits and drawbacks of the Bering Strait crossing for the Americas would only complement the current study by providing a better understanding of the big picture.

Part II.

China: Journey to a Global Identity

Part II

China:
Journey to a Global Identity

Although Chinese civilization, like all other civilizations, evolved throughout its historical journey, it nevertheless preserved a core set of features that characterize it as a single cultural tradition. Literally, much of the Chinese cultural heritage was rejected in earlier periods of modern China. The establishment of the People's Republic of China (PRC) at the end of the tormented first half of the century in 1949 and the ideological rupture along cultural rejection of the traditions reached its apex with the Cultural Revolution in the 1960s. But yet, modern China nevertheless retains many characteristics of its cultural heritage today due to genuinely pursuing a cultural rejuvenation process to adopt the abandoned and repressed elements of that heritage. In other words, much of the culture of contemporary China that still thrives has an explicit link to the civilization that emerged nearly as long ago as other cradles of civilization around the world, such as Egypt or

Mesopotamia. China's accomplishments on civilizational grounds are not less impressive than the magnificent Hellenistic Greek or the grandiose Latin Roman periods. The way Graeco-Roman civilization undeniably had shaped different parts of Europe, the features of China's traditional way of life promoted the cultural evolution of East Asia (Reagan, 2018).

The primary rationale behind the traditional Chinese culture's penetration to surrounding countries easily with a powerful impact on the historical development of Asia is partly due to its embedded values and institutions symbolizing its cultural system. Historically, China, one of the largest and most populous countries globally, subsequently had to have an unparalleled approach to address problems. Being an oversized country with ethnic and linguistic diversity and the associated disturbances of predominantly rural society with large urban centers vying for limited natural resources has always been problematic. The traditional Chinese system has met these challenges marvelously adequately for millennia to a great extent. Most certainly, the persistence of Chinese civilization and its intellectual, cultural, and artistic contributions to world civilization requires a thorough assessment of the educational system to decipher the critical features (Reagan, 2018).

One crucial factor regarding the history of Chinese culture and institutions is that the data and abundance of available historical sources make it much easier to capture the peculiar aspects of the country firmly. Moreover, like the western tradition, it is possible to reliably trace the data up to the early times of the Eastern Zhou dynasty (771-256 BCE), which coincides with approximately the Sophists period in the Hellenistic Greek period. Consequently, it is more straightforward to deepen our understanding of the Chinese political progress to some extent.

For instance, it would be inconceivable to examine traditional Chinese political and cultural development without repeated reference to Confucian thought. Undoubtedly, the traditional Chinese thought is essentially Confucian philosophy. Confucian thought undeniably played a critical role in forming Chinese traditions and institutions. The teachings of Confucius and notably as it was articulated and expanded by later Chinese philosophers Mencius and Chu Hsi inspired the Chinese civilization and culture and are at the source of the contemporary Chinese intellectual life and the Chinese peasantry. Confucian philosophy and moral thought combine ethical teachings and social obligations in 'five hierarchical relationships': sovereign and subject, parent and child, husband and wife, brother and brother, and friend and friend. Moreover, those relations are praised through five constant virtues: benevolence, justice, order, prudence, fidelity. It also furnished a persuasive justification for a highly stratified social order giving birth to a society particularly conservative and resistant to change.

For centuries, China has been a legendary puzzle in other parts of the world. Although it is considered one of the oldest civilizations, the PRC is equally a broadly new politico-territorial entity, with only 73 years of history. Since President Xi Jinping's arrival to power in 2013, Chinese interaction with the world has taken an assertive turn, getting away from the Deng Xiaoping era's slogan of keeping a low profile as the guiding principle in Chinese foreign policy (Feng, He, & Li, 2019; Zeng, 2020).

In recent times, along with China's economic and military rise, there has been considerable interest in academic circles in comprehending the foreign policy orientation of the PRC and its possible impact on international order (Beretta et al., 2017; Blackwill & Campbell, 2016; Breslin, 2010; Ding & Panda, 2021; Feng, He, & Xuetong, 2019; Garcia, 2022; Garver, 2016; Godehardt, 2014; Kaczmarski, 2015; Kochhar, 2018; Lanteigne, 2020; Larson & Shevchenko, 2019; Sun, 2021; Sutter, 2021; Tan, 2016; Turcsa´nyi, 2018; Zhang & Austin, 2013). There are ample examples of audacious Chinese foreign policy initiatives, particularly in the realm of economics. For instance, the ever-increasing investment and economic activities in Africa and Latin America created niche markets for Chinese firms. The well-known by now 2013 Belt and Road Initiative (BRI) is driven by a massive global development strategy (Garlick, 2020; Gerstl & Wallenbock, 2021), emphasizing infrastructure development and investments across 138 countries not only in Eurasia but also in Africa[47] and Latin America[48]. The 2015 establishment of the Asian Infrastructure Investment Bank (AIIB) with 57 countries on board was designed to support sustainable infrastructure and other productive sectors in Asia and beyond, including developed as well as developing countries. However, in the not very distant future, Chinese assertive foreign policy initiatives may extend into the military domain through building string of military bases around world and increasing power projection capabilities to maintain safeguarding the country's economic interests around the world, similar to the US practices after the WWII[49]. To this end, in 2017, China launched a national program targeting to elevate Chinese military to the "world class" level by 2049, the centenary of the PRC [50].

In international relations, power is an indispensable concept for comprehending the parameters of the world. In a sense, power is the most valuable currency of great-power politics, and states compete for it among themselves (Mearsheimer, 2001). Indeed, China's rise is one of the defining episodes in 21st-century world politics. As China's power increases, speculations and questions about what China's rise will mean for the world's future and how it would impact the current international order (Harnisch et al., 2016; Kachiga, 2021). The friendly/unfriendly rise of China creates challenges vis-à-vis the conceptual evolution of international relations theory (Pan & Kavalski, 2022). Consequently, Chinese foreign policy formulation will be instrumental in determining the future of international politics. To uncover and anticipate China's behavior, it is essential to know what Chinese leaders think about international relations and what kind of analytical lenses they use to process global events.

Undoubtedly, power matters in international politics; however, another crucial factor is knowing how China will utilize its power is even more important than how much power it possesses. Some scholars firmly believe that China will use its ever-expanding power to challenge US hegemony and the US-led liberal international order established after WWII (Friedberg, 2005, 2015; Mearsheimer, 2006a, 2010).

Some are more optimistic than others arguing that China's rise will occur within the existing liberal international order and will gradually become an integral part of the international system (Ikenberry, 2008). Nevertheless, on the other hand, plenty of other pessimists portrays a more bleak picture concerning that an increasingly assertive China may find itself in a conflictual situation with the reigning hegemon, the United States, falling into Thucydides's Trap (Allison, 2017) during the power transition in the international system (Organski & Kugler, 1980).

Central Eurasia is significant at the crossroads of the Eurasian continent, and it had a decisive influence on all the settled societies around it. A current historical interpretation from the Eurasianist school to the geopolitics of Halford Mackinder and Owen Lattimore to the contemporary world-system theorists regarded Central Eurasia as a key region of the Eurasian world system (Christian, 1994; Frank, 1992; Lattimore, 1962).

From the 17th to the mid-18th century, three empires of massive Eurasia, namely, the Manchu Qing (1644–1911), Tsarist Russia (1613–1917), and the Mongolian Zunghars (1671–1760)—competed for influence and power in the core of Eurasia (see Figure 10). The vastness of geography made communications, military campaigns, and economic relations all very difficult. At the end of this prelude to the Great Game of the late 19th century, only the Qing and Russians were left standing facing each other, while the Zunghars had vanished as an organized power. The binary division of Eurasia remained mostly intact until the demise of the Soviet system in 1991 (Perdue, 2005).

Figure 10. Eighteenth-century Eurasia

Note. (Keller, 2020)

Although no social process ever perfectly repeats the past, the Chinese decision-makers learned from history by building on past experiences or learning from their mistakes. Moreover, they use the past to explain and justify the present to address contemporary political needs. In a way, regardless of the ideological underpinnings, the continuity in foreign policy presents itself in an institutionalized way under different regimes.

The backward-looking tendency among Chinese academics and foreign policymakers first and foremost indicates respect for tradition and is also a method to challenge the prevalent theories, doctrines, and ideologies without disrupting the fundamentals of society (Grydehoj & Su, 2022). Hence the writing and rewriting of history constitute a key element in shaping the strategies pursued by China. Past experiences may offer some guidance to Chinese interested in negotiating a new identity for their nation in the 21st century.

In addition, China's geographical factors and geopolitical realities have also been influential in determination of its foreign policy orientation. Since Deng Xiaoping's initiation of the reform movement in the 1980s, the swiftness of economic, sociocultural, and political changes in China has been breathtaking. The Chinese citizen's adjustment to this rapidly changing socio-economic, political, and technological environment has been of varying degrees of success. Correspondingly, many confronted dilemmas and frustrations in maintaining connections to the threatened traditional core values associated with Chineseness (Veeck et al., 2011).

The chapters in Part II will address several aspects of Chinese foreign and economic policy vis-à-vis evolving Eurasian geopolitics. The chapters on the revitalization of the historical Silk Road, the Shanghai Cooperation Organization (SCO), and the Xinjiang Uyghur Autonomous Region (XUAR) will attempt to decipher the foreign policy orientation of China in Eurasia. It will pay close attention to the conditions that influenced the current period's foreign and military policymaking processes and its geopolitical expression in Eurasia.

Chapter IV

Pax Sinica along the Silk Road

Pax Sinica is a historiographical term, modeled after the original phrase Pax Romana. It refers, in Latin, to a Chinese-provided peace which in turn is used to describe an era of peace in East Asia sustained by Chinese hegemony. In historical terms, both the Pax Sinica of the Eastern hemisphere through Han China and the Pax Romana of the Western hemisphere through Rome signified a trans-regional order based on rules and regulations. This orderly world of the Pax Sinica generated a number of positive results such as the intensification of travel, ever-expanding trade relations, an increase in the overall living standards of the populace, the proliferation of cities, and a demographic upsurge in Eurasia along the ancient Silk Road. During this period, China was the dominant civilization not only in the Eastern hemisphere but also in the Middle hemisphere due to its political, economic, military and cultural influence. This chapter aims to reintroduce this historiographical term to elucidate the recent Chinese initiatives in Eurasia along the Silk Road to facilitate the integration and connectivity of the continent.

Some dramatic economic transformations and political intrusions affected the Eurasian geopolitical space in the final decades of the twentieth century. On the one hand, the economic rise of China attracted lots of attention and was labeled a success story by the Western world. On the other hand, in December 1991, fifteen new states emerged in Eurasia from the ashes of the Soviet empire.[51] All these newly independent former Soviet Union republics struggled to rebuild their economic base in an era of globalization. Consequently, this remarkable increase in independent states at the heart of Eurasia gave rise to a number of convoluted political, legal, environmental and economic problems.

Figure 11. *Eurasian Economic corridors*

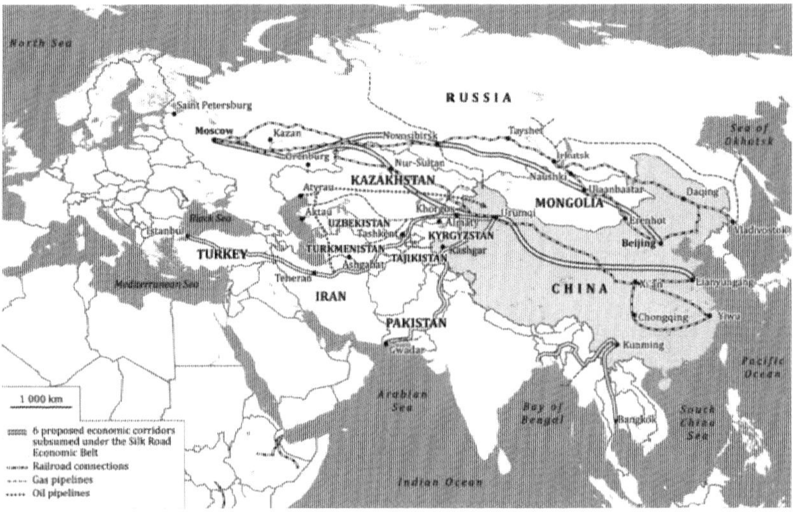

Note. (Pieper, 2022)

China and the newly independent former Soviet republics made some efforts to strengthen bilateral ties and improve cooperation on different fronts to overcome those convoluted problems. After the transitional years of the 1990s, the Shanghai Cooperation Organization (SCO) under the leadership and the financial backing of China became an essential component of the Eurasian political landscape. The organization established a new sort of cooperation among Eurasian nations ranging from the former Soviet space to Iran to Pakistan to India. The SCO member states have handled many issues related to geopolitics, Eurasian security, the economy, and regional politics.

Throughout its long history, China had intense commercial and cultural interaction with its hinterland. Indeed, in recent times, China's economic and diplomatic influence in Eurasia has been on the rise. Although China is now a global power, it has not always been one. Arguably, until the early 2000s, it was first a fast-growing regional power, and before the beginning of the reforms in 1979 a vast but isolated country, incapable of asserting itself vigorously in global affairs. However, up until the eighteenth century, China was by far the world's largest and most vibrant economy. At this junction, it is important to remember that the fundamentals of the British Industrial Revolution were established by transferring critical technologies from China to the West through the Silk Road.

In 2013, in Kazakhstan, President Xi Jinping revealed the commencement of the Belt and Road Initiative (BRI), confirming China's long-term strategic, security and economic objectives in Eurasia. The new Silk Road project(s), also known as BRI, is promoting infrastructure along with land and sea trade between Europe and Asia with a total investment from Beijing that could well exceed a trillion dollars. The initiative also forms the nexus of power, culture, and commerce which is now at the center of China's foreign policy. Currently, China's BRI, which has become the centerpiece of China's economic diplomacy in Eurasia, has already started to transform the outlook of the region. This foreign policy initiative uses Pax Sinica as modus vivendi for rewarding developments. Consequently, it would be fair to assert that Xinjiang and Central Asia play a crucial role in the success of this initiative.[52] On the other hand, the growing Uyghur demand for a separate homeland and continuing ethnic tension in Xinjiang pose some challenges to China's authority in the region.[53]

The magnitude of the BRI is indicated through some spectacular numbers and has far-reaching implications for Eurasia in particular and the globe in general. For instance, the territory in question comprises a substantial part of global trade generating more than half of global economic output and is home to three-quarter of the world's population while holding an estimated three-quarters of proven global energy reserves. Most certainly, the initiative would put China at the center of global economic gravity and create a genuine potential vis-à-vis the changing global geopolitical arrangement.

One of the arguments in this chapter is that the rise of China[54] alters the geopolitical landscape in Eurasia. The dynamics behind this changing perspective have been unveiled through a renewed interest in the old Pax Sinica. Notably, economically less developed and politically unstable areas of Eurasia may benefit from Pax Sinica-facilitated political or economic strategic planning, which in turn would help in maintaining much-desired stability and much-needed economic development in the region. However, inescapably, the concept also finds its applicability in the entirety of Eurasia highlighting the Chinese hegemonic posture. After presenting a comprehensive overview of geopolitics in regards to Eurasia and the Silk Road, this chapter will elucidate the concept of Pax Sinica from a historiographical point of view. The subsequent sections will delve into Chinese geopolitics within the framework of a more significant Eurasian geopolitical panorama designating Pax Sinica as a Chinese foreign policy motto to increase its influence and control over Eurasia.

Pax Sinica in Historical Context and the Ancient Silk Road

Throughout history, it is possible to observe a number of periods facilitated by a politically, economically, militarily or culturally dominant power. For instance, the Pax Assyriaca was set to describe an extended period of military-enforced peace in the Neo-Assyrian Empire during the 7th century BCE in regions that included mostly Mesopotamia and the current Levant. The Pax Mongolica was established in the 13th century after the initial invasions of the Mongolian armies and the creation of the extensive Mongolian Empire. The following peaceful time was called the Pax Mongolica where stability, peace, development of culture and economic growth ruled the land. It helped to diffuse different ideas through cultural expansion and trade routes all around Eurasia.

However, most certainly, the Pax Romana is the most acclaimed one, symbolizing a period of relative peace and stability across the Roman

Empire prevailing for over 200 years between 27 BCE and 180 CE. The Empire was to a great extent decentralized, allowing provinces to make and administer their laws while acknowledging Roman taxation and military authority. Rome's most magnificent and colossal infrastructure projects were built during the Pax Romana. Roads all over the Empire were constructed to maintain a harmonious unity. Subsequently, there was also spillover to other areas in the realm of arts, humanities, and social sciences. The Roman Empire was prosperous because it was peaceful, warfare banished to the frontiers which were protected by the army. The Pax Romana held sway over much of Western Europe, the Middle East and North Africa for centuries. The area in question was stable and economically developed, with little or no trace of devastation. Due to the Pax Romana, much-feared rebellions and large-scale violence were notably rare.

Along the same line of logic, it is possible to argue that the Pax Sinica was the Chinese version of the Pax Romana, lasting from 202 BCE – the foundation of the Han Dynasty by Liu Pang – to 195 CE, almost 400 years. The Pax Sinica allowed a notable part of the Eastern and Middle hemisphere to flourish. Interestingly, the Pax Sinica introduced by the Han Dynasty corresponded to the Pax Romana of the Western world. The Han emperors inaugurated a merit system[55] and a strong/stable central government much like in the Roman Empire in the West. During the Pax Sinica, under the tutelage of the Han Dynasty, several critical developments occurred such as the civil service and the first papermaking process and territorial expansion on the eastern front into Korea, Manchuria, and Vietnam by the Han emperor Han Wudi. Many symbolic and historical Chinese benchmarks such as the Great Wall of China were erected in this period. Long-distance travel and trade facilitated commerce in silk, spices, and tea with the Roman Empire which in turn created co-prosperity zones in Eurasia.

Moreover, the Silk Road played a pivotal role in cultural diffusion. For instance, Buddhism, which originated in India, reached the Middle Kingdom and ultimately arrived on the Korean Peninsula through a Chinese monk in 372 CE, when King Sosurim of Goguryeo was in power. The ancient Silk Road was instrumental in the diffusion of not only Buddhism but also Abrahamic religions such as Judaism, Christianity, and Islam. Consequently, it would be fair to assert that the Silk Road should not be envisioned just as a promoter of commerce between the East and the West in Eurasia but also culture, knowledge, and ideologies (Frankopan, 2017).

Chinese Geopolitics and the Rationale Behind Pax Sinica

The Chinese approach to 21st-century geopolitics in Eurasia and subsequently the basis of Pax Sinica is better understood through a survey of some aspects of recent Chinese political history, which in turn provides a guide to deciphering Chinese diplomatic tactics and initiatives. For instance, the "Century of Humiliation," in which the European powers shaped the world, has not been forgotten, but it is now overlooked by China and considered as an historical lesson. Most certainly, these traumatic historical experiences are shaping the current Chinese behavior in the international arena. China, by becoming a powerful challenger to the status quo of the United States in the international arena, has asserted one more time its Sinocentric worldview. Most certainly, Chinese geopolitics is going through some fundamental changes in this new chapter of adaptation to a world full of geopolitical puzzles.

To this end, the new "Long March" à la 21st century, initiated by Xi Jinping under the rubric of the Belt and Road motto, has revitalized the ancient trade roads by embracing the new Silk Road, which covers the entirety of Eurasia. Figuratively speaking, these Chinese initiatives have reversed the 500-year-old direction of imperialism from eastward expansion to westward expansion (Rousset, 2018).

China has grosso modo 14,500 km of coastline from the Bohai Gulf in the north to the Gulf of Tonkin in the south. Undoubtedly, there are some severe impediments in the way of the Chinese navy's access to the high seas. From Japan and Korea in the north to Malaysia and Indonesia in the south, an invisible line of American surveillance restricts the freedom of the Chinese navy (Emmers, 2010). Chinese uneasiness and resistance to that feeling of encirclement manifested itself in April 2018 through the most significant naval exercises since its independence with 48 ships including two aircraft carriers in the Taiwan Strait projecting its military might with the aim of asserting its sovereignty and territorial integrity in the South China Sea and beyond. Consequently, it should be clear at this juncture that China's opening to continental Eurasia represents a strategic alternative to the coastal geopolitical impasses that it endures.

Geopolitical frameworks are at the center of this multifaceted political strategy. Due to slowing economic growth year-on-year, many Chinese domestic industries find themselves in an overproduction situation. For instance, once the driving force of the country, the cement and steel industries are facing severe surpluses due to diminishing domestic demand for those materials. One venue to overcome those bottlenecks is to launch gargantuan infrastructure projects through the new Silk Roads in Eurasia, which in turn would facilitate and fortify Chinese political and cultural influence in those respective regions of the Silk Road(s) pathways (Bost et al., 2018).

The Strait of Malacca is very likely to be blockaded by the US in a political or military crisis. Due to the necessity to secure the flow of natural resources and particularly fossil fuels, Chinese policymakers are attempting to circumvent the Malaysian Peninsula through Eurasian land corridors. The port facility in Gwadar, in the Baluchistan region of Pakistan by the Arabian Sea, is a Chinese-subsidized construction mega project. The 3,218 km China-Pakistan Economic Corridor (CPEC) is one of the most significant projects under the BRI stretching from Kashgar in China's Xinjiang region to Pakistan's Gwadar Port. On the other side of the Indian subcontinent in and around the Andaman Sea, the 1,700-plus kilometer China-Myanmar Economic Corridor (CMEC), stretching from Kunming, the capital of Yunnan Province in China, to the seaport at Kyaukpyu in Myanmar's Rakhine State, is designed to avoid such geostrategic dilemmas (Tan & Grillot, 2014).

According to the Chinese master plan vis-à-vis the new Silk Road(s), significant investments are envisaged in all industries ranging from tourism to mining to manufacturing. Large-scale infrastructure undertakings such as railroads, bridges, tunnels, and dams will attempt to increase connectivity among the Silk Road countries. Moreover, energy projects in the domain of oil/natural gas pipelines and power plants will constitute another facade of this complex interdependence in Eurasia.

These transport corridors will give birth to new cities or the enlargement of existing ones. Moreover, they will magnify the erection of brand-new manufacturing businesses/assembly lines, and necessitate the construction of school systems, electricity grids, water systems, and health/hospital systems. This sort of development will indubitably entail an expansion of the labor force and overall population, which in turn will increase the population density in thinly populated areas and decrease the population density in overcrowded coastal parts of Eurasia (Bost et al., 2018).

The Khorgos development project is an excellent example to elucidate this sort of development. Khorgos sits across the border between Kazakhstan and China. Although this Special Economic Zone (SEZ) is located in one of the most remote areas of the globe, it is also a good illustration of effective Sino-Kazakh cooperation (Stevens, 2018).

The allocation of much-needed financial resources for the projects will originate mainly from Chinese backed international funds such as the New Development Bank (NDB),[56] the Silk Road Fund[57] and the Asian Infrastructure Investment Bank (AIIB)[58]. On the one hand, despite the disapproval and reservations of the US towards these initiatives in Eurasia, many rich first world countries have shown a genuine interest in taking part. The attractiveness of the projects and the high expected financial returns are the primary rationale behind their desire to get involved. On the other hand, developing countries in Eurasia see a window of opportunity to expedite their economic development, although in some cases, it also contains some elements of servitude to Chinese belligerent aspirations.

The new Silk Routes are to reach major industrial and commercial centers in Western Europe. To that end, China has already started a shopping spree for logistics facilities and ports – Piraeus in Greece (Stevens 2018) – in order to promote transport corridors between Asia and Europe. A cargo train from Shanghai runs for more than 12,000 kilometers to directly connect China to major European cities. Since 2011, China Railway Corporation (CRC) has run as many as 11,000 cargo trains to Europe, intensifying trade and connectivity across Eurasia. CRC currently runs 65 China Railway Express freight routes that reach 15 countries in Europe. For instance, the main routes consist of Chongqing to Duisburg, Zhengzhou to Hamburg, Suzhou to Warsaw, Yiwu to Madrid, Shenyang to Hamburg, Changsha to Hamburg, Daqing to Zeebrugge, Xiamen to Moscow, Nanjing to Moscow, and Tianjin to Minsk. The China-Europe cargo train connection allows the benefits of large volume, low freight rates and high speed, cutting the transportation time to one-third compared to shipping by sea and slashing the cost to one-fifth compared to air cargo (Suokas, 2018). Such an impressive undertaking at the Eurasia level is probably unique. Perhaps only the Trans-Siberian Railroad initiative between 1891 and 1916 could be comparable in scope and vision[59].

There are some significant social, cultural and ecological challenges to be faced with these Silk Road initiatives. Investor(s) will face possible geopolitical, economic and financial uncertainties and fallout. The successful advancement of these strategic investments may be affected by political unpredictability on the ground. For instance, the core of Eurasia is quite prone to such disturbances: the independence movement in Pakistani Baluchistan, the "renaissance" of the Taliban in Afghanistan, the rejuvenation of political Islam in Central Asia, the Kashmir problem between Pakistan and India, the Xinjiang and Tibet puzzles in China, the Crimea/Eastern Ukraine/Chechnya issue in Russia, and the Sunni/Shite struggle in the Middle East.

Contemporary Geopolitical Dynamics in Eurasia

Eurasian integration and connectivity is unfolding on many different levels. Multiple simultaneous processes are now pointing to a new Great Game à la 21st century: the China- induced new Silk Roads, the Russia-driven Eurasia Economic Union (EAEU), the Asia Infrastructure Investment Bank (AIIB), and the International North-

South Transportation Corridor (INSTC).

On one level, in the 21st century, geography is still indispensable for analyzing some hefty geopolitical, environmental, and socio-economic conflicts of contemporary Eurasia. In fact, geographical reasoning can provide valuable hints about the challenges that the world currently faces. Most certainly, China is not an exception to this criterion. On the contrary, it lies at the center of many global geopolitical maneuvers. For instance, the Strait of Hormuz, off the southeastern coast of Iran, represents one of the most critical geopolitical maritime choke points in the world, not only for Iran but all other Persian Gulf countries[60]. The strait is a must-go route and main artery for oil and natural gas shipments from all Gulf Cooperation Countries (GCC), Iraq and Iran to the rest of the world[61]. Consequently, it represents a critical geopolitical reality to take into consideration since the majority of oil imported into China originates from this region (Daojiong & Breslin, 2010).

Furthermore, there are also some fundamental transformations vis-à-vis geopolitically dormant parts of Eurasia such as the Arctic region. Due to global climate change and rising temperatures, academics, as well as policymakers, are discussing a possible future polar Silk Road to avoid the lengthy and costly Suez Canal option to reach major European industrial centers. The Arctic Ocean is melting at a startling pace with some serious geopolitical implications. On the one hand, the ecological balance in the region will change with the thinning of the ice. There will be implications for the global climate, too. The waters of the Arctic Ocean will absorb more heat from the sun, thus introducing more energy into the ocean. On the other hand, there are also some potent geopolitical entanglements of the Arctic's melting. This new phenomenon will make the Arctic Ocean navigable throughout the year. The sea route linking northeast Asia and Western Europe will shorten the shipping distance by over 4,000 kilometers and will lead to changes in the patterns of global trade and shipping (Gupta, 2009).

Apart from its significance in the domain of shipping routes, it is critical to understand that the Eurasian Arctic is also one of the most affluent regions in the world in terms of its fossil fuels – oil, natural gas, coal – and mineral resources. It also has immense geopolitical importance.

The recent inauguration of the Yamal Arctic gas terminal proclaimed a new era of cooperation between China and Russia to explore Arctic resources. Yamal contains natural gas reserves totaling the equivalent of more than four billion barrels of oil, and China National Petroleum Corporation (CNPC) and the Silk Road Fund hold a combined 29.9 percent stake in the project. The Yamal liquefied natural gas project has strategic significance for both countries and takes the BRI all the way to the inside of the Arctic Circle. The Arctic gas terminal is predicted to supply China with four million tons of LNG a year and expedite the country's transformation to clean energy sources. Shipping to China would take place via the Northern Sea Route, which in turn would allow ships to reach China in 15 days, shaving almost 20 days off the regular time using the traditional route through the Suez Canal. The shipping lane running between the Pacific and the Atlantic along Russia's northern coast offers valuable incentive for the Polar Silk Road envisioned by China and Russia ("The_Editorial_Notes", 2017).

By all accounts, trade between Europe and Asia largely exceeds transatlantic or transpacific trade. For the last five hundred years, Europeans have thought of Europe and Asia as two opposing ends of the world. Europe represented the modern, technological, progressive facade of the globe. Asia, on the other hand, was depicted as stagnant, backward, and undeveloped. However, it seems today that that sort of Eurocentric reading of the world has some serious flaws and the roles have been reshuffled to highlight a Sinocentric reading of international relations. Although Eurasia as a geopolitical framework is evolving as an integrated entity, it seems that political organization is a sine qua non for any further rewarding development. China was the first to propose and initiate such policy. The BRI is a gargantuan undertaking to redesign Eurasia according to its Sinocentric worldview. A Pax Sinica would be a first step in the direction of conceiving Eurasian identity in the 21st century by investing in common denominators around the four corners of Eurasia. It is essential to remember that the Eurasian supercontinent would host three-quarters of the world's population and more than two-thirds of its economic output. However, in the making of this Eurasian supercontinent, the BRI is presented as an attempt to replace the "West" with something new. A Pax Sinica in its desire to redesign the map of the world would also face a set of competing projects and initiatives from India, Japan, Russia, and Europe. Nonetheless, these distinctive/ competing assumptions and conceptualizations – from the liberalism of

Western Europe to the capitalism with Chinese characteristics of Beijing to the militarism of Russia – about future Eurasian political organization could also be a source of possible conflict. The new Eurasia-wide "Great Game" may also be a source of instability for an undetermined period. Most certainly, a possible loose form of association by all the major Eurasian powers under the rubric of a Pax Sinica would marginalize the US by pushing it away from the center of gravity of global political and economic affairs. However, on a positive note, it is important to remember that the Americas and Eurasia could be geographically connected through a possible Bering Strait crossing.

The Bering Strait crossing would link the entirety of Eurasia to the entirety of the Americas, and it can be seen as a natural extension of any BRI projects. There are some immense geopolitical benefits to such a project. It would bring about a profound and lasting change in the global economic and political outlook. The most valued function of the Bering Strait crossing and the extension of the associated railroad network would be to release the massive natural resources trapped underneath the tundra and permafrost for the benefit of global economic development. Moreover, the railroad project(s), the connection energy grids and the extension of pipeline systems would also be instrumental in building development corridors in those underdeveloped and sparsely populated regions of the world. The development of the resources and their rapid transportation to global markets would contribute not only to the overall development of the region but also would be valuable for resource-poor countries of northeast Asia such as Japan, Korea, and China (relative to its economic size). A rational and pragmatic US foreign policy would eventually realize the endless possibilities this would present to both sides of the Bering Strait. Consequently, future US administrations would explore the possible impact(s) of the Bering strait crossing as a formidable infrastructure project for the economic development of Eurasia and the Americas. A cohabitation of a Pax Sinica with a Pax Americana would only complement each other to create much desired global peace, stability, and prosperity. By doing this, the US would secure not only its primary role in a multipolar world but also the moral upper-hand in global politics as a responsible superpower (Maçães, 2018).

However, there are also some concerns and uneasiness vis-à-vis the BRI among the countries in which Chinese investment is taking place. The Pax Sinica envisaged by the BRI attempts to facilitate political and economic interaction among Eurasian countries and discover the full economic potentials of member nations that are so far lagging behind economically. China has always characterized the BRI as a win-win situation for all parties involved, presuming that both China and host countries would enjoy some Panglossian ramifications regarding economic prosperity. Notwithstanding, the reality on the ground may be quite different. China's BRI, through the trade infrastructure project(s), could be running into notable impediments due to the rising massive debt loads of the countries involved. At the time of its announcement in 2013, the overall cost of this trade initiative was calculated to be around $26 trillion in infrastructure investment (railways, power plants, ports, highways etc.) by 2030 in order to connect and expand the regional economies in Eurasia. Seemingly, China is the primary provider of billions of dollars in credit to drive these projects. The main competitors of China in the global arena concerning influence and power, such as the United States, Japan, and India, have displayed earnest anxiety vis-à-vis the new Eurasian economic system since it would diminish their weight in international politics. From the international development point of view, it may create some severe sustainability issues regarding the sovereign debt of, in particular, eight countries receiving infrastructure project funds from China, namely Pakistan[62], Djibouti[63], the Maldives, Mongolia, Laos[64], Montenegro, Tajikistan, and Kyrgyzstan. Consequently, some governments in Eurasia are portraying a gloomy picture amid complaints against China for generating a debt trap that dispossesses those countries involved from accessing critical assets ("A_Debt_Trap?", 2018).

China-Russia Axis in the Making through Regional Organizations

Russia is an influential global power with a vast territory, abundant resources and tremendous potential for development and remains a critical factor in China's strategic goals. In the decade(s) following the demise of the Soviet Union, territorial disputes have been wholly settled through negotiations, and a comprehensive strategic partnership of coordination has been established. Russia holds unique strategic value for China. Russia is expected to become a major strategic partner of China regarding the latter's peripheral diplomacy, maintaining Eurasian peace and stability, building a distinct international order and balancing ties with the US. Both China and Russia as emerging non-Western powers possess some common denominators, sharing similar strategic needs, interests, and ideas about global politics which in turn could form the foundation of their diplomatic relations. Therefore, it is possible to see the burgeoning Sino-Russian relationship within the context of Eurasia as a long-term strategy for both parties based on mutual benefits (Wang, 2017).

Russia as a critical Eurasian power possesses a puissant military but has struggled to rebuild its economic base. There are some significant difficulties in guaranteeing a stable domestic order due to demographic shifts, economic changes, and institutional weaknesses. However, economic power is only one variable defining a country's strength in the international arena, but some other variables such as military capabilities, geopolitical strength, and international standing are equally indispensable. On the other hand, another prominent Eurasian power, China, is characterized as an economic powerhouse and has captivated a great deal of attention across the globe. Relations between China and Russia have evolved dramatically in recent times. During the past decade, China and Russia have made some efforts to strengthen bilateral ties and enhance cooperation on a number of economic/political/diplomatic fronts. China wants to keep Russia engaged in Eurasia as a key regional actor, and the SCO represents a great framework to do so.

The configuration of the new Russia-China strategic partnership contains many common denominators from energy to trade to security. Notably, in recent times, it is possible to observe the entente at play between Russia and China on multiple grounds. The concerted drive to bypass the U.S. dollar, the push towards an alternative banking clearance mechanism,[65] the AIIB- and the NDB-involved infrastructure financing, the massive accumulation of gold reserves and the expanded politico-economic role of the SCO are all indications of a "Grand Rapprochement" in Eurasia (Escobar, 2018). However, Sino-Russian bilateral relations are more of an entente, a basic understanding of the structural realities of the current global order supported by mutual interests, rather than an alliance. Russian policymakers have the fear that robust Chinese economic and financial capabilities will drive Russia into second-tier status in Eurasia (Chandran, 2018).

As a result of this entente, the SCO was founded on June 15, 2001, in Shanghai by China, Russia, Kazakhstan, Kyrgyzstan, Tajikistan, and Uzbekistan. The SCO has been instrumental for China increasing its influence across Eurasia and formed the foundation of the BRI project of Beijing in 2013. The SCO, as an emerging regional organization, has become an essential part of both Russia's and China's strategy in Eurasia. Moreover, the evolution of the SCO is of broader significance to global geopolitics and geoeconomics.

Consequently, it would be fair to argue that the SCO has played a pivotal role in terms of advancing China's Eurasian policies in par with officially stated goal of peaceful rise. Most certainly, the SCO has provided some policy benefits for China and a window of opportunity on the way to launch a Pax Sinica in Eurasia. China's engagement with Central Asia needs to be evaluated in regard to its own national and international security concerns. China's discourse on the "three evils," namely fundamentalism, extremism, and secessionism, determines its foreign policy orientation vis-à-vis the region (Peyrouse, 2018). On the other hand, Moscow has activated a partnership agenda for cooperation between different Eurasian organizations such as the EAEU, the SCO, and ASEAN, but also with a wide range of major regional powers on a bilateral basis, particularly China, India, Pakistan, Turkey, and Iran. Although China has exhibited a strong desire and an apparent preference for developing a free trade agreement within the format of the SCO in Eurasia, Russia has displayed a very cautious approach due to China's dominant economic position within the organization and repeatedly declined to commit to such plans (Dragneva, 2018).

China's relations with the Central Asian states have also been based on the creation of a more comprehensive set of tools with which to address non-security issues, most notably increased economic and energy cooperation. The establishment of the SCO Business Council and Interbank Consortium was intended to coordinate and finance joint projects among regional entrepreneurs. The Chinese government has been especially committed to developing the trade potential of the SCO. Consequently, Chinese trade with Kazakhstan, Kyrgyzstan, and Uzbekistan has increased considerably since 2001. This development has not only allowed Chinese goods and services to compete with those of Russia and Europe but has also permitted greater access to Chinese markets by Central Asian countries. Moreover, China provides a great deal of financing and technical know-how to critical infrastructure projects such as the improvement of transportation links and pipelines (Baizakova, 2013; Lanteigne, 2010; Movkebaeva, 2013).

The compilation of rationales pointing to the pivotal nature of Eurasian geopolitics is overwhelming. China as an emerging Eurasian power in global politics seriously challenges the current status quo and American interests in Eurasia. This long-delayed but expected rise may be just a normal and healthy political outcome given the rapid and substantial global transformations taking place in recent decades. The various Silk Road schemes through the BRI project serve as a blueprint for China's ambitious geo-economic and geopolitical strategy of connecting itself to the global economy and strengthening its influence. In this regard, a Pax Sinica would necessarily unleash "Promethean" forces and lead to a more stable Eurasia over the long run. There is no doubt that securing stability and peace along the Silk Road would instigate a new age of renaissance in Eurasia with spectacular economic, commercial, cultural, and scientific breakthroughs.

A new Pax Sinica along the Silk Road has been conducive to Chinese efforts dedicated to deepening Eurasian connectivity and some degree of loose integration, urging all countries to operate in cooperation to create a more open Eurasian economic space. Eurasian connectivity and integration have a substantial potential taking into consideration its combined landmass, population, natural resource base, and economic scale. Despite a significant range of development gaps, Eurasia enjoys a massive, dynamic and competitive market with a wide range of opportunities for economic growth and comprehensive cooperation. The developed as well as the less-developed economies of Eurasia complement each other in such a way that a win-win situation could present itself for the entirety of the continent. This reciprocal leverage for each country is currently at the center of Eurasian cooperation schemes.

Against a backlash of unilateralism, protectionism, and hegemonic posture, the BRI and the Pax Sinica as a mechanism provide an invaluable opportunity to rejuvenate the ancient connectivity along the Silk Road by forging new possibilities for investment in many areas. Silk Road projects, through a path towards openness, innovation, prosperity, and peace in Eurasia without falling into the trap of a hegemonistic perspective, would be a reliable indication of the eagerness to promote cooperation and connectivity across Eurasia.

Although there is much remaining to be done, this study has mainly focused on Pax Sinica's fundamentals as a strategic concept in Eurasian geopolitics. It is not in the scope of this paper to provide an extended discussion of the possible impacts of the United States' approach to Eurasian geopolitics. Nevertheless, it is critical to bear in mind that in the decades since the collapse of the Soviet Union, the United States has retained the status of a prevailing power in the international state system. Although in recent years, this status has increasingly been brought into question, the American unipolar moment has never been achieved by any other state in modern times. Consequently, this article would benefit substantially from extending the analysis in that direction and analyzing Eurasian geopolitics from the American perspective by comparing and contrasting Pax Sinica with Pax Americana. Furthermore, an investigation of the potential benefits and drawbacks for other Eurasian powers such as the European Union, Korea, Japan, Turkey, India, Iran, Pakistan, and Russia would only be complementary to the current study by providing a better decipherment of the consequent Eurasian puzzle. Notably, a more detailed investigation of the Russian-driven organization EAEU in conjunction with the SCO would further enhance our understanding of current Eurasian geopolitical realities.

Chapter V

The Shanghai Cooperation Organization

The colossal economic transformations and political intrusions had been affecting brutally China and the Soviet Union in the final decades of the twentieth century. Currently, Russia is a gigantic power, struggling to rebuild its economic base in an era of globalization. On the other hand, the economic rise of China has attracted a great deal of attention and labeled as a success story by the Western world. China and Russia have made a number of efforts to strengthen bilateral ties and improve cooperation on a number of economic/political/diplomatic fronts. Since the mid-1990s, the Shanghai Cooperation Organization (SCO) has been an important feature of Eurasian politics and a vehicle to forge a new sort of cooperation between China and Russia. A number of issues related to geopolitics, security, the economy and regional politics have been handled by the SCO member states.

Since the end of the Cold War, several scholars have suggested that the regions of the world have gained increased importance in the current international system and they act as an emerging potent force in the process of globalization (Holm & Sørensen, 1995; Mittelman, 2000). The Westphalian state is referred as a system of political authority based on territory and autonomy and it has been the dominant form in the international system up to the 1990s (Caporaso, 2000). In the past decade, however, the underpinnings of this system have been challenged by the creation of new regional unions or the restructuring of already existing ones. Consequently, the international system has witnessed a cohabitation of multiple forms of governance at multi-level. Regions are the building blocks of this new international system and inherently, changes that take place within them affect the international system overall. To certain extend the regions and their development provides a context for the explanation of newly emerged systemic trends.

This chapter will argue that the 21st century saw the strengthening of the existing regional systems or the naissance of many loose and new regional systems. The chapter will discuss regional integration theories while providing examples from the Shanghai Cooperation Organization (SCO).

In distinction from European Union, the SCO as a regional system is characterized by the absence of democracy and the continuation of authoritarian leadership (Ambrosio, 2008). The nature of the regime in place limits the possibility of interest and preference formation from bottom-up. Consequently, regional integration theories utilized to explain European integration becomes blurry when applied to the SCO. Finally, the chapter will evaluate the development of the SCO over the past decade by taking in consideration Chinese and Russian approaches. Yet, the contention of this chapter is that since most of the developed conceptual framework as well as the case studies vis-à-vis the regional systems are Eurocentric, the application of these lenses to the growing number of regional systems in other parts of the globe remains at best problematic, and at worst elusive.

The Shanghai Cooperation Organization is a permanent intergovernmental international organization founded on 15 June 2001 in Shanghai by the People's Republic of China, the Russian Federation, the Republic of Kazakhstan, the Kyrgyz Republic, the Republic of Tajikistan and the Republic of Uzbekistan. The main goals of the SCO are strengthening mutual confidence and good neighborly relations between the member countries; promoting effective cooperation in politics, trade and economy, science and technology, culture as well as education, energy, transportation, tourism, environmental protection and other fields; making joint efforts to maintain and ensure peace, security and stability in the region. The Council of Heads of State Council (HSC) is the highest decision-making body in the SCO. It meets once a year to take decisions and give instructions on all important issues of the SCO activity.

The SCO is an emerging regional organization in Eurasia. It has become an important part of both Russia's and China's regional strategy towards Central Asia and the security and economic policies of the newly independent former Soviet Central Asian states—Kazakhstan, Kyrgyzstan, Tajikistan and Uzbekistan. Moreover, the development of the SCO is of wider significance to global politics, security and economics due to the fact that the core member states with 30 million km^2 forms one fifth of earth's landmass, have one fourth of global population and one sixth of global GDP. Russia and China are two of the most prominent states of the international system as permanent members of the UN Security Council.

At present, the SCO's full membership stretches from the Baltic Sea to the Pacific Ocean, covering most of the territory of the Eurasian continent. China, Russia, Kazakhstan, Kyrgyzstan, Tajikistan and Uzbekistan have all been full members of the SCO since its formation in 2001. India and Pakistan were admitted as full members in 2017, followed by Iranian membership in 2021 at the 21st summit of the SCO leaders in Dushanbe, Tajikistan. The three observer states are Mongolia, Afghanistan and Belarus, while Dialogue partners include Cambodia, Nepal, Sri Lanka, Turkey, Armenia and Azerbaijan. However, it would be fair to argue that in spite of these two categories of associate membership, the SCO is overpoweringly centered on its core full membership. The SCO's agenda now encompasses a wide range of issue areas from security to economic to cultural and humanitarian collaboration between its member states.

China's Approach to the SCO

China's rapid rise to global power status changed the parameters of the strategic chest game in global politics. Consequently, its relationship with Russia is also frequently renegotiated due to the fact that Russia is an important neighbor and a crucial resource base in a time of ever growing Chinese energy hunger (Eder, 2014). The development of the SCO has provided a number of regional policy benefits for China. First, the development of these links has served to facilitate China's policy of ensuring the stability of the country's vulnerable western frontier in and around Xinjiang. Despite the remoteness of the province and the considerable amount of resources required by China to maintain it, the area is vital to Chinese security interests, since it provides a buffer zone between China's core provinces and unstable greater Central Asia (Song, 2014). It contains natural resources deemed important to Chinese economic growth and it provides a wanted/desirable window into Soviet Central Asia that began to grow in importance after the collapse of the USSR. Retaining good relations with Russia and Central Asia is absolutely critical to guarantee the safety of China's Xinjiang region

(Lanteigne, 2010).

However, China has also demonstrated increasing reservations about the prospect of color revolutions being exported from the ex-Soviet territory to China itself. The Chinese government's view of those events—Georgian Rose Revolution in 2003, Ukrainian Orange Revolution in 2004, Kyrgyz Tulip Revolution in 2005—were that they were the outcomes of external intrusion intended to weaken the regimes. The Chinese government has been worried about Western attempts to destabilize its legitimacy, and the above mentioned Revolutions in the former Soviet space have further intensified those concerns (Lanteigne, 2010; Yuan, 2010).

Although the revolutions in Georgia and Ukraine took place in areas distant enough for China to be concerned about it, the Tulip Revolution just next to the Chinese unstable Xinjiang region created a good deal of internal discussions in Beijing. The SCO has been seen as promoting both regime security as well as state security in the wake of those revolutions. The SCO has uncompromisingly accentuated the non-interference in the internal affairs of the member states (Lanteigne, 2010).

Central Asian relations are a natural prolongation of Chinese strategy of developing more harmonious and friendly relations in the international system, otherwise known as peripheral diplomacy. This proclivity began in the 1980s, when the Chinese government began developing its policy of building a stable periphery in Asia and encouraging more cordial relations with its neighbors in order to facilitate its ongoing economic and security policy reforms, to gain insight from the newly industrializing economies in East Asia such as South Korea or Taiwan and to discourage any developments in terms of security threats on Chinese borders (Baizakova, 2013; Lanteigne, 2010).

To a certain extent, the SCO has confirmed China's new regional friendship policies, enhancing further the Chinese government's policy of presenting a more businesslike and congenial face both to its periphery and to the world as a whole, in keeping with its stated goal of peaceful development. Moreover, China's desire to obtain a responsible great power status has been linked with productive co-operation and engagement with international institutions such as the UN and regional economic and strategic organizations (Lanteigne, 2010).

Evidently, a fundamental element vis-à-vis China's peripheral diplomatic plan has been the aspiration to re-establish friendly relations with the Russian Federation. The relations between those two giants had been placed in a deep freeze for decades following the Sino-Soviet split in the 1960s after the Great Leap Forward catastrophe. Due to the extensive border between the two states—the world's sixth-longest international border with 4,195 km—any Chinese undertaking to create a stable periphery along its western frontier would not succeed without more cordial relations with the government in Moscow (Baizakova, 2013; Cheng, 2011; Dadabaev, 2013; Lanteigne, 2010; Movkebaeva, 2013).

However, the end of the Cold War did bring with it some major alterations to global politics. Russian or Chinese foreign policy concerns became increasingly closer to alignment, which in turn were influenced by both countries' concern about American power in Eurasia as well as a joint preference for the development of a multipolar international system rather than a system based on US hegemony. The SCO was a great vehicle to realize their strategic goals for both countries (Baizakova, 2013; Lanteigne, 2010; Zhuangzhi, 2004).

The government in Moscow in the 1990s sought to increase economic ties with the Asia-Pacific region based on the Russian Far East's energy supplies and its strategic location as a transport corridor, as well as it being both a destination for foreign laborers and a source of scientific expertise (Poussenkova, 2009). China has played an important role in that engagement process as it became worried after 9/11 that Russian regional interests were experiencing a strategic contraction, which allowed the USA swiftly to augment its presence in Afghanistan and elsewhere in the Eurasian region. However, China's relationship with Russia is not without its difficulties. There are a number of controversial issues on the table between two countries such as trade imbalances in favor of China, illegal and unregulated cross-border trade, high levels of Chinese immigration into the Russian Far East, and persistent historical distrust (Alexeeva, 2008; Arsenov et al., 2005; Barkovsky, 2006; Kangas, 2007; Kuhrt, 2012; Lanteigne, 2010; Rozman, 2008; Sullivan & Renz, 2010; Troyakova, 2007).

On the other hand, although both countries have shown some signs of anxiety to publicize their growing levels of harmonious relationship, equally, it is unlikely that the two countries will enter into an alliance comparable to one that existed before the Sino-Soviet split in the 1960s. China just wants to keep Russia engaged in the North East Asia as a key regional actor and the SCO represents a great framework to do so. Conversely, there are also signs of mounting tension between the respective Russian and Chinese governments' view vis-à-vis the direction of the SCO. Moscow envisions an Organization with significantly improved military capabilities and desires greater cooperation between the SCO and the Collective Security Treaty Organization (CSTO). However, Chinese government has been more inclined towards an Organization that develops into a more multifaceted community and has resisted adamantly any Russian efforts to link too narrowly both organizations (Cheng, 2011; Lanteigne, 2010).

The Soviet Central Asia is another point of friction between Russia and China within the framework of the SCO. The fascinating aspect of Central Asian system is that it became to exist as a region composed by nation-states along the Westphalian logic only after the end of the Cold War. Even more captivating phenomenon is that nation building and region building have developed simultaneously. In December 1991, five new Central Asian states—Kazakhstan, Kyrgyzstan, Tajikistan, Turkmenistan, and Uzbekistan— emerged after the collapse of the Soviet Union (Allworth, 1995). In modern times, these five countries have never enjoyed the status of independent actors in the international arena.

There are several features corresponding to the concepts of region / regionalism / regionalization highlighted in the first part this essay. First,

Central Asian states form a logical geopolitical unit. It is isolated by a range of high mountains, the Caspian Sea and steppes at the core of the Eurasian continent. Second, they share a common Muslim heritage, a common history and a common language—the only exception being Tajik—and similar social structures. Nowhere are the states of the former Soviet Union more closely bound with one another than in Central Asia.

Less than one year after their independence, these states engaged in the integration of their policies in the domains of the environment, energy, illicit drug trafficking, the economy and security. However, the dimensions of the ecological catastrophe in the region have important repercussions on all five states. The awareness of the issue gave birth to the signing of an agreement, in February 1992 dealing with the establishment of a basic institutional framework. The agreement is designed to govern activities of the two interstate Basin Water Management Bodies—Bassejnovoe Vodnoje Ob'edinenie-BVO. Over the past decade, many other agreements have been reached to form a common front with the aim of producing an effective regional response to the problem. Currently, the Interstate Council for the Aral Sea (ICAS) is designated as the principal regional organization responsible for formulating broad and long-term policies and implementing programs for addressing various aspects of the ecological crisis. On the other hand, the regional cooperation over the environmental issues initiated the creation of a "Central Asian Union" in 1993.

In the early years after the collapse of the Soviet system, the development of Central Asian relations has offered China the opportunity to establish a diplomatic and strategic foothold in an increasingly important region. With the overlap between NATO partners and the SCO membership, it was suggested that the Shanghai group might act as bridge between Chinese and Atlantic security interests. Obviously, the need for this connection has grown since 9/11 attacks in the US. The strategic engagement of global power gets in Central Asia due to its proximity to Afghanistan has presented to China a window of opportunity to get firmly engaged not only in the core of Eurasia but also well beyond. In addition, China's engagement with both Russia and Central Asia can be seen as an attempt to weaken further Western influence at the core of Eurasia. Although the Chinese government has insisted that it is not in a position to challenge Western interests in Central Asia, its growing diplomatic and political power cannot be discounted when examining the future of Central Asian foreign relations. There is no doubt that the 2005 closure of American air force base at Karshi-Khananbad (K2) in Uzbekistan and another closure in 2014 at Manas in Kyrgyzstan after more than 12 years of flying troops and cargo in and out of Afghanistan were indications of a power shift between the US, the SCO member states at the heart of Eurasia (Lanteigne, 2010).

China's relations with the Central Asian states have been also based on the creation of a more comprehensive set of tools with which to address non-security issues, most notably increased economic and energy cooperation. The establishment of SCO Business Council and Interbank Consortium intend to coordinate and finance joint projects among regional entrepreneurs. The Chinese government has been especially committed to developing the trade potential of the SCO. Consequently, Chinese trade with Kazakhstan, Kyrgyzstan and Uzbekistan has increased considerably since the 1990s. This development did not only allow Chinese goods and services compete with those of Russia and Europe but also permitted a greater access to Chinese markets by Central Asian countries. Moreover, China provides a great deal of financing and technical know-how to important infrastructure projects such as improvement of the transportation links and pipelines (Lanteigne, 2010; Movkebaeva, 2013).

However, it would be fair to assert that the SCO's image is largely associated with its anti-colonial and anti-imperial initiatives, and that's the reason why smaller member states enthusiastically participate in this organization. There is an increasing concern that smaller members of the SCO are not considered to be equal players but are only taken advantage of by economically and demographically superior China. This current perceived image of China complicates the process of SCO identity formation. Consequently, there is a need for a closer and more clearly defined SCO area identity formation based on shared visions and opportunities for all member states without distinction (Dadabaev, 2013).

Equally, it is important to remember that Central Asian energy resources also play a central role in the Chinese government's strategic calculations, especially as China is very much concerned with developing a steady external energy supply that cannot be easily interrupted by Western pressures or politics, or subject to any maritime interference or blockades—which may be the case for the fossil fuels imported from the Middle East through the Malacca strait. This explains why the Chinese government has been anxious to develop energy trade with the landlocked Central Asian states, while also ensuring that it has its own pipeline projects capable of transporting oil and natural gas from Kazakhstan and Turkmenistan to offset Western and Russian projects (Song, 2014). Undeniably China is seeking alternative energy resources in various regions around the globe but the proven reserves of Central Asia's Caspian region takes a central place in those strategic calculations. The country's increasing dependence upon imported oil and natural gas as a result of steady/continuous economic development has increased China's uneasiness about energy security/insecurity. As a logical outcome of those concerns, respective Chinese governments signed a number of energy development and transport agreements with Central Asian states since 1993, as the country became net oil importer for the first time (Lanteigne, 2010).

Russia's approach to the SCO

For Russia, the SCO is above all a framework for cooperation with China. The scale of cooperation between Moscow and Beijing reached unprecedented levels not just within the framework of the SCO but also on bilateral level (Lukin, 2006). For instance, the recent China/ Russia natural gas deal worth around $400 billion represents a major step not only in global energy markets but also in Eurasian geopolitics. Moreover, Russia and China held a series of joint large-scale military exercises, made a joint declaration on world order in the 21st century, and have used the SCO to counter US military presence in Central Asia. However, there is also some remarkable competition with and distrust vis-à-vis each other. The Russian military community views the promotion of cooperation with China within the framework of the SCO as indispensable, but remains divided over the extent of such strategic military cooperation in light of possible rivalry between the two (Laumullin, 2006).

Russian ambitions for economic cooperation within the SCO are limited to certain sectors and predominately to large-scale infrastructural and energy projects. The Russian leadership considers that the strength of the Chinese economy means that a free trade agenda in the SCO would lead to Chinese domination of the other member states' economies. This concern also plays an important role in Russia's approach to bilateral economic relations with China. Moscow is seen as restricting the development of the huge trade potential between the economically weak regions of Russia's Far East and North-Western China because of political considerations about growing Chinese influence in these regions. It is absolutely true that the Russian Far East (RFE) is considered as a region in crisis due to troubled economic conditions, corrupt governance, and problem-ridden cross-border relations with China, Japan, and both Koreas (Rozman, 2008). Due to some fears that the Russian Far East might disengage itself from the center and other regional/global powers may end up having a major grip in the region, Moscow started to show some genuine interest in those eastern border provinces. The region in question covers a large geographical area from Siberia to Russia's Pacific coast, forming the northeastern corner of Asia. Although the Far East constitutes one-third of Russia's total landmass, it has only 6.6 million residents—4.7 percent of the total population. The low population density, just over one person per square kilometer, makes the region one of the most sparsely populated places in the world. The scarcity of residents exists alongside a wealth of natural resources that have attracted the interest of the Russian central government as well as foreign investors. Evidently, Russian politicians, bureaucrats/technocrats are all concerned about the level of socioeconomic development in that region (Troyakova, 2007).

However, it would be fair to assert that the developmental troubles of the RFE partly related to the region's history and location. Moreover, the USSR did also neglect socio-economically the region until its collapse in 1991. After the disintegration of the Union, the RFE, like many other regions, was to a great extent abandoned by the financially struggling central government in Moscow Moscow's extended negligence to the region has left the RFE provinces economically underdeveloped, demographically challenged, and geographically exposed.

Yet Moscow has recently begun to focus specifically on revitalizing the RFE, as years of dynamic economic growth and surging global trade in neighboring China have pulled the international community's attention to developments in the Pacific Rim. This change in the international political and economic climate, especially in light of the RFE's rich supplies of natural resources and strategic location in the North Pacific, has brought about a rethinking of Moscow's policy in Russia's Far East (Alexeeva, 2008; Blank, 2011).

Certainly, the Russian Far East has many barriers to economic development. It is very important, for China and Russia, to establish a friendly and mutually beneficial relationship by following the converging interests of the two countries. While discussing long term prospects of cooperation in the Russian Far East with China, it is possible to envisage some scenarios of economic development that may be useful to policymakers. An active involvement of China in the economy of the Russian Far East seems to be the best way to accelerate the economic development of the region. It is possible to generate powerful arguments for such a policy regarding the region (Arsenov et al., 2005). First, the Chinese economy is very dynamic and shows remarkable strength not only in the region but also all over the world. According to some estimations done by the Russian Academy of Sciences, Gross National Product (GNP) of China will be more than twice the size of Japanese economy—another economic giant of the region—by 2015. Secondly, the length of territorial border between Russia and China in the Russian Far East makes possible the development of joint production facilities by creating "frontier zones" of economic interaction. Thirdly, this economic interaction could make the region more attractive for Chinese labor, which in turn would promote stable/friendly interstate and inter-regional Sino-Russian relations. Moreover, the relationship between China and Russia can also be a role model for a new type of relationship between great powers, characterized by mutual security, cooperation and mutual economic development.

There is no doubt that those two countries in question have different political/economic systems and social structures. Consequently, there are often misapprehensions regarding a number of issues. But, both sides by getting familiar with these situations may circumvent misreading each other. The strategic partnership between China and Russia should be forged on interests, rationality and rule of law by avoiding the sentiments of fantasizing or idealizing each other. The Russian Far East can present a good opportunity to create that environment where the mutual interests for both sides would come together.

Russian foreign policy under the leadership of Vladimir Putin has focused on recapturing the lost great power status after the collapse of the Soviet Union in 1991 (Billon & Khatib, 2005; Goldman, 2008; Perovic et al., 2009; Spechler, 2010). As part of this agenda, the reclaiming of Russia's place as the leading power in the former Soviet space has been seen as a priority. This focus on the post-Soviet space is interpreted by many as one part of a wider program aimed at recapturing the status of a 'great power'. Russia always considered Soviet Eurasia space as its privileged interest area. However, Chinese scholars (Yi-chong, 2006; Zhao, 2008; Zweig & Jianhai, 2005) persistently underline the centrality of Soviet Central Asia to Chinese energy security and describe Sino-Central Asian energy relations as "natural" and "inevitable". There is little doubt that China will eventually replace Russia as the dominant economic force in Central Asia (Eder, 2014).

The development and deepening of bilateral/multilateral cooperation with Commonwealth of Independent States (CIS) has always been a priority for Russia's foreign policy. In this context, the Russian decision makers view Central Asia as a pivotal region (Allison, 2004; Bahgat, 2006; Blank, 2006; Buszynski, 2005; Ebel, 2009; Jaffe & Soligo, 2009; Johnson, 2009; J. Mankoff, 2009; O'Hara, 2005; Specher & Specher, 2009). Consequently, the SCO is considered by Russian elites to be one of its key tools for expanding its relations with the Central Asian states. Moreover, the Russian leadership sees the SCO as an important element in its security policy in a number of respects. It views its own security as directly related to Central Asia, because Russia shares a long porous border with the region. Issues such as illegal narcotics and the activities of Islamic fundamentalist groups in Central Asia have been identified as major security challenges with the potentiality to spread north over the border into Russia. As well as engaging with Central Asia for security purposes, the Russian leadership also interprets economic cooperation as important for ensuring its predominant place in the region, and its position as the Central Asian Republics' most important trade partner. Russia values the SCO as a means for cooperation in infrastructure development and for coordination of its energy policies among itself, China, Kazakhstan and Uzbekistan. This focus on energy is also born out of the perceived need to increase Russia's role in the wider East Asian economy, in order to assert itself as an important energy supplier to the rapidly growing states of the region (Aris, 2011).

Since the revival of relations between Russia and China at the end of the Cold War, both countries have established a degree of solidarity on interpretations of the current contemporary international system, with both perceiving that alternative models to the Western liberal-democratic international system are necessary. Both countries want to show the real possibility of a "Eurasian integration" model that is independent from, and an alternative to, its political dialogue with the European Union (EU) and the North Atlantic Treaty Organization (NATO). The SCO can be viewed by Russia and China as having contributed to presenting their viewpoint on a number of significant international events, especially when this viewpoint is contrary to the position taken by the EU or the US.

In distinction from the EU, the SCO as a regional system is characterized by the absence of democracy and the continuation of Soviet style authoritarian leadership. The nature of the regimes in place limits the possibility of interest and preference formation from bottom-up. Consequently, regional integration theories utilized to explain European integration becomes blurry when applied to the Shanghai Cooperation Organization.

The emerging international system is characterized by regional diversity and not by uniformity. Consequently, it is fair to argue that since the regional differences in the structure of the world exist, such differences should matter theoretically also. Current state of field in regional integration theories indicates more "European exceptionalism" than 'a' regional integration theory. However, it might appear to be quite challenging task to develop a theoretical structure encompassing such regional diversity, but attempts has to be made.

Furthermore, the growth of regional systems after the Cold War suggests that it is plausible to treat regions as unit of analysis and generate middle range theories that can be tested. That would be useful to detect certain trends in systemic changes since the dominant theories of International Relations show certain limitation regarding that matter.

The SCO is a very loose organization: it is not a military-strategic alliance, nor a full-fledged economic union, nor is it a political organization in the conventional sense. Taking into account various aspects, the possibility of creating an effective regional organization out of the SCO—comparable to NATO in terms of military or the EU in terms of political/economic decision making—may be an impressive undertaking. No doubt that still the major issues/problems are mostly handled at the bilateral level. And even if the SCO did succeed in developing into such an effective organization, the China's extraordinary growth would confine the other member states into little more than a supply-base for China's natural resources (Laumullin, 2006). To this end, May 2014 Sino-Russian deal of $400-billion gas supply opens up a new market for Moscow as it risks losing European customers over the Ukraine/Crimea crisis.

Russian and Chinese leadership increasingly interprets the approach of leading Western powers towards the SCO as negative. Furthermore, both countries have encountered a number of disagreements with Western states and organizations over normative issues, which in turn gave birth to a number of criticisms about the 'double standards' of Western powers vis-à-vis international affairs. In that sort of global political context, both China and Russia would use the SCO as a valuable tool to assert themselves in global affairs.

Chapter VI

Uyghurs at Eurasian Crossroads

China's Belt and Road initiative, which has become the centerpiece of China's economic diplomacy in Eurasia, has already started to transform the outlook of the region. Consequently, it would be fair to assert that Xinjiang and Central Eurasia play a crucial role in the success of this initiative. On the other hand, the growing Uyghur demand for a separate homeland and continuing ethnic tension in Xinjiang pose some challenges to China's authority in the region.

This chapter is inspired by a geopolitical method for analyzing the significance of identity formation among Uyghurs at the Eurasian crossroads along the Silk Road. Geopolitics is essential to the understanding of the behavior of human societies organized into complex, geographically well-defined systems.

It would be reasonable to allege that the fundamental impulse behind this chapter is to cultivate a renewed interest in and awareness of the identities along the Silk Road at the Eurasian crossroads. Efforts to revitalize the ancient Silk Road at the core of Eurasia explain the logic behind why a better knowledge base is required vis-à-vis the region.

The Uyghur people find themselves at the center of the Chinese-masterminded Belt and Road Initiative (BRI) to create land connectivity across Eurasia, which in turn provides a positive sign that this research is very timely. It intends to offer a much-needed fresh look at the robust Uyghur culture, language, and perplexing geopolitical history of the region. By doing that, the project would generate an intellectual environment to decipher the complexities of the area and shed light on the bewilderment of Tarim Basin communities.

Moreover, the chapter would focus on the examination of the political, linguistic, cultural, and religious identities of the Uyghurs of Central Asia within the context of historical transformations and state policies. For instance, it is looking at the formation and consolidation of Uyghur ethnic identity during the 20th century. It will attempt to show how externally imposed borders in Central Asia by China, Russia, and Britain during the Great Game negatively affected Uyghur ethnic identity.

Geographical Characteristics

Xinjiang is one of five of the People's Republic of China's ethnic "autonomous" regions, the others being Inner Mongolia, Ningxia, Guangxi, and Tibet (Xizang). It is the largest administrative division[66] covering 1.65 million sq km, representing 18 percent of geographical China. If it were a country by itself, then it would be ranked as the 18th largest country in the world between Libya and Iran.

Figure 12. *The Xinjiang Region*

Note. (Millward, 2021)

Xinjiang's geopolitical environment, historical/ cultural mosaic, and religious amalgamation are just a miniaturized version of much larger geography ranging from Khiva, Bukhara, Samarkand on the Westernmost edge to the Jiayu Pass[67] in the easternmost edge of Central Eurasia on the East-West direction and from Kazakh steppes of the northernmost edge to the Khyber Pass[68]/Kashmir in the southernmost edge.

The XUAR has grosso modo 5600 km of international borders, namely with Mongolia, Russia, Kazakhstan, Kyrgyzstan and Tajikistan, Afghanistan (Wakhan Corridor), and through Kashmir with Pakistan and India. All disputes on international borders have been addressed (especially with Russia) except a territorial conflict over specific segments of the international border with the Indian part of Kashmir. The Aksai Chin region is an integral part of the XUAR and Tibet from the Chinese perspective. In recent times, violent skirmishes occurred between India and China in 2020-22 over territorial sovereignty.

On a topographical level, almost two-thirds of the area of the XUAR consists of inhabitable deserts and high mountains. Only about 1.8% of its territory is cultivable land, 34% of which is used for pasture, while forests occupy 2.2% of the regional area. The continental location and mountain system of the XUAR have a powerful impact on its hydrographic and climatic conditions. The region is surrounded by the Karakorum Mountain range bordering Pakistan and India; the Kunlun Mountain range demarcating the border with Tibet Autonomous Region of China; the Pamir Mountain range with Tajikistan and Afghanistan; Tien Shan mountains with Kyrgyzstan; the Altai mountains with Kazakhstan, Russia, and Mongolia. On the other hand, the Taklamakan desert occupies most of the central and eastern parts of the XUAR bordering Gansu and Qinghai provinces of the PRC.

Moreover, it is also possible to envisage a horizontal division of the region into two distinctive subregions: Dzungarian Basin, the region's northern half taking its name from nomadic Dzunghar people, and the Tarim Basin, the regions' southern half where most of the PRC's cotton production originates due to the availability of freshwater resources through the melting snow. Although most of the region's rivers disappear in the desert, the Irtysh River, the longest tributary river in the world (4,228 km), is the main tributary of the Ob reaching the Arctic Ocean.

In a general sense, a province officially allows unique social, religious, and even political rights for the ethnic minorities native to the area. However, when it comes to autonomous regions, these privileges are not always applied. There is no doubt that China has strategic issues at stake in Xinjiang. Throughout Chinese history, it was deemed that the region was pivotal and a vast buffer zone shielding the core of China from foreign attacks and influences. Evidently, the geopolitical events of the 19th century through worldwide western colonization proved that the real danger came from the eastern seashores. But equally, Xinjiang has long served as a critical trade route for Chinese commerce through the notorious Silk Road, connecting mainland China to Central Asia, the Middle East, and Europe.

Today, Chinese geopolitical strategists are looking back to the old Silk Road routes as a way to safeguard economic and energy security. The overwhelming naval presence of the United States and other western nations in the Info-Pacific region, especially around the maritime choke points, contributes to the feeling of encirclement. Consequently, land connection with the rest of Eurasia seems more strategically valuable and manageable, providing a safe alternative to the eastern seashore.

Central Eurasia possesses a vast amount of natural resources, which are indispensable for future Chinese economic development. In that sense, Xinjiang offers an essential passageway to the rest of Eurasia. This geopolitical aspect reinforces Beijing's perceptions about the need to keep this autonomous region and its native Uyghur population along with other ethnic minorities under control.

Moreover, some dramatic economic transformations and political intrusions affected China and Central Eurasia in the final decades of the twentieth century. Currently, the economic rise of China has attracted lots of attention and has been labeled a success story by any standards. On the other hand, Uyghurs of the Tarim Basin are struggling to keep their cultural and ethnic identity as well as their religious beliefs due to the pressures received from Beijing. Needless to say that all along with its long history, China had intense commercial and cultural interaction with that hinterland.

Demographic Characteristics

Some of the most significant transformations in Xinjiang since 1949 have been related to demographic and economic changes. The Xinjiang Statistical Yearbook 2020 provides comparative and comprehensive demographic data regarding the trends. The XUAR, with a population of slightly over 25 million in 2020, is home to 13 recognized ethnic groups, namely Uyghur, Han, Kazakh, Hui (Dungans for non-Chinese speakers), Mongolian, Kyrgyz, Xibo, Tajik, Uzbek, Daur, Manchurian, Tatar, and Russian (Cappelletti, 2020). According to the census in 2020, the primary ethnic group, Uyghurs, with 12 million people, forms approximately 45 percent of the total population. The second-largest ethnic group, the Han Chinese, accounted for 42 percent, with close to 11 million people.

Indeed, the rapid increase of the Han population since independence is noticeable. The demographic aspect has also been specified as the cause of instability and tension. In the early 1800s, the population under the Qing dynasty was roughly 60 percent Turkic and 30 percent Han Chinese. The first census of PRC in 1953 census indicates that the population of the XUAR was almost 5 million, of which 75 percent were Uyghur and 6 percent were Han Chinese. In 1964 census documented a radical change in the Uyghur to Han ratio. The Uyghur proportion did go down to 54 percent, and Han Chinese did go up to 33 percent. Following the economic reforms initiated by Deng Xiaoping throughout the 1980s and 90s witnessed another hike in the Han population and another decline in the Uyghur population. The census of 2000 points out to a 45 percent Uyghur versus 40 percent Han Chinese out of 18.5 million overall population of the XUAR (Toops, 2004).

Although in contemporary times, Xinjiang is divided almost equally between Uyghur and Han communities in terms of the percentage, the region is still home to significant other groups. However, most of those minorities share Islamic and Turkic cultural and linguistic heritage with Uyghurs. Among the eight prefectures of the region-Turpan, Hami, Aksu, Kashgar, Khotan, Altay, Tacheng, and Ili-five are autonomous prefectures where the majority of the population is other than the Han and Uyghur; Kizilsu (Kyrgyz), Changji (Hui), Bortala-Bayangol (Mongol) and Ili (Kazakh). The ethnic composition of the region has been distorted by the CCP officials reflecting the lessons learned from the concept of nationalities shaped in the Stalinian USSR (Cappelletti, 2020).

Until 1949, over three-quarters of Xinjiang's population lived in the South and only one-quarter in the North. The situation changed dramatically in the following decades because the CCP officials embraced a strategy emphasizing the economic development of the North and overlooking the Uyghur-dominated South. The PRC employed policies similar to the Soviet policy to populate Soviet Central Asia with a Slavic population, where the percentage of ethnic Russians gained significance in mainly Kazakhstan, Kyrgyzstan, and urban areas of other titular Soviet republics of the region. The sustained waves of migrants arriving from China's Han-populated heartland for settling in the region were encouraged by the CCP. By the end of the Cold War, the population of the northern part of the XUAR outpaced the population of the South.

State-sponsored migration to Xinjiang was not a new phenomenon, and it had been utilized as a Qing policy since the 18th century. Nevertheless, it has been more resolutely followed after 1949. The primary drive for the state-sponsored population transfer during the PRC times is related to the CCP's goals of fostering the economic and cultural development of the region as it is deemed underdeveloped. In addition, those policies of Han migration to the XUAR had the ultimate goal to sinicize the western borders of the PRC as much as possible to solidify the territorial revendications.

Moreover, another rationale behind the policy may be categorized as an attempt to decrease the population pressures on the densely populated eastern parts of the country. Indeed, those major demographic upheavals were not done overnight and followed meticulously executed phases. For instance, the earliest period witnessed the arrival of the People's Liberation Army (PLA) personnel and administrative officials. Likewise, the inauguration of the Great Leap Forward through the second five-year economic plan (1958-1962) resulted in the arrival of the Xinjiang Production and Construction Corps. Another benchmark was the initiation of the Cultural Revolution (1966-1976), with the arrival of a great number of volunteers to the rural areas of the XUAR. However, the one-child policy (1980-2015) imposed on Han Chinese had a somehow unfavorable impact on the trends vis-à-vis the state-sponsored migration to the region.

The amelioration of the transportation system and the railroad's arrival to Urumchi in 1962 has also been a catalyzer development regarding the arrival of Han Chinese from the heartland. It did also help to alleviate the heavily distorted sex ratio since the Han migration was male-dominated primarily. In a similar way of territorial engineering in the USSR and the PRC for ethnicities and minorities, the CCP officials initiated a social engineering project to improve the gender ratio imbalances by encouraging young women from the Han Chinese heartland. In addition, many incentives such as financial assistance, housing, employment, a transfer of hukou (household registration), marriage arrangements to established immigrants were made available to the target population.

Islam in Xinjiang

Prior to the arrival of Islam in Xinjiang, the region experienced a set of diverse religions, ranging from Manicheism, Buddhism, and Nestorian Christianity (Beller-Hann, 2008). Islam reached China during the Tang dynasty soon after its revelation (610-632 AD) in the Middle East through sea route and land route.

The maritime Silk Roads had been instrumental in Islam's expansion towards eastern regions. Muslim merchants reached from the Arabian

Peninsula through the Indian Subcontinent, Southeastern archipelagos of Indonesia, and the Philippines reached the Southeast coastal ports of China. On the other hand, the land route expansion of Islam was associated with the battle of Talas (751 AD), where the Abbasid and Tang armies faced each other, which was significant in terms of its far-reaching consequences. The defeat of Tang marked the end of its westward expansion and gave birth to the increased leverage of the Islamic control of Transoxiana along with the contemporary Xinjiang territory as Tang's influence in the region retreated.

The 1980s were geopolitically tumultuous by any standards for Central Asia. Nevertheless, the disastrous Soviet campaign in Afghanistan followed by the rise of the Taliban and simultaneous Islamic revivalism had some stupendous implications for Uyghurs in the XUAR.

By the time of the Tiananmen square events in 1989, the number of mosques in Xinjiang had increased to some 20,000. However, the overwhelming majority were located in the southern part of Xinjiang, where Uyghurs had the absolute majority (Wang 2004). A decade later, at the closing years of the 20th century, the number had reached 23,000 and continued to grow (Mackerras 2001: 292).

The February 5th, 1997, Ghulja riots were based on demands of equal treatment, religious and cultural freedom, and freedom of speech while insisting on an end to the daily racial discrimination with the cultural and economic marginalization of the Uyghur community of the XUAR. Those riots, which resulted in the death or imprisonment of hundreds of Uyghurs, gave perfect modus operandi to CCP for a crackdown on 'illegal religion' by targeting the separatists, religious fundamentalists, political activists. Moreover, after the events of 9/11 and China's decision to jump aboard the US bandwagon known as the 'war on terror,' repression of religious activities in Xinjiang deepened further as state campaigns began to speak of 'international terrorists' and 'jihadists' (Dwyer 2005: 53-57).

The contemporary forces of globalization and the gradual opening of the PRC had a significant impact on the XUAR as a critical border region at the junction of China, Inner Asia, the Middle East, and Europe (Zhao 2001: 220), and as holding a pivotal position at the crossroads of six cultural and geographic regions (Becquelin 2000: 65). It is a territory that has been affected by differing cultures and shifting politics on all sides. Moreover, the emergence of the independent Central Asian states in 1991 has dramatically altered the geocultural and geopolitical dynamics of the Eurasian landmass (Zhao 2001: 220).

Like the rest of the PRC, Xinjiang was prohibited against outside influences in the earlier decades and subsequently had limited access to religious ideologies in other Muslim societies. However, globalization has considerably increased the flow of ideas and feelings from outside of Xinjiang into the region (cf. Mackerras 2001: 301). The Uyghur community became exposed to a variety of information, images, concepts, and lifestyles (Kim 2005: 446). Imported Islamic materials, pilgrimage to Mecca, Islamic theological studies abroad, and increased access to media coverage of Muslim issues worldwide played a vital part in the revivalism of traditional Islamic proclivity in Xinjiang. Consequently, the seclusion of the Uyghur Muslims in Xinjiang has been alleviated in specific ways while forging closer religious connections with the outside, which strengthened the religious identity formation process and the sense of being distinct and unique vis-à-vis the Han Chinese identity.

The re-Islamization of the Uyghurs of the XUAR can be understood as a convenient vehicle to prompt resistance against the perceived oppressive policies of the PRC. There are plenty of examples during the colonization/decolonization era indicating a similar role played by Islam[69]. Moreover, it is also very well possible that the impression of unequal and unfair economic opportunities available to the Uyghur community precipitated a reinvigorated Islam in the region. Those reactions can partly be considered a natural reaction to the failure of China's economic policies to benefit all ethnic groups in the XUAR equally.

The Sources of the Unrest

The section below is keen to explore the sources of Uyghur discontentment and ethnic strife in Xinjiang. To this end, it will investigate the 20th century by dividing it into two equal parts as pre and post-independence of the PRC. However, a third period covering from 9/11 to the present requires cautious and vigilant scrutiny due to its unique transformational and transitional dynamics.

Pre-1949 Period

This Turkic Muslim minority with an estimated population of 11 million is the fifth most populous ethnic group among the 56 minority groups officially recognized by the Chinese government. The concept of Zhonghua minzu as the Chinese communist party defines it. The CCP treats the Uyghurs as an ethnic minority, not a nation. Uyghurs reside mainly in the Xinjiang autonomous region of northwest China – the largest administrative unit in the country with its 1.6 million km^2. Although Xinjiang is a province that officially allows unique social, religious, and even political rights for Uyghurs native to the region, these privileges are not always applied. The historical circumstances of the development of Uyghur identity can be revealed by examining the political formation in the late Qing and early republican eras (Brophy, 2016; Brophy, 2011).

Certainly, Tsarist Russia, Ottoman Turkey, and then the Soviet Union played a significant role in the creation of a specific group within the Muslims of Chinese Turkistan. Accordingly, it would be more suitable to identify Xinjiang not as a periphery but as an intersection of empires in many ways very similar to the Balkans or the Caucasus regions. In this tumultuous epoch at the turn of the Great century, the Russian, British, and Qing empires' geopolitical interests converged with some dramatic implications for Central Asian populations. By extending the implications of the Great Game to Xinjiang, China, along Russia became an actor while unveiling the connections to Ottoman Turkey and the British/Japanese disposition vis-à-vis Xinjiang.

There is no doubt that China has strategic issues at stake in Xinjiang. Throughout Chinese history, this province has been one of the largest buffer zones shielding the core of China from foreign attacks and influences. Equally, Xinjiang has long served as a critical trade route for Chinese commerce through the notorious historical Silk Road, connecting mainland China to Central Asia, the Middle East, and Europe. Currently, the Belt and Road initiative of Chinese President Xi Jinping gives some good indications about the importance and relevance of the core of Eurasia. Consequently, the exposing of the period between the 1880s and the 1930s would be valuable to better comprehend the contemporary geopolitical contests in Xinjiang. The examination of the history of the Soviet Central Asian republics and the history of Xinjiang within the framework of a larger Turkistan would provide the rationale behind the adoption of the Uyghur idea of nationhood from the Soviet Union to Xinjiang as a part of the Bolshevik revolutionary mission. Three distinct groups of Xinjiang Muslims – Kashgaris, Taranchis, and Dungans – moving back and forth across Russian and Chinese Turkistan were instrumental in the dissemination of the revolutionary or the reformist concepts. Moreover, the section(s) dedicated to Jadidism yields an exceptionally compelling account of the origins of Uyghur nationhood. No doubt, the Jadidist movement in Russian Turkistan has been the subject of considerable research (Skrine & Ross, 2005); however, much less is known about the impact of Jadidism on Chinese Turkistan.

At this junction, a detailed account of intellectual collaboration taking place between the Muslims of China and the Ottoman Turks would be valuable. Most certainly, the fall of the Qing Empire in 1912 and the start of the WWI in 1914 provided the necessary political vacuum and weak governance structures for pan-Turkic ideas to flourish among Muslims in Xinjiang. Certainly, it is possible to find its roots simultaneously in multiple sources, ranging from local Islamic tradition to transnational pan-Turkic ideas and Orientalism. The origins of Uyghur nationhood are closely connected to the redesigning of the Turkic past by the Uyghur intellectuals who flourished in the Russian Muslim and Ottoman avant-garde milieus.

The rise of Jadidism is just a reflection of the massive shift of power due to the decline/collapse of the Ottoman Empire, which led to the subordination of Muslims and deprived Central Asia of the intellectual and spiritual guidance of the Sublime Porte. Brophy marvelously diagnoses all the epic changes that were taking place within Xinjiang and the Uyghur nation. Most certainly, the movement did an excellent service to the development of the national self-consciousness of the Uyghurs and played a fundamental role in the formation and development of a national liberation ideology.

Most importantly, the movement reminded the Turkic/Muslim populace of the region of ideals such as freedom, national pride, great ancestors, and rich cultures that were put down in a dormant phase by the Qing Empire. The Jadidist action program became a model for future generations. The historical merit of the Jadids was their attempts to uplift society starting from the smallest, i.e., education and its development.

The study of Uyghurs at the heart of Eurasia is important in several ways. Firstly, such a study would provide numerous valuable insights into the interaction(s) that took place between China and the Russian Empire, and to a lesser extent with the Ottoman Empire, in the early twentieth century. Consequently, a better understanding of the evolving Uyghur identity would also shed light on Sino-Russian relations of the late Russian Empire/early Soviet period and the late years of the collapsing Qing Empire followed by the tumultuous years of rebellion/civil war.

Post-1949 Period

The contemporary occurrences of ethnic uneasiness in Xinjiang can be tied up to several factors such as, among others, the enduring culture of violence, regional autonomy system, and foreign influences. To some extent, all those factors contributed to the worsening of the conflict in the region.

Various autonomous regional structures around the world illustrate the fact that they have been erected to protect either the states' territorial integrity or the decaying rights of minorities. The in-place political system in Xinjiang has systematically prevented Uyghur attempts to initiate the desired autonomy and hence provoked and aggravated Uyghur discontentment.

The turbulent early decades of the PRC as an outcome of disastrous policies of the Great Leap Forward in 1958 and the Cultural Revolution in 1966 also took a heavy toll on Uyghurs in Xinjiang. The lack of true regional autonomy, repressive policies aiming at linguistic and cultural assimilation, and religious persecutions gave birth to the sentiment of estrangement among most Uyghurs in Xinjiang.

The arrival of Deng Xiaoping to the leadership position in 1978 and the transformation of the system through economic reforms created a honeymoon period for cultural tolerance in the country in the 1980s. On the other hand, Chinese officials argue that the derelict policies pursued by PRC in the 1980s in the region permitted the separatist organizations and Islamic extremists, influenced by the events taking place next door in Afghanistan against the Soviet invasion, to grow in number and become more influential.

However, the manifestations in Xinjiang in 1988 and 1989 and a violent uprising in 1990 opened the door for a policy swing by Deng Xiaoping, authorizing a clampdown in the province. Since those dying days of the Cold War until today, the repressive measures put in place for Xinjiang on language, culture, religion remained largely intact and meticulously observed.

Unfailingly punitive and oppressive reactions to the manifestations, along with wide-ranging maltreatment of religion, incubated violence and desperation among Uyghurs by shutting down the path for political solutions to the majority's apprehension in the region.

Although the decentralization of the economy has been pursued in many provinces of the country, Xinjiang has been mostly an exception to that policy. The state authority is still overwhelmingly omnipresent due to the region's disproportionate concentration of state enterprises and dependence on subsidies.

Moreover, massive Han migration for employment in the natural resources sectors contributed to the resentment of Uyghurs. The privileges given to Han officials at all levels of public life amplified the bitterness and grievance (Bovingdon, 2004). The situation on the ground looked very similar to the colonization of the land by Han Chinese and the Uyghurs being colonial subjects. Han immigration and state policies have perilously intensified the pressure on Uyghurs to assimilate linguistically and culturally, which in turn, evidently colliding with the straightforward protections mentioned in the constitution. Those Chinese policies enforced the sense of detachment between Uyghurs and Hans in Xinjiang, and it is probably one of the most significant sources of conflict indicating a profound Uyghur discontent with Chinese rule in Xinjiang.

International Influences

Although Uyghur discontent cannot be associated exclusively with international influences, there are still several ways that the international aspects were felt heavily vis-à-vis the politics and policies in the Xinjiang Uyghur Autonomous Region (XUAR). Evidently, with its wide-ranging ethnic minorities, religions, and federal structure, the USSR furnished a model to observe and learn for CCP officials. Consequently, the

Chinese planners have meticulously analyzed Leninist interpretation of nationalism and territoriality, Stalinist purges, Khrushchevian thaws, or Gorbachevian glasnost to apply them to peripheral regions of the PCR. The minzu system of regional autonomy management had been constantly updated and adapted with one eye on Soviet experiences. The preferential policies put in place to protect distinct ethnic identities and the institutionalization of those policies followed the example set by the USSR. In crude terms, the way the Soviets planners designed a model "Homo Sovieticus, " the Chinese planners pursued devising a Homo Sinocus. To this end, the preferential policies while recruiting professionals or students among non-Han populations scrutinized the Soviet model. Particularly the too-fast and too-late policy initiatives of the Gorbachev era and the following period of disintegration of the USSR was eye-opening for the PCR. They have unquestionably studied the Soviet example to avoid precipitating the crises that faced Moscow.

After following the events of Tiananmen Square in 1989, several countries in the West got interfered mainly regarding the Tibetan culture and identity, which is another autonomous region and the second-largest administrative unit of the PRC after Xinjiang. The catchphrase was the protection of human rights and democratic values. During the Clinton Presidency in the 1990s, human rights were pivotal regarding the US foreign policy orientation. Such policies to protect human rights worldwide by the only remaining superpower encouraged Uyghurs to expect to find allies in their endeavor. Moreover,

Following the end of WWII, until the establishment of the PRC,

It was apparent that the Kuomintang (KMT) was on the losing end of the struggle between Nationalists and communists. Several foreign governments have sought to influence politics in Xinjiang, with the US and the USSR mounting the most consistent efforts, such as sending agents to Xinjiang and Tibet for an intelligence assessment.

In the 1960s, the US government supported Uyghur language broadcasts geared towards China. Even the rapprochement of the 1970s between the two countries did not subdue American intervention in Xinjiang (also in Tibet). Hence, the establishment of Radio Free Asia (RFA) in 1996 and the Uyghur service starting in 1998, broadcasting information critical of the Chinese state had been interpreted as a hostile act by the PRC.

The Soviet Union was even more involved than the United States, sending advisors and intelligence officers to Xinjiang in the 1930s. The establishment of a communist regime in China did not change Kremlin's desire to retain political and commercial leverage in the region. Moreover, the Sino-Soviet Split during the Khrushchev era accelerated those activities. For instance, the 1962 departure of 60,000 Uyghur and Kazak dissidents from Xinjiang to Kazakh SSR became a showcase to illustrate the far superior living conditions in the USSR compared to Xinjiang. Daily Uyghur-language broadcasts from Tashkent, Uzbek SSR, were used to rebuke the Chinese cultural and linguistic policies against the Uyghurs in Xinjiang. The main goal from the Soviet perspective was to incite Uyghurs for further self-determination with the ultimate goal of creating a so-called East Turkistan. Of course, the violent Sino-Soviet border conflict of 1969 near Zhenbao (Damansky) Island on the Ussuri River, near Manchuria, did open the possibilities for further border incursions into Xinjiang the same year. Moreover, the demise of the Soviet system in 1991 inadvertently opened pandora's box for Chinese politics in Xinjiang. The emergence of fully independent states by various Turkic ethnic groups in West Turkistan gave further motivation to Uyghurs expecting political change.

Non-governmental organizations (NGOs) have also been instrumental in uplifting the Uyghur spirit for further autonomy and have given Uyghurs greater international visibility. After the independence of Soviet Central Asia, Uyghurs established formal political organizations in Kazakhstan and Kyrgyzstan bordering Xinjiang. Like any other NGOs, those groups were motivated to influence global and Chinese policies for greater international stature for the independence movement. However, Chinese officials tried to overcome those influences by using international organizations such as the SCO to pressure the respective countries to rein on those movements. On the other hand, the dynamic and politically active Uyghur diaspora across the globe provides support and funds for resistance to Chinese policies in Xinjiang.

The high-profile multilateral interventions of the 1990s, such as Bosnia and Kosovo, broadly inspired Uyghurs with a significant impact on Xinjiang politics while alarming the Chinese officials. Moreover, allegedly the accidental bombing of the Chinese embassy in Belgrade on May 7, 1999, had been interpreted by the Uyghurs and Tibetans as a sign that the international community would equally support their causes. However, 9/11 and the subsequent invasions of Afghanistan and Iraq considerably reduced the likelihood of international intervention on Uyghurs' behalf. Nevertheless, the geopolitical chess game in Central Asia required the Chinese support of the US for a successful campaign against al-Qaeda and the Taliban in Afghanistan. Moreover, coincidentally the admission of the PRC to the WTO on December 11, 2001, exactly three months after the 9/11 terrorist attack following a lengthy and challenging 13 years of negotiation, opened more conciliatory US policies vis-à-vis Xinjiang.

Along with this policy change, several organizations, such as the Eastern Turkistan Islamic Movement (ETIM), declared a terrorist organization by the US. To Beijing's satisfaction, Uyghurs became a victim of realpolitik among great powers.

Conclusion

Numerous studies have been completed highlighting the significance of actors outside of the state in various global issue areas. Yet, the preponderance of research in world politics remains state centric and the prevailing theories in international relations generally overlook the activity of entities outside of the state. Both realism and institutionalism analyze international politics only at the systemic level. Both theories consider states the main actors in an anarchical system and share a good deal when it comes to understanding the nature of global politics.

However, it may be necessary to draw a line between geopolitics and the realist school of international relations. Somewhat, geopolitics has been corrupted by its sporadic association with realist thinking of IR. Realism is bestowed in power politics, which is one of the most ambivalent terms in the lexicon of international relations. IR scholars utilize the notion of polarity to explain the distribution of power in the international system. The balance of power[70] and balancing/bandwagoning[71] are just some foreign policy options for states searching for security to navigate in a treacherous anarchic world. Both realism and geopolitics contain balance-of-power theories; however, their descriptions and use differ by subject. For realism, the relative physical strengths of nations or coalitions are determined by physical-balance relationships. In contrast, the geopolitical balance of power relies on spatial positions or patterns. In geopolitical terms, security derives more from position than from power. In addition, realists describe international politics as a model of billiard balls in which states are the only important actors (Waltz, 1979). From the realist point of view cooperation is not expected to be either extensive or durable (Carr, 1939; Grieco, 1990; Morgenthau, 1948; Walt, 1987; Waltz, 1979).

There is no doubt that states are very important actors in world politics and fundamentally constitute the international system. To this day, the nation-state has prevailed over all other actors in world politics, to an extent that "international relations" not world politics is the conventional title given to this field of study since the formation of Westphalian international system (Krasner, 1999; Lyons & Mastanduno, 1995). Indeed, it is also possible to locate common denominators between geopolitics and the realist model of IR. For instance, history and geography can be conducive to determining the power's operation, range, and capacity to plan/implement. Although the geopolitical study of power in time and space pertaining to foreign policy and military action is essential in understanding international relations, military history, and the development of states and state systems; the excessive reliance upon power is unfamiliar to geopolitics. If geopolitics means that geography is an essential factor in understanding a country's foreign and security policy, then geopolitics is critical. For example, comprehending the Chinese and Russian strategic and foreign policies in historical terms would be arduous and problematic without considering their geographic factors.

The spatial positioning of states is the main emphasis and concern of geopolitics, unlike the concept of power attributed to states in realism. Consequently, the 21st-century geopolitical model necessitates a clear departure from any association with the realist model and its power description. The independent variables of geopolitical thinking are remarkably distinct from the realist model. Most certainly, Realism as a dominant paradigm in IR offers invaluable tools to analyze the international system. However, the geopolitical model also can make its separate contribution to deciphering the central tenets of the international system.

Throughout most parts of the 20th century, geopolitics was at the core of international relations thinking; however, it was widely assumed to have lost relevance with the end of the Cold War. Scholars, while dismissing geopolitical considerations, moved on toward issue areas such as transnational actors, global governance, the impact of domestic politics, international development, international organizations, trade liberalization, feminist perspectives, nuclear nonproliferation, psychological explanations of international conflict, human rights, international law, and environmental changes (Gourevitch, 2002; Martin & Simmons, 2001; Maxfield, 2002; Mitchell, 2002; Raustiala & Slaughter, 2002; Risse, 2002; Schmitz & Sikkink, 2002; Simmons & Martin, 2002 ; Stein, 2002; Tickner, 2002).

Conflict among states had become less common after the demise of the Soviet Union, but new types of violence were on the rise. While the pertinence of the state was not abrogated, its grandstanding as an explanatory power seemed to lose ground vis-à-vis other actors. Within that context, the geopolitical analysis also considered *démodé* as a vestige of the old Cold War times and charged with strangely missing the evolving international relations.

That having been said, in recent times, geopolitics has been reincarnated as a powerful tool to analyze perplexing international puzzles (Agnew, 1985, 1995; Agnew, 2003; Kaplan, 2012; Sicherman, 2002). Many episodes of unfolding dramas of rising strategic competition across Eurasia, ranging from Ukraine to Syria to the Caucasus, to name a few, create intriguing puzzles to tackle for international relations. The formation of an encouraging zeitgeist following the Cold War all but evaporated while opening an unchartered path for a gloomy panorama of the international system. The salient matter is that the return of geopolitics (Mead, 2014) is also activated a seismic geopolitical shift regarding the great power rivalries in Eurasia. In a way, the heavyweights of Eurasian geopolitics, Russia, and China, act as force multipliers for each other in Eurasia and beyond. The arrival of Cold Warlike developments has been scrupulously observed by academics as well as policymakers and political leaders. Consequently, it would be fair to assert that the 21st-century international system is witnessing a gradual reactivation and intensification of geopolitical thinking (Atkinson & Dodds, 2000).

Geopolitics' recent re-emerged popularity in common parlance highlights the fact that location does matter. The main assumption is that geography is an important independent variable for an analytical model analyzing the possible outcomes of political control of space by states. The classical realist Hans Morgenthau labeled the geographical factors and natural resources as critical elements in the determination of the national power and the fate of nations. To some extent, the significance of geography as a driver of state behavior originates from its durability in time. Put it differently, the politico-administrative units such as kingdoms, empires, and the nations or the rulers at the helm of those units do exist only very temporarily based on Fernand Braudel's concept of *Longue Durée*[72]; on the other hand, geographical attributes such as rivers, oceans, mountains, steppes, forests, and desserts remain subject only to gradual slow-motion environmental alterations. Along this line of logic, the centuries-long clashes in Eurasia from Eastern Europe to the South China Sea through the Caucasus and Central Asia should not be without warning and random.

Although the future structure of polarity and the prevalence of strategic stability in the international system are still through a transformational phase, the balance of power is never stagnant, functioning as a dynamic correlation of forces in a perpetual state of constant change. Evidently, in a sense, wars are the best decisive tools to reconfigure the existing political equilibrium with the aim of revising the international system. Certainly, it is difficult to clearly predict the outcome of the current reconfiguration process. The new system may favor the American-led western world along with like-minded peripheral East Asian countries or the axis of continental Eurasian powers. However, as we witness the post-communist honeymoon period of Russia with the West is over following the 2014 and 2022 crisis in Ukraine, the Sino-Russian rapprochement and entente within the Eurasian regional context is also an influential force not to take lightly.

China and Evolving Eurasian Geopolitics

The value of geopolitical concepts can be seen in Chinese foreign and security policy discussions. In geopolitical terms, China represents the elements of both rimland (coastal China) and heartland (Chinese Central Asia). China's reassertion of its sovereignty over part of Central Asia between 1937–1945 was a response to Japan's conquest of much of China's coastal rimland leading to the transformation of dynamics between the Kuomintang and other regional forces in different parts of the country (Lin, 2008). Such alteration of the geopolitical context transformed modern China from a maritime economy ingrained in East Asian trade to a continental one based on overland trade routes through Eurasia. Consequently, this transformation of the Chinese geopolitical setting accompanied fundamental political and cultural consequences, which was the dominant theme during the communist era. The Chinese geopolitical drive into Central Asia was renewed after the demise of the Soviet Union as Russia ceased to dominate the region (Banuazizi & Weiner, 1994; Walsh, 1993). President Xi Jinping's policy initiative to rejuvenate the ancient Silk Road in 2013 was just another manifestation of those transformations by unveiling the ambitious program to knit together modern continental Eurasia. During the annual meetings of the Boao Forum[73] for Asia (BFA), President Xi has always been very resolute about China's commitment to advancing a cohesive partnership for a prosperous cohabitation in Eurasia (Jinping, 2018).

The geopolitical expression of the Belt and Road initiative assigns an intrinsic value to the road itself through a manifestation of cultural expression for political goals. For example, the seven expeditions of Zheng He[74] between 1405 and 1433 extended China's political sway over maritime Asia for half a century (Dreyer, 2007). While exploring Southeast Asia, India, the Persian Gulf, and the east coast of Africa, Zheng He visited some thirty states using navigational techniques and ships that were well ahead of their time and well before European explorers. Each expedition implicated tens of thousands of government troops and operated more than a hundred ocean-going vessels. The Chinese fleet was 90 times bigger than that of the Portuguese navigator Vasco de Gama and capable of transporting 150 times the number of marines. As a result of these expeditions, more than sixteen states between Java and the Persian Gulf sent tributes to the Ming court (Tsai,

1996). In addition, numerous envoys from foreign countries journeyed to China to pay homage to the Ming emperor. He was commemorated in 2005, while his seven expeditions were proudly spotlighted in the 2008 Beijing Olympics. Yet, the use of spatial elements in the past had been politically immensely valuable, such as population settlement patterns or territorial extension, with geopolitical implications opening the path to making further territorial claims or extending political influence. For instance, the Russian diaspora[75] in the former Soviet states and, to a lesser extent, the Chinese diaspora[76] in Southeast Asia could play a pivotal role in meddling in the internal affairs of those respective countries.

The geopolitical analysis can be a valuable tool to shed light on the development of China's international relations in the last 500 years since the beginning of the *Age of Exploration*. For example, Ming China's relations with Mongolians in the mid-15th Century were contentious.

The Mongols were considered a constant threat to the citizens. At the same time, the Ming Dynasty was unable to maintain military dominance on the steppe resulting in the subsequent shift to a defensive policy of wall building. It can also be interpreted as continuing resentment following the Mongolian Yuan[77] rule between 1271 and 1368 and subsequently giving birth to xenophobic[78] behavior by alienating them on cultural or trade grounds. Indeed, these factors play a crucial role in China's assessment of foreigners and, more importantly, its relationship with the outside world. Due to conflictual relations with the Mongols, Ming China renounced the voyages to the

Indian Ocean after 1433 and concentrated on conflict to the North and neglecting, at their peril, the potential threats originating from southern borders. Consequently, in 1498, when the Portuguese embarked on their voyages to the East, they encountered little resistance to their advancement, which opened the path eventually leading to the Century of Humiliation. In Mackinderian terms, China appeared to be more of a continental power than an oceanic one due to the changing geopolitical balance between the oceans and the heartland.

Figure 13. *Fifteenth-century China*

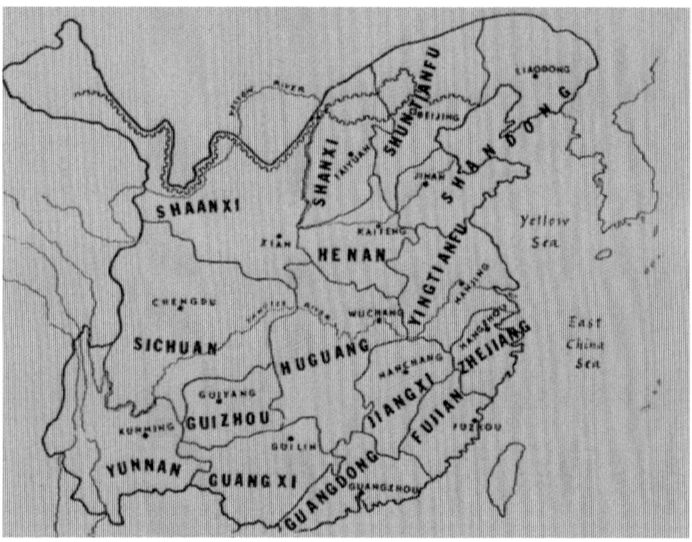

Note. (Tsai, 1996)

In geopolitical terms, continental Eurasia represents a great opportunity for China to escape from the overwhelming US military and strategic presence in the Western Pacific. In economic terms, China considers Eurasian developing countries as a suitable and lucrative destinations for the excess capacity of its industrial production. Consequently, keep providing the country with much expected full employment and high annual economic growth rates to pull millions out of poverty and create a robust middle class. In political terms, the Chinese economic development furnishes a functioning alternative to the western ones and a role model in the long haul for the developing Eurasian countries. However, an economic downturn or crisis situation would be considered unstabilizing, not only detrimental to Chinese leadership in the Eurasian region but also an existential threat to the CCP leadership's hold on power and China's cohesiveness.

Russia and Evolving Eurasian Geopolitics

Eurasia has been pivotal to relations between Europe and Asia across space and time. Indeed, being the crossroads of civilizations contributed to the cultural and ethnic diversity of the region. Eurasia lost its geostrategic value against the US liberal world order with the disintegration of influential Eurasian connecting politico-administrative units (the fall of the Ottoman Empire[79] in 1922 and the Soviet Union in 1991). Today, Russia, like China, is a major revisionist power in Eurasia, with significant implications for the realignment of the global order and the capacity to design new relationships across the region.

In historical terms, Russia is located on the margins of Europe proper, and Russian society experienced the transformational political, economic, and societal events of Western Europe only partially and belatedly. For instance, the Renaissance, the Reformation, and the Revolutions shaping the modern European value system have impacted the Russian identity to a much lesser level. The geographical vastness/remoteness of the country, along with the intriguing Cyrillic alphabet, and the cohabitation of hundreds of different ethnic groups and languages, are just the manifestation of a few easily observable realities enhancing and promoting the distinctiveness of Russia and Russians. Russians also have questioned their ambivalent position vis-à-vis European or Asian characteristics of their identity. Indeed, another point of view focused on Russian exceptionalism, a unique Slavic civilization destined to provide the world with a "third" way[80].

The re-emergence of Eurasianist doctrines after the disappointing and tumultuous decade following the disintegration of the Soviet Union was a sort of confirmation that Russia holds a unique place between Europe and Asia. The Cyrillic alphabet appears mysterious to the uninitiated, as does the odd system of dual dates for key historical events. Russia is huge and geographically remote, with over one hundred ethnic groups and many languages.

The Euroasianist approach emphasizes aspects of Russian culture resulting from the centuries-long interaction and fusion of Slavic elements with Turko-Muslim identities throughout the vast geography. Moreover, Eurasianism rejects the idea that Russia is on the periphery of Europe and considers it a forte originating from the country's geographical peculiarity. The Eurasianist discourse has been appealing in Russian politico-military circles because it did provide a comprehensible framework to grasp the realities behind the collapse of the Soviet Union. Eurasianism's call for a civilizational definition of Russia is another manifestation of geopolitical thinking as a conceptual framework to understand the regionalism in Eurasia (Laruelle, 2012).

Russia's Eurasianist orientation has been materialized through the resistance against the US-led liberal world order and a general rejection of Europe, the West, and capitalism which was considered disastrous for the rest of humankind. The Eurasian geopolitical framework plays a vital role for Russia by overcoming the feeling of failure following the collapse of the Soviet Union and by providing the necessary lebensraum[81] for Russian national security, foreign policy, and Russia's role in the 21st-century international politics. Moreover, the idea that Russia is holding a central geographical position in Eurasian space, naturally and inevitably, involves an imperial form of political organization. In a sense, regional organizations such as the Shanghai Cooperation Organization, Collective Security Treaty Organization, or Eurasian Economic Union play a pivotal role in achieving strategic and geopolitical goals.

The dismemberment of the Soviet Union has had a substantial impact on the geopolitical features of the Russian Federation. The Eurasian periphery of the Russian heartland has experienced some revolutionary geopolitical changes since the disintegration of the Soviet Union. This periphery now represents the zone of convergence among the heartland, the maritime realm, South Asia, and East Asia. The former satellite regions of the Eurasian rimland have become the subject of political maneuvering against Russian geopolitical interest.

In contrast to the Tsarist or Soviet territorial expansion era, Moscow has now focused on preventing the erosion of its influence over neighboring states. Regardless, Russia remains an intimidating state to reckon with, the largest political landmass in the world, extending for nine thousand km from west to east across eleven time zones and a north-south width of 2,500 to 4,000 km from its the Arctic north to the Black Sea, the Caucasus, and the mountains of southern Siberia. No other national state possesses Russia's spatial depth. An analysis of Russia's geopolitical features pinpoints the ingrained strength allowing it to recuperate so quickly from the decade of political and social instability and economic disarray that followed the demise of the USSR. Regaining its status as a major power that controls the Eurasian heartland enables Russia to pressure on the Eurasian periphery, especially in Syria, Iran, and Ukraine, thus wielding global influence once more (Cohen, 2005).

In recent times, from the Russian perspective, a significant challenge has been the maintenance of Russian dominance in Ukraine and the prevention of further expansion of NATO in Scandinavia or near abroad . Consequently, Russia found itself strategically exposed to NATO's eastward expansionist policies in the European theater. In those terms, further deepening and Eurasian connectivity presented itself as a viable alternative to the US lead western alliance system.

In concluding remarks, geopolitical thinking, preoccupied with borders, resources, flows, territories, and identities, provides a framework for critical analysis and understanding, which is essential in 21st-century international relations. Geopolitics offers a good range of tools to decipher the global landscape by utilizing geographical descriptions and metaphors, such as iron curtain, Third World[82], or rogue state[83].

Many factors are at play to vindicate the essentiality of a geopolitical framework. This is particularly more nuanced in Eurasia. For instance, think about the impact of the rising temperatures and the environmental change taking place in the vastness of Siberia's north by 2050, which would permit the spread of crops and people to the Arctic coast and the use of its coastal waters for east-west shipping. Undoubtedly, the recent unfolding events in the South China Sea, Ukraine, Syria, Kashmir, Afghanistan, and Korean Peninsula are clear indications of the continued relevance of geopolitics in Eurasia and global politics.

Based on the discussions that have underpinned this book, it is evident that Eurasia is set to face multiple geopolitical fault-lines that set the stage for great power rivalry. The future two volumes on evolving Eurasian geopolitics will delve into different geographies in Eurasia. The second volume will explore geopolitical contours of South Asia and West Asia and finally the third volume will investigate geostrategic calculations in Northeast Asia and Southeast Asia. Moreover, along the geographical focus there are several issues ranging from security dilemmas/paradoxes to nuclear proliferation to territorial disputes in Eurasia will be the subject matter of the following volumes.

For instance, the security dilemma[84] reflects the difficulty that states have in ascertaining if the military postures of rival states are driven by defensive intentions or offensive ones. A closely related term is that of the security paradox, in which a state's attempts to acquire more defensive weaponry are taken as evidence of hostile intentions by its rival, resulting in a vicious circle of escalating mutual hostility that thereby leads to the paradoxical effect of reduced security for both.

Within Eurasia, the patterns of interaction that are described by the security dilemma are reflected in the current patterns of Sino-American interaction on the one hand and the Russo-American interaction on the other. The US stands as the status quo superpower in the Indo-Pacific region whilst retaining numerous allies and security partners in the region. At the same time, in committing itself to the security of these allies through the forward deployment of the US military in the Indo-Pacific region, the US defense posture has also alarmed China over the prospect of a US-led effort to geostrategically encircle China.

The utility of the geopolitical security dilemma as an analytical tool is reflected elsewhere in the Asia Pacific region. In Northeast Asia, North Korea has come to regard its missile and nuclear programs as an instrument of regime survival; nonetheless, these same capabilities are regarded as offensive capabilities by the ROK, Japan, and the US. Yet, by adopting coercive security and diplomatic policies in response, the US and Japan (along with past ROK Presidencies) have increased the extent of the North Korean leadership's paranoia.

Another important issue that is closely related to security dilemma tensions concerns the issue of nuclear proliferation[85]. Without its missile and nuclear programs, North Korea could plausibly be ignored by the bulk of the international community. At the same time, however, North Korea's ongoing progress with its nuclear missile program has deeper ramifications. Were Japan to respond to the North Korean or Chinese threats to its security by developing an independent nuclear arsenal, such a development, in conjunction with Japan's ambivalence in acknowledging its wartime legacy, is certain to spark off a regional nuclear arms race.

Moreover, a further issue of importance concerns maritime territorial disputes in the Indo-Pacific region. This overlaps with related issues such as the ability to control the critical SLOCs upon which national pride, energy security, freedom of mercantile navigation, and naval power projection intersect. Although the prospect of territorial land disputes has a comparatively low probability of leading to armed skirmishes or conflict, nonetheless, the possibility of such developments occurring must be considered in light of the territorial disputes between India-Pakistan-China as well as between Thailand and Cambodia.

In contrast to territorial disputes, a dispute of sovereignty is far more serious insofar as a state's right to exist itself comes under challenge. Under such circumstances, such a state will have its back to the wall and thus be forced to fight to survive. A dispute of sovereignty arguably describes the armed standoff on the Korean Peninsula, given that both Seoul and Pyongyang do not recognize the diplomatic legitimacy of the other side. Nonetheless, the prospect of such a situation leading to armed conflict is low, given that the leaders of both

Koreas are aware of the extensive devastation that would result from a conflict.

A rather more serious political fault-line in this regard is the status of Taiwan. China has consistently rejected the status of Taiwan as an independent country and, on multiple occasions in the past, made fairly explicit threats of force to prevent such an outcome. This is further complicated by a growing demographic of Taiwanese who were born after the separation of Taiwan from the mainland, who have little emotional connection to China, and who have since embraced the democratization of Taiwan (in contrast to the continued authoritarianism in China). Moreover, with the Trump Administration's increasingly acrimonious trade war with China taking place alongside a rapprochement of sorts with Taiwan in a US attempt to counter the rise of China, such a convergence of events leads to the possibility of strategic miscalculation occurring over Taiwan.

Moreover, transnational security issues concern the full spectrum of security issues that may transcend national boundaries. In this regard, such issues take the form of transnational organized crime (involving activities such as human trafficking, sexual slavery, the narcotics trade, piracy, and the trade-in illicit firearms), terrorism (for instance, terrorist organizations that operate on border areas) as well as the environmental impact of pollution.

In addition, the onset of climate change and global warming is likely to have multiple severe impacts on maritime states, low-lying island nations, and ecological systems. Rising sea levels will inflict havoc on low-lying coastal communities, and climate change will lead to more extreme weather conditions such as typhoons, hurricanes, tropical storms, and cyclones. This will, in turn, impact agricultural outputs that will imperil global food chains.

Notes

01 The term iron curtain was coined after WW II in the heydays of the Cold War. The analogy portrayed a very real sense of a geographical division cutting across continental Europe. Metaphorically speaking, a curtain made of iron not only contains light from filtering through it but also prevents any other flows such as people or goods through complete isolation. The geographical imaginations of the iron curtain have been instrumental for Winston Churchill and, later, Ronald Reagan making reference to light/darkness or evil empire concepts and highlighting the deep divisions in Europe along with liberal democracies of the West and fascist/communist regimes of the East.

02 Pivotal land and sea corridors show as choke points, these being straits, passages, canals, channels, and river estuaries whose positions exert impact over an extended distance beyond their immediate locations.

03 The Great Game refers to Russian and British geopolitical thinking in Central Asia and Afghanistan in the late 19th century. Lord Curzon (Viceroy of India, 1899–1905) was a firm believer in British territorial expansion in Central Eurasia, subsequently reluctant to abide by all earlier treaties with Afghanistan. According to Curzon, Central Eurasian geography was a chessboard where the Great Game was played for world dominance. The revival of British expansionism and occupation of southern Afghanistan, namely, the vital Khyber Pass, prompted Tsarist Russia to respond in a similar manner.

04 The Belt and Road Initiative suggested in 2013 consists of two pillars: the Silk Road Economic Belt and the Twenty-First-Century Maritime Silk Road. Xi Jinping raised the first in his speech during his visit to Nursultan then Astana, Kazakhstan, in March 2013, and the second was proposed in November 2013 during a speech given in Jakarta, Indonesia, marking the birth of this grand geopolitical strategy.

05 The middle-income trap points out a situation where a middle-income country is unsuccessful in convergence in transitioning its economic development path to a high-income status as a result of rising costs and declining competitiveness. Many economies in the developing Third World have been confined to a middle-income trap distinguished by the stagnation of GDP per capita and a sluggishness in their economy's competitiveness. Investment, innovation, and timely structural reforms are the main pillars to upgrading a middle-income economy into a high-income economy.

06 Balance of power refers to the configuration of regional states composed of varying numbers, from one to five normally, positioned for equilibrium or disequilibrium among them depending upon state policies and upon the wider

political environment. The outcomes are thus: unipolar, bipolar, or multipolar, and their arrangements accommodative (more stable) or hostile (more unstable). Most scholars visualize the classical balance as multipolar and accommodative and as more stable. Yet the present unipolar pattern of the United States as hegemon has proven peaceful, since it appears to be accommodative to the major Great Powers. In classical geopolitical terms, security derives more from position than from power, the alignments of checkerboards a prominent instance. For further information see Kissinger, H. (1994). *Diplomacy*. Simon & Schuster. , Kissinger, H. (2001). *Does America Need a Foreign Policy? Towards a Diplomacy for the 21st Century* Simon & Schuster. , Levy, J. S., and William R. Thompson. (2005). Hegemonic Threat and Great Power Balancing in Europe, 1495–2000. *Security Studies, 14*(1). , Posen, B. R. (1984). *The Sources of Military Doctrine: France, Britain, and Germany between the World Wars*. Cornell University Press. , Vasquez, J. A., & Elman, C. (Eds.). (2003). *Realism and the Balance of Power: A New Debate*. Prentice Hall. , Walt, S. M. (2002). The Enduring Relevance of the Realist Tradition. In I. Katznelson & H. V. Milner (Eds.), P*olitical Science: State of the Discipline*. W. W. Norton.

07 *La mission civilisatrice* was one of the mottoes of French colonial expansion under the Third Republic, referring to the period from the late 1870s all the way to the beginning to the decolonization period in and around World War II. For further information see Hobsbawm, E. J. (1987). *The Age of Empire, 1875–1914*. Pantheon.

08 This American slogan first revealed in 1845 indicated a political philosophy to support 19th century US territorial expansion. According to the central tenets of this approach, the United States was destined – by God – to advance democracy and capitalism across the entire North American continent.

09 This Anglo-Saxon foreign policy motto originated from Rudyard Kipling's poem about the Philippine-American War (1899-1902) encouraging the American colonization of the Philippines and supporting imperialism as a noble enterprise of civilization. To some extent, it is conceptually related to the American policy of Manifest Destiny, which is a space concept within geopolitics when shorn of its nationalistic and religious connotations, the term refers to the inevitability of a country occupying outlying territorial spaces. Such an expansion often manifests as a right or obligation to civilize and develop the new lands.

10 This imperialist foreign policy motto of the German Empire was adopted at the end of the 19th century after the German reunification with the intention of turning Germany into a first-rate global power through new overseas colonies. The intellectual origins of the phrase belong to German Foreign Secretary Bernhard von Bülow.

11 The concept refers to regions under domination by an outside adjacent or nearby Great Power, examples being Middle America by the United States and Eastern Europe by Russia during the Cold War. A shatterbelt structure would replace these influence spheres in that a rival outside competitor would intrude into the area.

12 The main argument was that the USSR would attempt to extend its territories across Eurasia for ideological reasons. Therefore, to alleviate the perceived threats originating from the Soviet advances, the US and its regional allies would erect "rimland dykes" along the continent's periphery to contain the Soviet expansion. For a detailed account see Daalder, I. H. (2022). The Return of Containment: How the West Can Prevail Against the Kremlin. *Foreign Affairs*(March). , Gaddis, J. L. (2005). *Strategies of Containment: A Critical Appraisal of American National Security Policy During the Cold War.* Oxford University Press; Revised edition. , Kennan, G. F. (1947). The Sources of Soviet Conduct. *Foreign Affairs, 25*(4). , Kennan, G. F. (2012). *American Diplomacy: Sixtieth-Anniversary Expanded Edition.* University of Chicago Press. , Larson, D. W. (1989). *Origins of Containment: A Psycological Explanation.* Princeton University Press. , Ngoei, W.-Q. (2019). *Arc of Containment: Britain, the United States, and Anticommunism in Southeast Asia.* Cornell University Press.

13 Huntington and others have asserted that previous ideological and nationalistic competitions among nations and blocs of the Cold War have shifted onto different social and cultural dimensions of conflict.9 Now, rival "civilizations" struggle in armed strife. Wars will be fought in march lands or frontiers that separate the various civilizations, particularly in borders showing contemporary hostility.

14 For further information and discussion on regionalism and regions see Erdem, C. (2015). Sino-Russian Strategic Partnership: The Shanghai Cooperation Organization. In E. Sorhun, Ü. Hacıoğlu & H. Dinçer (Eds.), *Regional Economic Integration and the Global Financial System* (pp. 257-273). Hershey, PA: IGI Global.

15 Before the demise of the Soviet system in 1991, the USSR was composed of 15 Soviet Socialist Republics (SSR): Armenia, Azerbaijan, Belorussia (now Belarus), Estonia, Georgia, Kazakhstan, Kirghizia (now Kyrgyzstan), Latvia, Lithuania, Moldavia (now Moldova), Russia, Tajikistan, Turkmenistan, Ukraine, and Uzbekistan.

16 The five Central Asia states cover approximately 4 million km2 at the center of the Eurasian continent, with Kazakhstan occupying 2,717,000 km2, Kyrgyzstan - 198,500 km2, Tajikistan - 143,100 km2, Turkmenistan - 488,100 km2, and Uzbekistan - 448,800 km2. In geographical terms, Central Asia can be divided into two main areas: the Turan Plain and the mountain zone. The deserts of Kara-Kum and Kizil-Kum cover the western and north-western parts of the basin within the Turan Plain. The eastern and southeastern parts include the Tian-Shan and the Pamir Mountains. The alluvial and mountain valleys and arid and semi-arid steppes constitute the remainder. Mountains occupy 93% of Tajikistan and 87% of Kyrgyzstan. Although the widely known oases of the region, such as the Fergana Valley, Horezm, Tashauz, Mary, Zerafshan, Tashkent-Chimkent, and others, constitute only a fraction of the total area, they have served as centers of civilization since early times.

17 This is the historical name of the geographic area covering from the Caspian Sea in the west to Xinjiang in the east and from Kazakh steppes in the north to Afghanistan and Iran in the south.

18 In 1552, the Russian Tsar—Ivan the Terrible—conquered Kazan, the capital of the Volga Tatars. This historical date marked the beginning of Russian eastward expansion. During the succeeding three centuries, Russia absorbed 4.5 million square kilometers of Muslim lands including the vast territories of Central Asia. For further details see Allworth, E. A. (Ed.). (1967). *Central Asia: A century of Russian Role.* Columbia University Press. , Becker, S. (2009). *Russia's Protectorates in Central Asia: Bukhara and Khiva, 1865–1924* (2 ed.). Routledge. , Brower, D., & Lazzerini, E. (Eds.). (1997). *Russia's Orient: Imperial Borderlands and Peoples, 1700-1917.* Indiana

University Press. , Geiss, P. G. (2003). *Pre-Tsarist and Tsarist Central Asia: Communal Commitment and Political Order in Change.* Routledge. , Pierce, R. A. (1960). *Russian Central Asia, 1867-1917: A Study in Colonial Rule.* University of California Press. , Sagadeev, A. (1993). Russia and the Great Power Ideology. *Central Asian Survey, 12.* , Sahadeo, J. (2010). *Russian Colonial Society in Tashkent, 1865-1923* Indiana University Press. , Sokol, E. D. (1954). *The Revolt of 1916 in Russian Central Asia.* Johns Hopkins University Press.

19 In 1901, the Russian-American Commercial Treaty was not renewed with the expectation that Russia could be self-sufficient in cotton production.

20 Guberniia of the Steppe refers to a geographic area covering the northern part of Kazakhstan, which shows different characteristics and independent from the rest of traditional Central Asia.

21 Prior to Soviet rule, the mahalla was an urban neighborhood, ward, or community of several hundred residents typically organized around Islamic practices. Each mahalla usually had at least one mosque. Through the mosque, mahalla residents organized holidays, weddings, funerals, circumcisions, memorial days, and other social events. Some mahallas were organized around ethnic and religious backgrounds such as Iranian or Jewish. Marriages were arranged through networks of neighbors and relatives. Spatial factors were important to the cohesion of mahalla. For instance, the proximity of resident families to one another contributed to the reproduction of specific practices, which came to be associated with the mahalla tradition. These included collective participation in security, sanitation, and water use. After the collapse of the Soviet Union in 1991, the region went through dramatic and drastic changes regarding the governability issue affecting the lives and relations of individuals not just within the state structure and local communities but also in the families. Within that context, Mahalla (local community organizations) has been promoted as a traditional institution unique to the country by the Uzbek government and portrayed as an essential unit of society. The Mahallas have existed for centuries in the Uzbek culture and managed to survive the Soviet period. Uzbek leadership has used the mahalla as a forum for defining ideology of transition driven by the values of cultural traditionalism and socio-economic modernization. But on the other hand, the mahalla structure can also be used by central government as a mechanism to exercise control over the population, repress dissent, force resettlement, and/or persecute religious minorities. For further information , see Abramson, D. M. (1998). *From Soviet to Mahalla: Community and Transition in Post-Soviet Uzbekistan* [PhD Dissertation, Indiana University]. Bloomington.

22 In October 2003, Putin gave a crushing blow to Yukos, Russia's largest oil company owned by oligarch Mikhail Khodorkovsky to set up an example and discipline the rest of the commodity magnates to go along with the strategic decisions made by Moscow. That was the most obvious assertion of power by Putin's inner circle composed of former special service officers.

23 This Turkic word "Aksakal" means "White Beard" referring to the elderly and wise people in the community. They served as decision-makers, advice-givers, and problem-solvers. Mahalla associations are headed generally by Aksakals.

24 The United States has fought five major wars since the end of WWII, namely Korea, Vietnam, the Gulf War, Iraq, and Afghanistan (only the Gulf War in 1991

can really be classified as a clear success).

25 The transboundary environmental crisis in the Aral Sea basin is considered the most prominent man-made environmental catastrophe. The Soviet policymakers and environmentalists had recognized a possible human-induced environmental change in the Aral Sea basin in the 1980s. The general tendency among scholars and experts vis-à-vis the environmental crisis in the Aral Sea basin has been associated with the technical/scientific/managerial aspects. Many studies done by scholars indicate that technical/scientific/managerial expertise is well documented in the region. For further information on the issue see Akiner, S., Tideman, S., & Hay, J. (Eds.). (1998). *Sustainable Development in Central Asia.* St. Martin's Press. , Atabaki, T., & O'Kane, J. (1998). *Post-Soviet Central Asia.* Tauris Academic Studies. , Baker, R., & Kocheleva, N. (1996). Environment versus Development: The Case of the Aral Sea. In R. Baker (Ed.), *Readings in Comparative and International Affairs Vol:35.* Indiana University Press. , Bedford, D. P. (1996). International Water Management in the Aral Sea Basin. *Water International, 21*(2), 63-69. , Belyaev, A. V. (1995). Water Balance and Water Resources of the Aral Sea Basin and its Man-Induced Changes. *GeoJournal, 35*(1), 17-23. , Bochniarz, Z. (1992). Water Management Problems in Economies in Transition. *Natural Resources Forum*(February), 55-63. , Bos, M. G. (Ed.). (1996). *The Inter-Relationship Between Irrigation, Drainage and the Environment in the Aral Sea Basin.* Kluwer Academic Publishers. , Chalidze, F. (1992). Aral Sea Crisis: A Legacy of Soviet Rule. *Central Asia Monitor, 1.* , Dorman, S. (1991). Who Will Save the Aral Sea? *Environmental Policy Review, 5*(2), 45-54. , Fergus, M. (1999). The Aral Sea Environmental Crisis: Problems and a Way Forward. *Asian Affairs, 30*(1), 35-44. , Feshbach, M. (1995). *Ecological Disaster: Cleaning up the hidden legacy of the Soviet regime.* The Twentieth Century Fund Press. , Feshbach, M., & Friendly, J. A. (1991). *Ecocide in the USSR: Health and Nature under Siege.* Basic Books. , Fierman, W. (Ed.). (1991). *Soviet Central Asia: The Failed Transformation.* Westview Press. , Glantz, M. H. (Ed.). (1999). *Creeping Environmental Problems and Sustainable Development in the Aral Sea Basin.* Cambridge University Press. , Glantz, M. H., Rubinstein, A. Z., & Zohn, I. (1993). Tragedy in the Aral Sea Basin: Looking back to plan ahead? *Global Environmental Change, 3*(2), 174-198. , Kiessling, K. L. (1998). Conference on the Aral Sea: Women, Children, Health and Environment. *Ambio, 27*(7), 560-564. , Kobori, I., & Glantz, M. H. (Eds.). (1998). *Central Eurasian Water Crisis: Caspian, Aral, and Dead Seas, Water Resources Management and Policy.* United Nations University Press. , Kotlyakov, V. M. (1991). The Aral Sea Basin: A Critical Environmental Zone. *Environment, 33*(1). , Levintanus, A. (1992). Saving the Aral Sea. *Environmentalist, 12*(2), 85-91. , Micklin, P. P. (1988). Desiccation of the Aral Sea: a water management disaster in the Soviet Union. *Science, 241*(4870), 1170-1177. , Micklin, P. P. (1991). *The Water Management Crisis in Soviet Central Asia.* University of Pittsburgh Center for Russian and East European Studies. , Micklin, P. P. (2000). Managing Water in Central Asia. In E. Herzig (Ed.), *Central Asian and Caucasian Prospects.* The Royal Institute of International Affairs. , Spoor, M. (1998). The Aral Sea Basin Crisis: Transition and Environment in Former Soviet Union. *Development and Change, 29*, 409-435. , Tanton, T. W., & Heaven, S. (1999). Worsening of the Aral Basin Crisis: Can There Be A Solution? *Journal of Water Resources Planning and Management*(November/December), 363-368. , Uitto, J. I., & Schneider, J. (Eds.). (1997). *Freshwater Resources in Arid Lands.* United Nations University Press.

, Vinogradov, S. (1996). Transboundary Water Resources in the former Soviet Union: Between Conflict and Cooperation. *Natural Resources Journal 36*(Spring). , Vinogradov, S. (2001). Managing Transboundary Water Resources in the Aral Sea: In Search of a Solution. *International Journal of Global Environmental Issues, 1*, 345-362. , Zaletaev, V. S., & Novikova, N. M. (1995). Changes in Biota of the Aral Region as a Result of Anthropogenic Impacts between 1950 and 1990. *GeoJournal, 35*(1), 23-29.

26 In the last 100 years, the population of Central Asia has increased by 15 times, and the irrigated land has increased by three times. The region's population will reach 80 million by 2025 and above the 100 million thresholds by 2050. As a result, there has been absolute and relative overpopulation in the region in and around fertile agricultural areas. At the same time, it has been impossible to place the rampant native population of the region in manufacturing jobs which in turn gave birth to a socially explosive situation. For example, the civil war in Tajikistan—a country with the least irrigated land available per inhabitant among all Central Asian republics—or extensive narcotic trafficking can be explained, to a certain extent, by an impoverished and unemployed population that is susceptible to a variety of ideological influences. See: Rotar, I. (1998, 23.12.1998). Okolo Dicietka "Spornih Territorii" v Srednei Azii [Nearly Dozen of "Disputed Territories" in the Middle Asia] *Nizavisimaya Gazieta.* These examples illustrate the close correlation between agricultural output, water resources, and employment in Central Asia. There are ample cases worldwide with the same characteristics viewed as a significant threat to national and regional security.

27 For instance, the Islamic Movement of Uzbekistan (IMU), with its goal of overthrowing the Karimov government in Uzbekistan to create an Islamic state under Sharia, used the tormented Tajikistan as a base to operate across the region. The heavy casualties suffered during the early stages of the American military campaign in and around the northern stronghold of the group in Mazar-i-Sharif were certainly considered beneficial by Karimov or other secular governments of the region.

28 The Caspian Pipeline Consortium (CPC) constructed a 1,500-kilometer pipeline from the oil-rich fields of western Kazakhstan (Tengiz, Kashagan, and Karachaganak) to ship the oil out to the Russian Black Sea port at Novorossiysk.

29 In the case of Ukraine, Gazprom reduced its flow of gas by 125 million cubic meters on January 1st, 2006, over a pricing dispute. Gazprom wanted to increase the price that Kiev paid for its gas from 50 to 230 per 1000 cubic meters, to be in line with international market pricing. The move was widely interpreted as Moscow's punishment of the pro-western stance of the newly elected Ukrainian President Viktor Yushchenko. One of Kiev's responses to the Russian ultimatum to cut off volumes was the threat of a sharp increase in the transit fees it charged Gazprom for shipping large amounts of gas through Ukraine to Western Europe, and this threat also contributed to the escalation in the conflict. The Ukrainian Russian gas dealings in turn' contributed to the undoing Yushchenko by stimulating a vote of no confidence in the Parliament, which led to a reorganization of the Ukrainian government under a coalition in which Yushchenko's party lost its ruling status in favor of a more pro-Russian grouping.

30 Georgia is another country that has elected a pro-Western government interested in joining the eastward expansion of NATO and the EU. Georgia is also a transit country for the BTC pipeline, which was sponsored by the US in a policy of promoting competition and energy security through multiple pipelines for Caspian energy resources. At present, only Azeri oil and gas are being transported in the pipeline, but there has been considerable discussion of extending the pipeline around or under the Caspian Sea in order to tap into Kazakh supplies. The BTC pipeline was routed through Georgia because the shorter route through Armenia was not possible due to the existing tensions between Armenia and Azerbaijan over the disputed territory of Nagorno-Karabakh. But Georgia itself is also vulnerable to Russian pressure via its frozen domestic conflicts. Abkhazia to the Northwest and Ossetia to the North are regions not fully under the control of the Georgian government/ residents of those regions expressed an interest in separation from Georgia. Georgians suspect that Russia has ambitions to absorb both rebellious regions. Russian Georgian relations have been tense since independence and have worsened since the election of Mikhail Saakashvili as Georgia's President. Recently, when Georgia arrested several Russians for spying, Russia banned all Georgian exports to Russia and mobilized its troops on the Georgian border. In January 2006 Russia cut the supply of gas to Georgia, forcing it to scramble to find alternative resources.

31 Until its dissolution in 1991, the USSR's number of underground nuclear tests conducted in Novaya Zemlya (see Figure 5) was around 130.

32 The Ilulissat Declaration was made in Ilulissat, Gronland, in 2008 as an outcome of the Arctic Ocean Conference by the five coastal states of the Arctic Ocean. The climate change, the protection of the marine environment, maritime shipping safety, and division of emergency responsibilities if new shipping routes are opened.

33 On April 18th, 2012, Putin has facilitated an agreement between Russian oil giant Rosneft and Exxon Mobile regarding the oil exploration in the Arctic region. The main goal of that agreement was to show the Russian presence/interest/claim in the region and maintain Russian position as the top producer.

34 Russia's seven newest icebreakers have multi-mission capabilities and are fueled by nuclear reactors capable of breaking through ice twice as thick as its diesel competitors. Russia has numerous icebreakers in its military fleet, including the largest and most powerful icebreaker in the world.

35 Essentially still 2 million people in 16 non-self-governing territories (NSGT) around the globe live under virtual colonial rule. The UN prepared list indicates that those territories are: Montserrat, Saint Helena, Anguilla, British Virgin Islands, United States Virgin Islands, Gibraltar, Cayman Islands, Falkland Islands (Malvinas), Turks and Caicos Islands, French Polynesia, American Samoa, Guam, Pitcairn, New Caledonia, Tokelau. Evidently, mostly Anglo nations (New Zealand, the United Kingdom, the United States) and France are some of the countries controlling those territories.

36 The name of the Strait originates from Vitus Bering, a Danish explorer in the service of the Russian Empire who entered the region in 1728. The International Date Line (established in 1884, 17 years after the sale of Alaska to the Americans by Tsar Alexander II) passes through the Bering Strait between Russian and American Diomede Islands, which in turn leaves the Russian and American sides usually on

different calendar days.

37 Up to 21st century, the RFE lacked officially defined boundaries; generally speaking, the term "Siberia and the Far East" was often used for all regions remaining in the eastern part of the Urals. However, in 2000, during the President Putin's first term, the Russian Federation went through a new territorial reorganization which gave birth to larger federal districts. At that occasion, the Far Eastern Federal District (FEFD) was formed, including Chukotka Autonomous Okrug, Kamchatka Oblast with Koryak Autonomous Okrug, Amur Oblast, Magadan Oblast, Primorsky Krai, the Sakha (Yakutia) Republic, Khabarovsk Krai, and Sakhalin Oblast, and Jewish Autonomous Oblast. Since 2000, the designation "Far East" has frequently been used by Russians about the FEFD. In that sense, the Far East covers an area of 6.2 million square kilometers, which is in turn approximately one-third of Russia's total area.

38 At the turn of the Century, Russian Tsar Alexander III and Tsarevich Nicholas II, showing a spectacular vision; leadership and dedication, initiated the Trans-Siberian railroad (1891-1916), covering more than 9,000 km which also included the southern the Chinese branch connecting Chita and Vladivostok through Harbin in Manchuria. The Trans-Siberian is the longest railroad line in service. Currently, the Line is still further expanding into various parts of Siberia and the RFE.

39 The nominal global GDP in 2021 was $94 trillion. The total GDP of the four nations of the Northeast Asia would be, *grosso modo*, $25 trillion (Russia $1.6 trillion, Japan $5.1 trillion, Korea $1.8 trillion, China $16.9 trillion). Moreover, if the above figures are calculated in Purchasing Power Parity (PPP) terms instead of USD denominated nominal values, and then it would amount to 39 trillion USD.

40 It is preferable to use the term Northern Sea Route instead of Northeast (NEP) or Northwest (NWP) Passage to avoid Eurocentric geopolitical classifications. The Northeast Passage is, from the European and northern Atlantic point of view, the shipping route to the Pacific Ocean, along Russian and Norwegian coasts. On the other hand, the Northwest Passage refers to the route through the Canadian coast. Technically speaking, the Northern Sea Route, as it is defined in Russian law and does not include the Barents Sea and therefore does not reach the Atlantic Ocean. However, since the NSR has a significant overlap over the majority of the NEP, sometimes the NSR term has been used to refer to the entirety of the Northeast Passage.

41 The Sino-Soviet split took place between 1960 and 1989. It started during Nikita Khrushchev years and lasted until the visit of Mikhail Gorbachev to Beijing in 1989. The deterioration of political and ideological relations between those two largest communist countries was instrumental for Sino-American rapprochement in the early 1970s and facilitated by disastrous policies of Mao Zedong through Great Leap Forward (1958-1962) and the Cultural Revolution (1966-1976).

42 The Aigun Treaty of 1858 between the Russian Empire and the Qing Dynasty forged the current configuration of the Sino-Russian border along the Amur River, modifying the almost two-century-old Nerchinsk Treaty of 1689. Russia gained access to further 600,000 sq. km on the left bank of the Amur, known as Priamurye, which did belong to China up to that time. Furthermore, the year 1860 saw the signing of the Convention of Beijing, again, in very advantageous terms to

Russia, gaining complete control over the Primorye region down to Vladivostok. From the Chinese point-of-view, both treaties are considered as unequal, illustrating the western imperialist period, infamous the "Century of Humiliation."

43 Tartary Strait is dividing the Russian island of Sakhalin from the Eurasian continent and connecting the Sea of Okhotsk with the East Sea. It is 4–20 m deep and 7.3 km wide at the narrowest point.

44 BRIC is an acronym coined in 2001 by the former chairman of Goldman Sachs Asset Management, Jim O'Neill for Brazil, Russia, India, and China.

45 OBOR is considered the most substantial overseas investment initiated by a single country. China is planning to invest up to $900bn in infrastructure projects to ranging from ports to high-speed railways to gas pipelines to increase Chinese access to those markets. For further information see Hancock, T. (2017). China encircles the world with One Belt, One Road strategy. *Financial Times, May 4th*

46 The EAEU is an integrated single market—Russia, Belarus, Kazakhstan, Kyrgyzstan, Armenia, Tajikistan—of 183 million people and a GDP of $2 trillion in nominal values.

47 China gradually became the biggest investor in Africa in the years following the 2008 financial crisis. As a result, thousands of Chinese enterprises in Africa make a remarkable impact on the continent's economic transformation. Although China does not have the historical ties, language, or relative geographical proximity, such as the U.S. and the former colonial countries of the U.K. and France, it was still able to get its position of prominence in a relatively short time. In addition, these commercial opportunities gave birth to 1 million Chinese citizens making Africa their permanent home since 2000. For a detailed account see Abegunrin, O., & Manyeruke, C. (2020). *China's Power in Africa: A New Global Order.* Palgrave Macmillan. , Alden, C., Alao, A., Chun, Z., & Barber, L. (Eds.). (2018). *China and Africa Building Peace and Security Cooperation on the Continent.* Palgrave Macmillan. , Alden, C., & Large, D. (Eds.). (2019). *New Directionsin Africa-China Studies.* Routledge. , Brautigam, D. (2015). *Will Africa Feed China?* Oxford University Press. , Dent, C. M. (Ed.). (2011). *China and Africa Development Relations.* Routledge. , Rotberg, R. I. (Ed.). (2008). *China into Africa: Trade, Aid, and Influence.* Brookings Institution Press. , Taylor, I. (2006). *China and Africa Engagement and compromise.* Routledge. , Zhang, X., Wasserman, H., & Mano, W. (Eds.). (2016). *China's Media and Soft Power in Africa: Promotion and Perceptions* Palgrave Macmillan.

48 Since 2000, China has increased its engagement significantly with Latin America and the Caribbean region in terms of diplomatic and economic ties by signing bilateral partnership agreements along with the establishment of comprehensive strategic partnerships with Argentina, Brazil, Chile, Ecuador, Mexico, Peru, and Venezuela. For further details see Fornes, G., & Mendez, A. (2018). *The China-Latin America Axis: Emerging Markets and their Role in an Increasingly Globalised World.* Palgrave Macmillan. , Gallagher, K. (2016). *The China Triangle: Latin America's China Boom and the Fate of the Washington Consensus.* Oxford University Press. , Jenkins, R. (2019). *How China is Reshaping the Global Economy: Development Impacts in Africa and Latin America.* Oxford University Press.

49 As of 2021, approximately 800 US foreign military bases are spread across 80 countries worldwide. Japan has the highest number with 120 operational bases,

followed by Germany with 119 and South Korea with 73. For a detailed account, see Hussein, M., & Haddad, M. (2021). Infographic: US military presence around the world. Al Jazeera. Retrieved April 23, 2022, from https://www.aljazeera.com/news/2021/9/10/infographic-us-military-presence-around-the-world-interactive

50 In 2017, the PLA established its first overseas military base in the Horn of Africa, geopolitically significant-Djibouti. Since then, there have been many reports highlighting possible future Chinese military installations at various strategically relevant sea lines of communications, such as in the Atlantic Ocean (Equatorial Guinea) and the Indo-Pacific region (United Arab Emirates-UAE and the Solomon Islands).

51 Eurasia is considered a single continent circumventing the social construct dating back to antiquity. Eurasia in geographical terms refers to the entirety of the European and Asian landmass. In that sense, Eurasia encompasses approximately 55 million sq. kilometers, which corresponds to slightly over one-third of the earth's total land area containing three-quarters of the global population.

52 Xinjiang is one of the People's Republic of China's ethnic "autonomous" regions, a province that officially allows special social, religious, and even political rights for the ethnic minorities native to the region. However, in the region, these privileges are not always applied. There is no doubt that China has strategic issues at stake in Xinjiang. Throughout Chinese history, this province has been one of the vast buffer zones shielding the core of China from foreign attacks and influences. However, equally, Xinjiang has long served as a key trade route for Chinese commerce through the notorious Silk Road, connecting mainland China to Central Asia, the Middle East, and Europe. Today, Chinese strategists are looking back to the old Silk Road routes as a way to safeguard economic security. Central Asia possesses vast energy resources, which are indispensable for future Chinese economic development. In that sense, Xinjiang offers an essential passageway to Central Asia. This geopolitical aspect reinforces Beijing's perceptions about the need to keep the Uyghurs and other ethnic minorities under control.

53 The large Uyghur diaspora in Central Asia comprises approximately 300,000 people based mainly in Kazakhstan and Kyrgyzstan.

54 For further information of the rise of China see Beckley, M. (2011). China's Century? Why America's Edge Will Endure. *International Security, 36*(3). , Christensen, T. J. (2006). Fostering Stability or Creating a Monster? The Rise of China and U.S. Policy toward East Asia. Ibid., *31*(1). , Mearsheimer, J. J. (2006b). China's Unpeaceful Rise. *Current History, 105*(690). , Ross, R. S. (2009). China's Naval Nationalism: Sources, Prospects, and the U.S. *Response. International Security, 34*(2). , Schweller, R. L., & Pu, X. (2011). After Unipolarity: China's Visions of InternationalOrder in an Era of U.S. Decline. Ibid., 36(1). , Weiss, J. C. (2013). Authoritarian Signaling, Mass Audiences, and Nationalist Protest in China. *International Organization 67*(1).

55 In China, the institutions of higher learning outrank similar western institutions of higher learning by centuries. The earliest aspects of Chinese civilization can be traced back at least as far as five thousand years and perhaps considerably further. The first documented information on the establishment of the education system goes back to the Yu period (2257–2208 BCE), namely Shangyang, the imperial central academy. By the time of the Shang dynasty (C. 1700–1100 BCE), schools

and other social institutions of a complex culture had developed as well as had the foundations for the examination system in use throughout the history of imperial China to appoint government officials. The imperial examination system probably requires closer scrutiny due to its unique place in Chinese education thought. Although written examinations to assist the selection process of government officials were used as early as the Han period (206 BCE to 220 CE), it was only during the Tang dynasty (618 CE to 907 CE) that they came to play an indispensable role in the appointment of such officials. Undoubtedly, China was well ahead of its time in terms of the development of a professional civil service based on talent rather than on birth. The main intent of the imperial examination system was to assure the quality of the civil service by leaning towards a more merit-based system. Another intent was to standardize the common body of knowledge for everybody. Moreover, the imperial civil service examination was also able to establish the possibility for upward social mobility within the Chinese society by allowing individuals with modest backgrounds to attain governance or power positions. This social class mobility was based on intellectual skill and talent. The early Chinese state revolved around literate and well-trained officials for the harmonious functioning of the empire. For instance, the nine-rank system - Three Kingdoms (220–280 AD) and the Northern and Southern dynasties (420–589 AD) - was used as a civil service nomination system to classify and assess officials according to their proclivities. The nine Rank System was ultimately replaced by the imperial examination system for the civil service during the Sui dynasty period (581–618 AD) to elect talented individuals from the general populace.

56 The NDB is a BRICS multilateral development bank established on July 15, 2014, by Brazil, Russia, India, China and South Africa. The bank was seeded with US$50bn initial capital, with the intention to increase capital to US$ 100bn. The bank will be headquartered in Shanghai. Each country will have one vote and no country will have power of veto.

57 Launched in February 2014, the China-led US$40bn Silk Road Infrastructure Fund invests in BRI projects. The fund is capitalized mainly by China's foreign exchange reserves and is intended to be managed like China's sovereign wealth fund.

58 Founded in October 2014, the AIIB aspires to be a global development bank with 21 Asian member countries with registered capital of US$100bn.

59 At the turn of the Century, Russian Tsar Alexander III and Tsarevich Nicholas II, showing spectacular vision, leadership and dedication, initiated the Trans-Siberian Railroad (1891-1916), covering more than 9,000 km which also included the southern Chinese branch connecting Chita and Vladivostok through Harbin in Manchuria. The Trans-Siberian is the longest railroad line in service. Currently, the line is still further expanding into various parts of Siberia and the RFE.

60 The Strait of Hormuz is a geostrategically important strait connecting the Persian Gulf with the Arabian Sea (Indian Ocean). The Strait is only 33 to 95 km wide throughout its length. Iran and Oman are the countries surrounding the Strait of Hormuz and share territorial rights over its waters. Nearly 17 million b/d of crude oil and refined products passed through the Strait in 2013 (about 30% of all seaborne traded oil and 20% of the total oil produced globally). A substantial amount of another fossil fuel, liquefied natural gas (LNG), also moves through the

Strait of Hormuz. Around 3.7 trillion cubic feet (Tcf) of LNG was transported from Qatar via the Strait of Hormuz in 2013, corresponding to more than 30% of global LNG trade.

61 The Gulf Cooperation Council (May 25, 1981) is a loose regional intergovernmental political and economic union consisting of all Arab states of the Persian Gulf, except for Iraq. It was founded in 1981 against the backdrop of the Islamic Revolution in Iran. The member states of the GCC are Bahrain, Kuwait, Oman, Qatar, Saudi Arabia, and the United Arab Emirates (UAE).

62 The soaring Pakistani foreign debt is mostly fueled by loans from China to finance the China–Pakistan Economic Corridor (CPEC), which is a wide range of infrastructure projects built by Chinese construction companies throughout Pakistan.

63 Djibouti is facing a high risk of debt distress since its public debt rose from 50 percent of its GDP in 2014 to 85 percent in the following two years. China inaugurated its first overseas military base in Djibouti in 2017, and it represents a critical step in the global ambitions of China's military. It most certainly changes the local politics and challenges the current power balance in the Horn of Africa. Djibouti is the third smallest country on the continent, but due to its unique geographical location in the Gulf of Aden is home to the military bases of the US, France, Great Britain, Japan, Saudi Arabia, and China. The only Japanese military base in the world was established in that particular country.

64 Most certainly, the initiative has immeasurably improved the economic and social provisions within Laos. The construction of the China-Laos railway has been instrumental in uplifting the economy of this landlocked country. But at the same time, the $6.7 billion China-Laos Railway project represents almost half of Laos's GDP.

65 Russia and China are attempting to link their national payment system. China's UnionPay system and Russia's Karta Mir system would be linked to avoid problems arising while using American payment systems such as Visa and MasterCard.

66 There are 34 administrative divisions in PRC: 23 provinces, five autonomous regions, four municipalities, and two special administrative regions.

67 The Jiayu pass is located in the Gansu province of the PRC, and it is the first pass at the Western end of the Chinese Great Wall. But equally, it is also a critical pass on the ancient Silk Road in terms of connecting the heartland of Han China and the Xinjiang region.

68 The Khyber Pass is a historical connection point linking Afghanistan (Nangarhar province) and Pakistan (Khyber Pakhtunkhwa province) through a mountainous area, and it did play a pivotal role during the 19th-century Great Game due to its strategic military location. Moreover, the Khyber Pass is located on a noteworthy trade route between Central Eurasia and South Asia.

69 From another angle, the manifestation of the use of Islam as a tool for resistance to the oppressive forces can be illustrated through the history of Jadidism in Central Asia at the turn of the Great century. However, this time, Jadidism as a powerful political movement gave birth to a range of new socio-political reforms among Muslim intellectuals of Central Asia, mainly among the Uzbeks and the

Tajiks, but also to a lesser extent among Kazakhs from the very end of the 19th century to the first decades of the 20th century. Jadidism, no doubt, was inspired heavily by several reformist revolutions that took place in different parts of Eurasia—Russia, Turkey, Iran, India—between 1905 and 1913. The Jadidist idea of reforming the traditional educational system of Muslim religious schools and cultural institutions in Central Asia became a powerful political tool to fight against the region's economic, moral, and political backwardness. The movement also promoted a national consciousness growth and formed the essence of national-liberation ideology vis-à-vis Turkistan's struggle for independence against Russian colonialism. For further information on Jadidism see Bazarbayev, K., & Ashimkhanovna, A. Z. (2012). Jadids Movement in Central Asia in the Late 19th and the Early 20th Centuries. *Asian Social Science, 8*(8). , Crews, R. D. (2006). *For Prophet and Tsar: Islam and Empire in Russia and Central Asia.* Harvard University Press. , d'Encausse, H. C. (1966). *Reforme et revolution chez les musulmans de russie l'empire: Bukhara, 1867-1924 [Reform and Revolution among the Muslims of the Russian Empire: Bukhara, 1867-1924].* Armand Colin. , Devlet, N. (1990). *İsmail Bey Gaspirali [İsmail Bey Gaspirali].* Türk Dünyası Araştırmaları Enstitüsü Yayınları. , Devlet, N. (1996). İsmail Gaspıralı dönemi ve Ruslarla uzlaşma [The Reconciliation Process with the Russians at the time of Ismail Gaspirali]. *Türk Dünyası Dil ve Edebiyat Dergisi, 2,* 403-408. , Dudoignon, S., & Hisao, K. (Eds.). (2001). *Islam in Politics in Russia and Central Asia (Early Eighteenth to Late Twentieth Centuries).* Kegan Paul. , Habletimoğlu, N. (1997). *Çarlık Rusyası'nda Türk Kongreleri 1905-1917 [Turkish Conventions in Tsarist Russia, 1905-1917].* Ankara Üniversitesi Basımevi. , İsmetullah, H. (2004). İsmail Bey Gaspıralı'nın Türkistan'ı Uyandırma Yolundaki Teşebbüsleri [Ismail Bey Gaspıralı's Attempts to Awaken Turkistan]. *İsmail Bey Gaspıralı İçin, 9*( ), 583-595. , Kanlıdere, A. (1997). Kazan Tatarları Arasında Tecdid ve Cedit Hareketi (1809-1917). *Türkiye Günlüğü Dergisi, 46*(Summer). , Karlybaev, M. (2002). L'instruction musulmane et les ishan chez les Karakalpaks du XIXeme siecle. *Cahiers d'Asie centrale, 10,* 177-191. , Khalid, A. (1999). *The Politics of Muslim Cultural Reform: Jadidism in Central Asia.* University of California Press. , Lazzerini, E. J. (1992). Beyond Renewal: The Jadid Response to Pressure for Change in the Modern Age. In J. A. Gross (Ed.), *Muslims in Central Asia: Expressions of Identity and Change.* Duke University Press. , Mardin, S. (1983). *Jön Türklerin Siyasi Fikirleri 1895-1908 [Political Ideas of the Young Turks, 1895-1908].* İletişim Yayınları. , Ortaylı, l. (1968). *Çarlık Rusyasında Türkçülük hareketleri ve Gaspirali Ismail Bey [Pan-Turkism movements in Tsarist Russia and Gaspirali Ismail Bey].* Anadolu Matbaası. , Özdemir, E. (2009). Kazak Kültürel Hayatında Tatarların Etkisi ve Kazak Ceditçiliği'nin Gelişimi [The Influence of Tatars in Kazakh Cultural Life and the Development of Kazakh Jadidism]. Bilig, 48, 157-176. , Qosimov, B. (1996). Sources littérarires et principaux traits distinctifs du djadidisme turkestanais (début du XXe siècle). *Cahiers du monde russe, 37*(1-2), 107-132.

70 A configuration of regional states composed of varying numbers, from one to five normally, positioned for equilibrium or disequilibrium among them depending upon state policies and upon the wider political environment. The outcomes are thus: unipolar, bipolar, or multipolar, and their arrangements accommodative (more stable) or hostile (more unstable). Most scholars visualize the classical balance as multipolar and accommodative and as more stable. See Mearsheimer, J. J. (2001). *The Tragedy of Great Power Politics.* W.W. Norton. , Walt, S. M. (1987). *The Origins of Alliances.* Cornell University Press. , Waltz, K. N. (1979). *Theory of International*

Politics. Addison-Wesley.

71 Balancers locate either as peripheral-within-regions or outside-of-region states, not intertwined within major power alliances and thus able to bandwagon or align with a dominant side of a regional balance or balance against a dominant side, evening the power distributions within the region. See Schweller, R. L. (1997). New Realist Research on Alliances: Refining, Not Refuting. *American Political Science Review, 91*(4). , Walt, S. M. (1985). Alliance Formation and the Balance of World Power. *International Security, 9*(4).

72 French historian Fernand Braudel introduced the term to indicate a perspective on history extending further into the past than human memory and the archaeological record. In crude terms, the effects of events occur so slowly that it is largely invisible to those who experience them. See in French or its English translation Braudel, F. (1969). *Ecrits Sur L'Histoire*. Flammarion. , Braudel, F. (1982). *On History [Writings on History]* (S. Matthews, Trans.; 2014 ed.). University of Chicago Press.

73 Boao Forum for Asia (BFA), formally inaugurated in 2001, takes place annually in the Hainan province of China to host the gathering of global elites, and it is modeled on the World Economic Forum in Davos, Switzerland. The BFA provides a platform to understand China's economic worldview and a better understanding of China's priorities in the Eurasian region.

74 Until Zheng He's grand expeditions, the Chinese trade junks, despite crisscrossing the Southeast Asian waters, seldom went beyond the Malacca Straits, leaving, in general, the Indian Ocean to the West Asians. Malacca and Sumatra thus became the terminal ports for Chinese maritime traders. However, before the founding of the Ming dynasty, hundreds of thousands of Chinese, primarily from Fujian and Guangdong, had been engaging in trade and commerce of all sorts in Southeast Asia. Chinese communities were known to have existed in just about every major Southeast Asian port city when the last Yuan emperor lost his mandate of heaven. By the end of the fourteenth century, Chinese maritime technology had developed to a level unsurpassed in the world. The Chinese had replaced Indians and Arabs in dominating the maritime trade of Southeast Asia in the fifteenth century. For more see Pelliot, P. (1933). Les Grands Voyages Maritimes Chinois au Début XVe Siècle *T'oung Pao 30*. , Tsai, S.-s. H. (1996). *The Eunuchs in the Ming Dynasty*. State University of New York Press.

75 After the demise of the Soviet Union, approximately 25 million ethnic Russians (out of 290 million Soviet population in 1991) found themselves living outside of the Russian Federation, with significant numbers in Ukraine and Kazakhstan. For more see Barington, L. W., Herron, E. S., & Silver, B. D. (2003). The Motherland is calling: Views of Homeland among Russians in the Near Abroad. World Politics, 55(2). , Flynn, M. (2007). Reconstructing 'Home/lands' in the Russian Federation: Migrant Centred Perspectives of Displacement and Resettlement. *Journal of Ethnic and Migration Studies 33*(3). , Heleniak, T. (2004). Migration of the Russian Diaspora after the Break-up of the Soviet Union. *Journal of International Affairs, 57*(2). , Kosmarskaya, N. (2005). Post Soviet Diaspora. In M. Ember, C. R. Ember, & I. Skoggard (Eds.), *Encyclopaedia of Diasporas: Immigrant and Refugee Cultures around the World*. Springer. , Lebedeva., N. M. (1995). *Novaya Russkaya Diaspora [New Russian Diaspora]* Institut Etnologii i Antropologii.

76 The Chinese diaspora is generally used to refer to close to 50 million ethnic Chinese living outside of mainland China, the special administrative regions of Hong Kong/Macau, and Taiwan. The origins of the diaspora can be traced back to the tormented events in the19th century Chinese history coinciding with the Century of Humiliation and subsequent several migration waves. Three-quarters of the Chinese diaspora is located in Southeast Asia, making up important segments of the populations of Thailand, Malaysia, Indonesia, and Singapore. Although the Southeast Asian Chinese diaspora represents a relatively small part of the overall general population, it controls around 60% of the region's private corporate wealth. For more see Barrett, T. C. (2012). *The Chinese Diaspora in South-East Asia: The Overseas Chinese in Indochina.* I.B.Tauris. , Tan, C.-B. (Ed.). (2012). *Handbook of the Chinese Diaspora.* Routledge , Yeoh, B. (2013). Chinese Migration to Singapore: Discourses and Discontents in a Globalizing Nation-State. *Asian and Pacific Migration Journal, 22*(1).

77 Traditional Chinese historians characterized the Mongol-ruled Yuan Dynasty as having ruined Chinese territory by annihilating the Chinese population, eroding the proper operation of government by discontinuing the civil service examinations, and enabling the development of more despotic rule in Ming China. For more, see Dreyer, E. L. (1982). *Early Ming China, A Political History, 1355-1435.* Stanford University Press. , Grousset, R. (1970). *The Empire of the Steppes: A History of Central Asia* (N. Walford, Trans.). Rutgers University Press. , Ming, H. H. (2016). *From the Mongols to the Ming Dynasty: How a Begging Monk Became Emperor of China, Zhu Yuan Zhang.* Algora Publishing. , Twitchett, D., & Mote, F. W. (Eds.). (2008). *The Cambridge History of China: The Ming Dynasty, 1368-1644, Part 2* (Vol. 8). Cambridge University Press.

78 The contemporary usage of the term xenophobia coincides with the Boxer Rebellion of 1899 in China. At the turn of the Great Century, European powers had begun to overrun and occupy parts of East Asia. The expansion of European power and culture eastward had been glorified through geopolitical concepts such as French "mission civilisatrice" or Anglo-American "white man's burden." European were firmly convinced of their rectitude, superior genetics, morality, and divine motivations throughout their colonial expansion. Consequently, they were puzzled by the contentious reception in an inhospitable China throughout the Boxer Rebellion when rebels revealed their mission to attack and exterminate all foreigners. European colonialism considered people encountered in foreign lands to be barbarians due to their cultural inferiority, which provided the moral justification for using deplorable tactics when the native population did not obey or accept the European colonizers. As a result, eight colonial nations in China got united in their outrage to suppress the uprising violently. For further info see Makari, G. (2021). *Of Fear and Strangers: A History of Xenophobia.* W. W. Norton & Company.

79 For further information on the decline and fall of the Ottoman Empire see Fromkin, D. (2009). *A Peace to End All Peace: The Fall of the Ottoman Empire and the Creation of the Modern Middle East* Holt Paperbacks. , İnalcık, H., & Quataert, D. (Eds.). (1997). *An Economic and Social History of the Ottoman Empire, Vol. 2: 1600-1914.* Cambridge University Press. , Karpat, K. H. (2002). *The Politicization of Islam: Reconstructing Identity, State, Faith, and Community in the Late Ottoman State.* Oxford University Press. , Kinross, L. (1979). *Ottoman Centuries* (10 ed.). William Morrow

Paperbacks. , Rogan, E. (2016). *The Fall of the Ottomans: The Great War in the Middle East* Basic Books

80 For instance, Nikolai Gogol, one of Russia's earliest and most original writers, expressed a messianic view in his novel Dead Souls conceptualizing a speeding troika, a carriage drawn by three horses, as a metaphor for Russia. Furthermore, the uniqueness of the Russian national identity has been pointed out in the writings of well-known Russian literary giants such as Gogol, Tolstoy, and Dostoyevsky, offering various depictions of the Russian soul. See Dostoyevsky, F. (2015). *The Brothers Karamazov* (C. Garnett, Trans.). Lerner Publishing. , Gogol, N. V. (1997). Dead Souls (R. Pevear & L. Volokhonsky, Trans.; 2 ed.). Vintage. , Tolstoy, L. (2005). *A Prisoner In The Caucasus*. Kessinger Publishing.

81 The term lebensraum (living space) was coined by Friedrich Ratzel in 1897 and was used as a political motto in Germany in reference to the unification of the country and the acquisition of colonies, following similar English and French examples. It was popularized in early twentieth-century Germany and became a geopolitical motto for imperial expansion. After Adolf Hitler's rise to power, the concept was used as a critical policy tool and main ideological principle to establish the Nazi worldview and its ensuing drive for military conquests and racial policy. For more on the issue, see Bernhardi, F. v. (2019). *Germany and the Next War*. Wentworth Press. , Haushofer, K. (2002). *An English Translation and Analysis of Major General Karl Ernst Haushofer's "Geopolitics of the Pacific Ocean": Studies on the Relationship Between Geography and History*. Edwin Mellen Press. , Ratzel, F. (1987). *La Géographie politique: Les concepts fondamentaux [Political Geography: Fundamental Concepts]*. Fayard.

82 The geographical term 'Third World' (*Tiers Monde*) was coined in 1952 by the French demographer, anthropologist, and historian Alfred Sauvy. The concept has been used to differentiate unaligned countries from either the Communist Soviet-led communist countries or the US-led capitalist countries during the Cold War. Since its conception, the term has had a continuous relevance in international relations by being one of the most important and expressive concepts of the 20th century. Although there was widespread criticism after the end of the Cold War, to this day, it remains one of the most used terms in studies pertaining to international development. See Sauvy, A. (1952). Trois mondes, une planète. *L'Observateur, 118*.

83 The geographical term 'rogue state' refers to the dangerously unpredictable way of conducting foreign policy while disregarding international law or diplomacy, which in turn represents a conceived potential threat to the international order. See Chomsky, N. (2000). *Rogue States: The Rule of Force in World Affairs* (Second Printing ed.). South End Press.

84 For further information on international security see Biddle, S. (2006). *Military Power: Explaining Victory and Defeat in Modern Battle* Princeton University Press. , Brooks, S., & Wohlforth, W. (2008). *World Out of Balance: International Relations and the Challenge of American Primacy*. Princeton University Press. , Christensen, T., & Snyder, J. (1990). Chain Gangs and Passed Bucks: Predicting Alliance Patterns in Multipolarity. *International Organization, 44*(2). , Debs, A., & Monteiro, N. P. (2014). Known Unknowns: Power Shifts, Uncertainty, and War. Ibid., *68*(1). , Fearon, J. (1995). Rationalist Explanations for War. Ibid., *49*(3). , Gilpin, R. (1981). *War and Change in World Politics*. Cambridge University Press. , Glaser, C. (1997). The Security

Dilemma Revisited. *World Politics 50*(1). , Ikenberry, G. J. (2019). *After Victory: Institutions, Strategic Restraint, and the Rebuilding of Order After Major Wars* (Revised ed.). Princeton University Press. , Katzenstein, P. (1996). *The Culture of National Security: Norms and Identity in World Politics.* Columbia University Press. , Snyder, G. (1984). The Security Dilemma in Alliance Politics. *World Politics, 36*(4).

85 For further details on the issue see Brands, H., & Palkki, D. (2011). Saddam, Israel, and the Bomb: Nuclear Alarmism Justified? *International Security, 36*(1). , Fuhrmann, M. (2009). Spreading Temptation: Proliferation and Peaceful Nuclear Cooperation Agreements," (Summer): 7-41. Ibid., *34.* , Gavin, F. (2009/10). Same As It Ever Was: Nuclear Alarmism, Proliferation, and the Cold War. Ibid.(3). , Holsti, O. R. (1990). Crisis Decision Making. In P. E. Tetlock, J. L. Husbands, R. Jervis, P. C. Stern, & C. Tilly (Eds.), *Behavior, Society, and Nuclear War* (Vol. 1). Oxford University Press. , Hymans, J. (2011). Veto Players, Nuclear Energy, and Nonproliferation: Domestic Institutional Barriers to a Japanese Bomb. *International Security, 36*(2). , Jervis, R. (1989). *The Meaning of the Nuclear: Statecraft and the Prospect of Armageddon.* Cornell University Press. , Kroenig, M. (2013). Nuclear Superiority and the Balance of Resolve: Explaining Nuclear Crisis Outcomes. *International Organization,, 67*(1). , Lieber, K. A., & Press, D. G. (2006). The End of MAD? The Nuclear Dimension of U.S. Primacy. *International Security, 30*(4). , Lieber, K. A., & Press, D. G. (2020). *The Myth of the Nuclear Revolution: Power Politics in the Atomic Age.* Cornell University Press. , Monteiro, N. P., & Debs, A. (2014). The Strategic Logic of Nuclear Proliferation. *International Security, 39*(2). , Mueller, J. (2010). Think Again: Nuclear Weapons. *Foreign Policy, 177* , Sagan, S. D. (1996/97). Why Do States Build Nuclear Weapons? Three Models in Search of a Bomb. *International Security, 21*(3)., Sechser, T. S. (2013). Crisis Bargaining and Nuclear Blackmail. *International Organization, 67*(1). , Tannenwald, N. (2005). Stigmatizing the Bomb: Origins of the Nuclear Taboo. *International Security, 29*(4). , Waltz, K. N. (1990). Nuclear Myths and Political Realities. *American Political Science Review, 84*(3).

Bibliography

"A_Debt_Trap?". (2018). Is China's $26 Trillion New Silk Road A Debt Trap? *Oilprice.com*. Retrieved October 24, 2018, from https://oilprice.com/Energy/Energy-General/Is-Chinas-26-Trillion-New-Silk-Road-A-Debt-Trap.html

"The_Editorial_Notes". (2017). Arctic Ice Silk Road takes shape. *The Strait Times*. Retrieved November 3, 2018, from https://www.straitstimes.com/asia/east-asia/arctic-ice-silk-road-takes-shape-china-daily

Abegunrin, O., & Manyeruke, C. (2020). *China's Power in Africa: A New Global Order*. Palgrave Macmillan.

Abramson, D. M. (1998). *From Soviet to Mahalla: Community and Transition in Post-Soviet Uzbekistan* [PhD Dissertation, Indiana University]. Bloomington.

Adler, E., & Barnett, M. (Eds.). (1998). *Security Communities*. Cambridge University Press.

Agnew, J. (1985). *Western Geopolitical Thought in the Twentieth Century* St. Martin's.

Agnew, J. (1995). *Mastering Space: Hegemony, Territory and the International Economy*. Routledge.

Agnew, J. (2003). *Geopolitics: Re-visioning World Politics* (2 ed.). Routledge.

Akaha, T. (Ed.). (1997). *Politics and Economics in the Russian Far East: Changing ties with Asia-Pacific* Routledge.

Akiner, S., Tideman, S., & Hay, J. (Eds.). (1998). *Sustainable Development in Central Asia*. St. Martin's Press.

Alden, C., Alao, A., Chun, Z., & Barber, L. (Eds.). (2018). *China and Africa Building Peace and Security Cooperation on the Continent*. Palgrave Macmillan.

Alden, C., & Large, D. (Eds.). (2019). *New Directionsin Africa-China Studies*. Routledge.

Alexeeva, O. (2008). Chinese Migration in the Russian Far East. *China Perspectives, 2008*(3), 20-32.

Allain, M. A. (2011). Canada's Claim to the Arctic: A Study in Overlapping Claims to the Outer Continental Shelf. *Journal of Maritime Law & Commerce, 42*(1), 1-47.

Allison, G. (2017). *Destined for War: Can America and China Escape Thucydides's Trap?* Houghton Mifflin Harcourt.

Allison, R. (2004). Strategic Reassertion in Russia's Central Asia Policy. *International Affairs, 80*(2), 277-293.

Allworth, E. A. (Ed.). (1967). *Central Asia: A century of Russian Role*. Columbia University Press.

Allworth, E. A. (1995). *Central Asia: One Hundred Thirty Years of Russian Dominance, A Historical Overview* (3rd ed.). Duke University Press.

Ambrosio, T. (2008). Catching the 'Shanghai Spirit': How the Shanghai Cooperation Organization Promotes Authoritarian Norms in Central Asia. *Europe-Asia Studies, 60*(8), 1321-1344.

Anderson, A. (2009). *After the Ice: Life, death, and Geopolitics in the New Arctic*. Smithsonian Books.

Aris, S. (2011). *Eurasian Regionalism: The Shanghai Cooperation Organisation*. Palgrave Macmillan.

Arsenov, V. I., Artemkina, E. V., & Zaboev, A. I. (2005). Rossiya v sisteme mejdunarodnih evroaziatiskih transportnih koridorov: sovremennoy sostoyanie, problemi, perspektivi i konkurentosposobnost [Russia in the System of International Eurasian Transport Coridors: Current State, Problems, Perspectives and Competitiveness] *Rossiskiy Vneshneekonomicheskiy Vestnik*(1).

Aslund, A. (2011). Revisiting the End of the Soviet Union. *Problems of Post-Communism, 58*(July–August/September–October).

Atabaki, T., & O'Kane, J. (1998). *Post-Soviet Central Asia*. Tauris Academic Studies.

Atkinson, D., & Dodds, K. (Eds.). (2000). *Geopolitical Traditions: Critical Histories of a Century of Geopolitical Thought*. Routledge.

Auslin, M. R. (2020). *Asia's New Geopolitics: Essays on Reshaping the Indo-Pacific*. Hoover Institution Press.

Baev, P. K. (2004). Assessing Russia's Cards: Three Petty Games in Central Asia. *Cambridge Review of International Affairs, 17*(2).

Bahgat, G. (2006). Central Asia and energy security. *Asian Affairs, 37*(1), 1-16.

Baizakova, K. I. (2010). Energy Security Issues in the Foreign Policy of the Republic of Kazakhstan. *American Foreign Policy Interests, 32*.

Baizakova, K. I. (2013). The Shanghai Cooperation Organization's Role in Countering Threats and Challenges to Central Asian Regional Security. *Russian Politics & Law, 51*(1), 59-79.

Baker, R., & Kocheleva, N. (1996). Environment versus Development: The Case of the Aral Sea. In R. Baker (Ed.), *Readings in Comparative and International Affairs Vol:35*. Indiana University Press.

Banuazizi, A., & Weiner, M. (Eds.). (1994). *The New Geopolitics of Central Asia and Its Borderlands*. Indiana University Press.

Barington, L. W., Herron, E. S., & Silver, B. D. (2003). The Motherland is calling:

Views of Homeland among Russians in the Near Abroad. *World Politics, 55*(2).

Barkovsky, A. N. (2006). Obrechen li Rossisky Dalny Vostok na sudbu tranzitnoy territoriy? [Is the Russian Far East Doomed to be a Transit Territory?] *Rossiskiy Vneshneekonomicheskiy Vestnik*(3).

Barrett, T. C. (2012). *The Chinese Diaspora in South-East Asia: The Overseas Chinese in Indochina.* I.B.Tauris.

Barylski, R. V. (1995). Russia, the West, and the Caspian Energy Hub. *Middle East Journal, 49*(2).

Bazarbayev, K., & Ashimkhanovna, A. Z. (2012). Jadids Movement in Central Asia in the Late 19th and the Early 20th Centuries. *Asian Social Science, 8*(8).

Becker, S. (2009). *Russia's Protectorates in Central Asia: Bukhara and Khiva, 1865–1924* (2 ed.). Routledge.

Beckley, M. (2011). China's Century? Why America's Edge Will Endure. *International Security, 36*(3).

Bedeski, R. E., & Swanstrom, N. (Eds.). (2012). *Eurasia's Ascent in Energy and Geopolitics: Rivalry or partnership for China, Russia and Central Asia?* Routledge.

Bedford, D. P. (1996). International Water Management in the Aral Sea Basin. *Water International, 21*(2), 63-69.

Beller-Hann, I. (2008). *Community Matters in Xinjiang: Towards a Historical Anthropology of the Uyghur.* Brill.

Belyaev, A. V. (1995). Water Balance and Water Resources of the Aral Sea Basin and its Man-Induced Changes. *GeoJournal, 35*(1), 17-23.

Belyi, A. (2003). New dimensions of energy security of the enlarging EU and their impact on relations with Russia. *Journal of European Integration, 25*(4).

Bennett, M. M. (2015). How China Sees the Arctic: Reading Between Extraregional and Intraregional Narratives. *Geopolitics 20*(3).

Beretta, S., Berkofsky, A., & Zhang, L. (Eds.). (2017). *Understanding China Today: An Exploration of Politics, Economics, Society, and International Relations.* Springer.

Bernhardi, F. v. (2019). *Germany and the Next War.* Wentworth Press.

Biddle, S. (2006). *Military Power: Explaining Victory and Defeat in Modern Battle* Princeton University Press.

Billon, P. L. (Ed.). (2005). *The Geopolitics of Resource Wars: Resource Dependence, Governance and Violence.* Routledge.

Billon, P. L., & Khatib, F. E. (2005). From Free Oil to 'Freedom Oil': Terrorism, War and US Geopolitics in the Persian Gulf. In P. L. Billon (Ed.), *The Geopolitics of Resource Wars: Resource Dependence, Governance and Violence* (pp. 109-138). Routledge.

Black, J. (2016). *Geopolitics and the Quest for Dominance.* Indiana University Press.

Blackwill, R. D., & Campbell, K. M. (2016). *Xi Jinping on the Global Stage Chinese*

Foreign Policy Under a Powerful but Exposed Leader.

Blank, S. (2011). Russia's Geo-economic Future; The Security Implications of Russia's Political and Economic Structure. *Journal of Slavic Military Studies, 24*(3), 351-395.

Blank, S. J. (2006). The Eurasian Energy Triangle: China, Russia, and the Central Asian States. *Brown Journal of World Affairs, XII*(2).

Bliakher, L. E., & Vasil'Eva, L. A. (2010). The Russian Far East in a State of Suspension. *Russian Politics & Law, 48*(1), 80-95.

Blunden, M. (2012). Geopolitics and the Northern Sea Route. *International Affairs, 88*(1).

Bochniarz, Z. (1992). Water Management Problems in Economies in Transition. *Natural Resources Forum*(February), 55-63.

Bogoyavlenskiy, V. (2010). Uglevodorodnye Bogatstva Arktiki i Rossiyskii Geofizicheskii Flot: Sostoyanie i Perspektivy [Hydrocarbon Resourses of Arctic and Russian Geophysical Fleet: Status and Perspectives] *Morskoy Sbornik, 1962*(9), 53-62.

Bogoyavlenskiy, V., & Laverov, N. (2012). Strategiya Osvoeniya Morskih Mestorozhdenii Nefti i Gaza Arktiki [Exploration Strategy of Offshore Oil and Gas Fields in the Arctic] *Morskoy Sbornik, 1983*(6), 50-58.

Bolt, P. J., & Cross, S. N. (2018). *China, Russia, and Twenty-First Century Global Geopolitics.* Oxford University Press.

Borgerson, S. G. (2008). Arctic meltdown: The economic and security implications of global warning. *Foreign Affairs, 87*(2).

Bos, M. G. (Ed.). (1996). *The Inter-Relationship Between Irrigation, Drainage and the Environment in the Aral Sea Basin.* Kluwer Academic Publishers.

Bost, d. F., Carroué, L., Colin, S., Laporte, A., Pihet, C., Sanmartin, O., & Teurtrie, D. (2018). *Images économiques du monde 2019 -Les nouvelles routes de la soie : vers une mondialisation chinoise? [The Economic Images of the World 2019 -The New Silk Roads: Towards Chinese Globalization?].* Armand Colin.

Bovingdon, G. (2004). *Autonomy in Xinjiang: Han Nationalist Imperatives and Uyghur Discontent* (Policy Studies, Issue.

Brady, A.-M. (2017). *China as a Polar Great Power.* Cambridge University Press.

Braker, H. (1989). Soviet Policy toward Islam In A. Kappeler, G. Simon, G. Brunner, & E. Allworth (Eds.), *Muslim Communities Reemerge: Historical Perspectives on Nationality, Politics, and Opposition in the Former Soviet Union and Yugoslavia.* Duke University Press.

Brands, H., & Palkki, D. (2011). Saddam, Israel, and the Bomb: Nuclear Alarmism Justified? *International Security, 36*(1).

Braudel, F. (1969). *Ecrits Sur L'Histoire.* Flammarion.

Braudel, F. (1982). *On History [Writings on History]* (S. Matthews, Trans.; 2014 ed.).

University of Chicago Press.
Brautigam, D. (2015). *Will Africa Feed China?* Oxford University Press.
Brecher, M. (1963). *The new states of Asia, a political analysis*. Oxford University Press.
Breslin, S. (Ed.). (2010). *Handbook of China's International Relations*. Routledge.
Broache, M. (2010). Re-Examining Russian Energy Power. *Journal of International Affairs, 63*(2).
Brooks, S., & Wohlforth, W. (2008). *World Out of Balance: International Relations and the Challenge of American Primacy*. Princeton University Press.
Brophy, D. (2016). *Uyghur Nation: Reform and Revolution on the Russia- China Frontier*. Harvard University Press.
Brophy, D. J. (2011). *Tending to Unite? The Origins of Uyghur Nationalism* Harvard University]. Cambridge, Massachusetts.
Brower, D. (1997). Islam and Ethnicity: Russian Colonial Policy in Turkestan. In D. Brower & E. Lazzerini (Eds.), *Russia's Orient: Imperial Borderlands and Peoples, 1700-1917*. Indiana University Press.
Brower, D., & Lazzerini, E. (Eds.). (1997). *Russia's Orient: Imperial Borderlands and Peoples, 1700-1917*. Indiana University Press.
Brzezinski, Z. (1998). *The Grand Chessboard: American Primacy and Its Geostrategic Imperatives*. Basic Books.
Brzezinski, Z. (2004). *The Choice—Global Domination or Global Leadership*. Basic.
Buitrago, S. R. d. (2020). China's Aspirations as a "Near Arctic State": Growing Stakeholder or Growing Risk? In J. Weber (Ed.), *Handbook on Geopolitics and Security in the Arctic. The High North Between Cooperation and Confrontation*. Springer.
Burg, S. (1986). Central Asian Elite Mobility and Political Change in the Soviet Union. *Central Asian Survey 5*(3.4).
Burke, D. C. (2020). *Diplomacy and the Arctic Council*. McGill-Queen's University Press.
Burley, A.-M., & Mattli, W. (1993). Europe Before the Court: A Political Theory of Legal Integration. *International Organization, 47*(1), 41-76.
Buszynski, L. (2005). Russia's New Role in Central Asia. *Asian Survey, 45*(4), 546-565.
Byers, M. (2009). *Who owns the Arctic? Understanding sovereignty disputes in the North*. Douglas and McIntyre.
Byers, M. (2013). *International Law and the Arctic*. Cambridge University Press.
Campbell, I. W. (2022). Russian Rule in Central Asia. In R. Isaacs & E. Marat (Eds.), *Routledge Handbook of Contemporary Central Asia*. Routledge.
Caporaso, J. A. (1998). Regional Integration Theory: Understanding Our Past and Anticipating the Future. In W. Sandholtz & A. S. Sweet (Eds.), *Supranational Governance: the Institutionalization of the European Union* (pp. 334-351). Oxford

University Press.

Caporaso, J. A. (2000). *The European Union : dilemmas of regional integration.* Westview Press.

Cappelletti, A. (2020). *Socio-Economic Development in Xinjiang Uyghur Autonomous Region: Disparities and Power Struggle in China's North-West.* Palgrave Macmillan.

Carlisle, D. (1994). Soviet Uzbekistan: State and Nation in Historical Perspective. In B. Manz (Ed.), *Central Asia in Historical Perspective.* Westview Press.

Carr, E. H. (1939). *The Twenty Years' Crisis, 1919-1939: An Introduction to the Study of International Relations.* Macmillan.

Chalidze, F. (1992). Aral Sea Crisis: A Legacy of Soviet Rule. *Central Asia Monitor, 1.*

Chandran, N. (2018). 'Serious' rivalry still drives China-Russia relations despite improving ties. *CNBC-Asia politics.* Retrieved November 5, 2018, from

Chapman, B. (2011). *Geopolitics: A Guide to the Issues.* Praeger.

Checkel, J. T. (1999). Norms, Institutions, and National Identity in Contemporary Europe. *International Studies Quarterly, 43*(1), 84-111.

Cheng, J. Y. S. (2008). A Chinese View of China's Energy Security. *Journal of Contemporary China, 17*(55), 297-317.

Cheng, J. Y. S. (2011). The Shanghai Co-operation Organisation: China's Initiative in Regional Institutional Building. *Journal of Contemporary Asia, 41*(4), 632-656.

Choi, Y. J., & Caporaso, J. A. (2002). Comparative Regional Integration. In W. Carlsnaes, T. Risse, & B. A. Simmons (Eds.), *Handbook of International Relations* (pp. 480-499). Sage Publications.

Chomsky, N. (2000). *Rogue States: The Rule of Force in World Affairs* (Second Printing ed.). South End Press.

Christensen, T., & Snyder, J. (1990). Chain Gangs and Passed Bucks: Predicting Alliance Patterns in Multipolarity. *International Organization, 44*(2).

Christensen, T. J. (2006). Fostering Stability or Creating a Monster? The Rise of China and U.S. Policy toward East Asia. *International Security, 31*(1).

Christian, D. (1994). Inner Eurasia as a Unit of World History. *Journal of World History, 5.*

Chun, H. (2008). Russia's energy diplomacy toward Europe and Northeast Asia: a comparative study. *Asia Europe Journal, 7*(2), 327-343.

Chung, C. P. (2018). What are the strategic and economic implications for South Asia of China's Maritime Silk Road initiative? *The Pacific Review, 31*(3).

Cohen, S. B. (2005). The Eurasian Convergence Zone: Gateway or Shatterbelt? *Eurasian Geography and Economics, 36*(1).

Cohen, S. B. (2009). *Geopolitics: The Geography of International Relations.* Rowman & Littlefield Publishers.

Crews, R. D. (2006). *For Prophet and Tsar: Islam and Empire in Russia and Central Asia.* Harvard University Press.

d'Encausse, H. C. (1966). *Reforme et revolution chez les musulmans de russie l'empire: Bukhara, 1867-1924 [Reform and Revolution among the Muslims of the Russian Empire: Bukhara, 1867-1924]*. Armand Colin.

d'Encausse, H. C. (1978). *L'Empire éclaté : la révolte des nations en URSS [The Shattered Empire: The Revolt of the Nations in the USSR]*. Flammarion.

d'Encausse, H. C. (1988). *Islam and the Russian Empire: Reform and Revolution in Central Asia*. I.B. Tauris & Co.

Daalder, I. H. (2022). The Return of Containment: How the West Can Prevail Against the Kremlin. *Foreign Affairs*(March).

Dadabaev, T. (2013). Shanghai Cooperation Organization (SCO) Regional Identity Formation from the Perspective of the Central Asia States. *Journal of Contemporary China, 23*(85), 102-118.

Dalby, S. (2003). Geopolitical Identities: Arctic Ecology and Global Consumption. *Geopolitics, 8*(1), 181-202.

Daojiong, Z., & Breslin, S. (2010). Oiling the wheels of foreign policy? Energy security and China's international relations. In S. Breslin (Ed.), *Handbook of China's International Relations*. Routledge.

Davis, S. (2003). *The Russian Far East: The Last Frontier Postcommunist States and Nations*. Routledge.

Debs, A., & Monteiro, N. P. (2014). Known Unknowns: Power Shifts, Uncertainty, and War. *International Organization, 68*(1).

Deniston, B. (2013). The Pacific Development Corridor: Maglev Across the Bering Strait. *Executive Intelligence Review, 40*(36).

Dent, C. M. (Ed.). (2011). *China and Africa Development Relations*. Routledge.

Dent, C. M. (2016). *East Asian Regionalism* (2nd ed.). Routledge.

Deutsch, K. W. (1957). *Political community and the North Atlantic area; international organization in the light of historical experience*. Princeton University Press.

Devlet, N. (1990). *İsmail Bey Gaspirali [İsmail Bey Gaspirali]*. Türk Dünyası Araştırmaları Enstitüsü Yayınları.

Devlet, N. (1996). İsmail Gaspıralı dönemi ve Ruslarla uzlaşma [The Reconciliation Process with the Russians at the time of Ismail Gaspirali]. *Türk Dünyası Dil ve Edebiyat Dergisi, 2*, 403-408.

Ding, A. S., & Panda, J. P. (Eds.). (2021). *Chinese Politics and Foreign Policy under Xi Jinping: The Future Political Trajectory*. Routledge.

Dodds, K., & Nuttall, M. (2016). *The scramble for the poles: The geopolitics of the Arctic and the Antarctic*. Polity Press.

Dorman, S. (1991). Who Will Save the Aral Sea? *Environmental Policy Review, 5*(2), 45-54.

Dostoyevsky, F. (2015). *The Brothers Karamazov* (C. Garnett, Trans.). Lerner Publishing.

Douglas, R. (2007). Russian-American Team: World Needs Bering Strait Tunnel! . *Executive Intelligence Review, 34.*

Dragneva, R. (2018). The Eurasian Economic Union: Putin's Geopolitical Project. *Russia Political Economy Project.*

Dreyer, E. L. (1982). *Early Ming China, A Political History, 1355-1435.* Stanford University Press.

Dreyer, E. L. (2007). *Zheng He: China And the Oceans in the Early Ming Dynasty, 1405-1433.* Pearson College Div.

Dudoignon, S., & Hisao, K. (Eds.). (2001). *Islam in Politics in Russia and Central Asia (Early Eighteenth to Late Twentieth Centuries).* Kegan Paul.

Ebel, R. E. (2009). *The Geopolitics of Russian Energy: Looking Back, Looking Forward.*

Eder, T. S. (2014). *China-Russia Relations in Central Asia: Energy Policy, Beijing's New Assertiveness and 21st Century Geopolitics.* Springer.

Edgar, A. (2004). *Tribal Nation: The Making of Soviet Turkmenistan.* Princeton University Press.

Emmers, R. (2010). *Geopolitics and Maritime Territorial Disputes in East Asia.* Routledge.

Emmerson, C. (2010). *The Future History of the Arctic.* The Bodley Head.

Erdem, C. (2015). Sino-Russian Strategic Partnership: The Shanghai Cooperation Organization. In E. Sorhun, Ü. Hacıoğlu, & H. Dinçer (Eds.), *Regional Economic Integration and the Global Financial System* (pp. 257-273). IGI Global.

Erdem, C. (2016). The Eurasian Corridor through the New Silk Road: Differing Geopolitical Perceptions. *Acta Via Serica, Winter*(Inaugural), 51-69.

Escobar, P. (2018). Back in the (Great) Game: The Revenge of Eurasian Land Powers. *Consortium News.* Retrieved November 2, 2018, from

Fairhall, D. (2010). *Cold front: conflict ahead in Arctic waters.* I. B. Tauris.

Farrell, M., Hettne, B., & Langenhove, L. v. (Eds.). (2005). *Global politics of regionalism: theory and practice.* Pluto Press.

Fawcett, L. L. E., & Hurrell, A. (1995). *Regionalism in world politics : regional organization and international order.* Oxford University Press.

Fawn, R. (Ed.). (2005). *Realignments in Russian Foreign Policy.* Taylor & Francis.

Fearon, J. (1995). Rationalist Explanations for War. *International Organization, 49*(3).

Feng, H., He, K., & Li, X. (2019). *How China Sees the World Insights From China's International Relations Scholars.* Palgrave Macmillan.

Feng, H., He, K., & Xuetong, Y. (Eds.). (2019). *Chinese Scholars and Foreign Policy: Debating International Relations.* Routledge.

Fergus, M. (1999). The Aral Sea Environmental Crisis: Problems and a Way Forward. *Asian Affairs, 30*(1), 35-44.

Feshbach, M. (1995). *Ecological Disaster: Cleaning up the hidden legacy of the Soviet regime.* The Twentieth Century Fund Press.

Feshbach, M., & Friendly, J. A. (1991). *Ecocide in the USSR: Health and Nature under Siege*. Basic Books.

Fierman, W. (Ed.). (1991). *Soviet Central Asia: The Failed Transformation*. Westview Press.

Flynn, M. (2007). Reconstructing 'Home/lands' in the Russian Federation: Migrant Centred Perspectives of Displacement and Resettlement. *Journal of Ethnic and Migration Studies 33*(3).

Fornes, G., & Mendez, A. (2018). *The China-Latin America Axis: Emerging Markets and their Role in an Increasingly Globalised World*. Palgrave Macmillan.

Forsyth, J. (1992). *A History of the Peoples of Siberia 1581-1990*. Cambridge University Press.

Frank, A. G. (1992). The Centrality of Central Asia. *Comparative Asian Studies, 8*.

Franklin, S. (2004). Russia in time. In S. Franklin & E. Widdis (Eds.), *National Identity on Russian Culture: An Introduction*. Cambridge University Press

Frankopan, P. (2017). *The Silk Roads: A New History of the World*. Vintage Books.

Friedberg, A. L. (2005). The future of US–China relations: Is conflict inevitable? *International Security, 30*(2).

Friedberg, A. L. (2015). The debate over US-China strategy. *Survival 57*(3).

Friedman, G. (2008). *The Methodology of Geopolitics: Love of One's Own and the Importance of Place*

Fromkin, D. (2009). *A Peace to End All Peace: The Fall of the Ottoman Empire and the Creation of the Modern Middle East* Holt Paperbacks.

Fuhrmann, M. (2009). Spreading Temptation: Proliferation and Peaceful Nuclear Cooperation Agreements," (Summer): 7-41. *International Security, 34*(1).

Gaddis, J. L. (2005). *Strategies of Containment: A Critical Appraisal of American National Security Policy During the Cold War*. Oxford University Press; Revised edition.

Gallagher, K. (2016). *The China Triangle: Latin America's China Boom and the Fate of the Washington Consensus*. Oxford University Press.

Garcia, Z. (2022). *China's Western Frontier and Eurasia: The Politics of State and Region-Building*. Routledge.

Garlick, J. (2020). *The Impact of China's Belt and Road Initiative From Asia to Europe*. Routledge.

Garver, J. W. (2016). *China's Quest: The History of the Foreign Relations of the People's Republic of China*. Oxford University Press.

Gavin, F. (2009/10). Same As It Ever Was: Nuclear Alarmism, Proliferation, and the Cold War. *International Security, 34*(3).

Geiss, P. G. (2003). *Pre-Tsarist and Tsarist Central Asia: Communal Commitment and Political Order in Change*. Routledge.

Gentes, A. A. (2008). *Exile to Siberia, 1590-1822*. Palgrave Macmillan.

Gerhardt, H., Steinberg, P. E., Tasch, J., Fabiano, S. J., & Shields, R. (2010). Contested Sovereignty in a Changing Arctic. *Annals of the Association of American Geographers, 100*(4), 992-1002.

Gerstl, A., & Wallenbock, U. (Eds.). (2021). *China's Belt and Road Initiative: Strategic and Economic Impacts on Central Asia, Southeast Asia, and Central Eastern Europe.* Routledge.

Gilpin, R. (1981). *War and Change in World Politics.* Cambridge University Press.

Gilpin, R. G. (1986). The Richness of the Tradition of Political Realism. In R. O. Keohane (Ed.), *Neorealism and Its Critics* (pp. 301-322). Columbia University Press

Glantz, M. H. (Ed.). (1999). *Creeping Environmental Problems and Sustainable Development in the Aral Sea Basin.* Cambridge University Press.

Glantz, M. H., Rubinstein, A. Z., & Zohn, I. (1993). Tragedy in the Aral Sea Basin: Looking back to plan ahead? *Global Environmental Change, 3*(2), 174-198.

Glaser, C. (1997). The Security Dilemma Revisited. *World Politics 50*(1).

Gleason, G. (1986). Sharaf Rashidov and the Dilemmas of National Leadership. *Central Asian Survey, 5*(4).

Glenn, J. (1999). *The Soviet Legacy in Central Asia* Macmillan Press.

Godehardt, N. (2014). *The Chinese Constitution of Central Asia: Regions and Intertwined Actors in International Relation.* Palgrave Macmillan.

Gogol, N. V. (1997). *Dead Souls* (R. Pevear & L. Volokhonsky, Trans.; 2 ed.). Vintage.

Goldman, M. I. (2008). *Petrostate: Putin, Power, and the New Russia.* Oxford University Press.

Goldthau, A. (2008). Resurgent Russia? Rethinking Energy Inc. *Policy Review, 147*(February & March), 53-63.

Gourevitch, P. (2002). Domestic Politics and International Relations. In W. Carlsnaes, T. Risse, & B. A. Simmons (Eds.), *Handbook of International Relations.*

Gowa, J. (1989). Bipolarity, multipolarity, and free trade. *The American Political Science Review, 83*(4), 1245-1256.

Grant, S. D. (2010). *Polar Imperative: A History of Arctic Sovereignty in North America.* Douglas and McIntyre.

Gresh, G. F. (Ed.). (2018). *Eurasia's Maritime Rise and Global Security: From the Indian Ocean to Pacific Asia and the Arctic.* Palgrave Macmillan.

Grieco, J. (1993). Understanding the Problem of International Cooperation: the Limitations of Neoliberal Institutionalism and the Future of Realist Theory. In D. Baldwin (Ed.), *Neorealism and Neoliberalism: The Contemporary Debate.* Columbia University Press.

Grieco, J. (1995). The Maastricht Treaty, Economic and Monetary Union, and the Neorealist Research Programme. *Review of International Studies, 21*, 21-40.

Grieco, J. M. (1990). *Cooperation among Nations: Europe, America, and Non-Tariff Barriers to Trade*. Cornell University Press.

Groisman, P., & Gutman, G. (Eds.). (2013). *Regional Environmental Changes in Siberia and Their Global Consequences Springer.*

Grousset, R. (1970). *The Empire of the Steppes: A History of Central Asia* (N. Walford, Trans.). Rutgers University Press.

Grydehoj, A., & Su, P. (2022). *China and the Pursuit of Harmony in World Politics: Understanding Chinese International Relations Theory*. Routledge.

Gupta, A. (2009). Geopolitical Implications of Arctic Meltdown. *Strategic Analysis, 33*(2), 174-177.

Haas, E. B. (1961). International Integration: The European and the Universal Process. *International Organization, 15*(3).

Haas, E. B., & Whiting, A. S. (1975). *Dynamics of international relations*. Greenwood Press.

Hableti̇moğlu, N. (1997). *Çarlık Rusyası'nda Türk Kongreleri 1905-1917 [Turkish Conventions in Tsarist Russia, 1905-1917]*. Ankara Üniversitesi Basımevi.

Hancock, T. (2017). China encircles the world with One Belt, One Road strategy. *Financial Times, May 4th*

Harnisch, S., Bersick, S., & Gottwald, J.-C. (Eds.). (2016). *China's International Roles Challenging or supporting international order?* Routledge.

Hauner, M. (1989). Central Asian Geopolitics in the Last Hundred Years: A Critical Survey from Gorchakov to Gorbachev *Central Asian Survey, 8*(1).

Haushofer, K. (2002). *An English Translation and Analysis of Major General Karl Ernst Haushofer's "Geopolitics of the Pacific Ocean": Studies on the Relationship Between Geography and History*. Edwin Mellen Press.

Heinrich, A. (2008). Under the Kremlin's Thumb: Does Increased State Control in the Russian Gas Sector Endanger European Energy Security? *Europe-Asia Studies, 60*(9), 1539-1574.

Heleniak, T. (2004). Migration of the Russian Diaspora after the Break-up of the Soviet Union. *Journal of International Affairs, 57*(2).

Hettne, B., Inotai, A., & Sunkel, O. (1999). *Globalism and the New Regionalism*. Palgrave Macmillan.

Hill, F., & Gaddy, C. G. (2003). *The Siberian Curse: How Communist Planners left Russia out in the Cold* Brookings Institutions Press.

Hobsbawm, E. J. (1987). *The Age of Empire, 1875–1914*. Pantheon.

Hoffmann, S. (1963). Discord in Community: The North Atlantic Area as a Partial International System. *International Organization, 17*(3), 521-549

Holm, H. H., & Sørensen, G. (1995). *Whose World Order?: Uneven Globalization and the End of the Cold War*. Westview Press.

Holsti, O. R. (1990). Crisis Decision Making. In P. E. Tetlock, J. L. Husbands, R.

Jervis, P. C. Stern, & C. Tilly (Eds.), *Behavior, Society, and Nuclear War* (Vol. 1). Oxford University Press.

Honneland, G. (2020). *Russia and the Arctic: Environment, Identity and Foreign Policy* (2 ed.). I.B. Tauris.

Howard, R. (2009). *The Arctic Gold Rush: The New Race for Tomorrow's Natural Resources*. Continuum.

Hu, L., & Chen, T.-S. (2008). China's Energy Security and Geo-Economic Interests in Central Asia. *Central European Journal of International and Security Studies, 2*(2), 42-55.

Hudgins, S. (2003). *The Other Side of Russia: A Slice of Life in Siberia and the Russian Far East.* Texas A&M University Press.

Huntington, S. P. (1993). The Clash of Civilizations? *Foreign Affairs, 72*

Huntington, S. P. (1997). *The clash of civilizations and the remaking of world order.* Touchstone.

Hussein, M., & Haddad, M. (2021). Infographic: US military presence around the world. *Al Jazeera*. Retrieved April 23, 2022, from https://www.aljazeera.com/news/2021/9/10/infographic-us-military-presence-around-the-world-interactive

Hymans, J. (2011). Veto Players, Nuclear Energy, and Nonproliferation: Domestic Institutional Barriers to a Japanese Bomb. *International Security, 36*(2).

Ikenberry, G. J. (2008). The Rise of China and the Future of the West—Can the Liberal System Survive? *Foreign Affairs, 87*(1).

Ikenberry, G. J. (2019). *After Victory: Institutions, Strategic Restraint, and the Rebuilding of Order After Major Wars* (Revised ed.). Princeton University Press.

İnalcık, H., & Quataert, D. (Eds.). (1997). *An Economic and Social History of the Ottoman Empire, Vol. 2: 1600-1914*. Cambridge University Press.

İsmetullah, H. (2004). İsmail Bey Gaspıralı'nın Türkistan'ı Uyandırma Yolundaki Teşebbüsleri [Ismail Bey Gaspıralı's Attempts to Awaken Turkistan]. *İsmail Bey Gaspıralı İçin, 9*( ), 583-595.

Jaffe, A. M., & Soligo, R. (2009). Energy Security: the Russian connection. In D. Moran & J. A. Russell (Eds.), *Energy Security and Global Politics: The Militarization of Resource Management* (pp. 112-135). Routledge.

Jakobson, L., & Peng, J. (2012). *China's Arctic Aspirations* (SIPRI Policy Paper, Issue.

Jenkins, R. (2019). *How China is Reshaping the Global Economy: Development Impacts in Africa and Latin America.* Oxford University Press.

Jervis, R. (1989). *The Meaning of the Nuclear: Statecraft and the Prospect of Armageddon.* Cornell University Press.

Jinping, X. (2018). *Xi Jingping: Important Speeches at the BOAO Forum For Asia Annual Conference* Foreign Languages Press.

Johnson, T. H. (2009). Central Asia: energy resources, politics, and security. In D.

Moran & J. A. Russell (Eds.), *Energy Security and Global Politics: The Militarization of Resource Management* (pp. 135-155). Routledge.

Jordan, B. B., & Jordan-Bychkov, T. G. *Siberian Village: Land and Life in the Sakha Republic* University of Minnesota Press.

Kachiga, J. (2021). *The Rise of China and International Relations Theory*. Peter Lang Publishing.

Kacowicz, A. M. (1998). *Zones of peace in the Third World : South America and West Africa in comparative perspective*. State University of New York Press.

Kaczmarski, M. (2015). *Russia–China Relations in the Post-Crisis International Order*. Routledge.

Kanet, R. E. (Ed.). (2010). *Russian Foreign Policy in the 21st Century*. Palgrave Macmillan.

Kangas, R. (2007). The Changing Face of the Russian Far East: Cooperation and Resource Competition Between Japan, Korea, and China in Northeast Asia. *Perspectives on Global Development & Technology, 6*(1-3), 441-460.

Kanlıdere, A. (1997). Kazan Tatarları Arasında Tecdid ve Cedit Hareketi (1809-1917). *Türkiye Günlüğü Dergisi, 46*(Summer).

Kaplan, R. D. (2012). *The Revenge of Geography: What the Map Tells Us about Coming Conflicts and the Battle Against Fate*. Random House.

Karagiannis, E. (2006). The Challenge of Radical Islam in Tajikistan: Hizb ut-Tahrir al-Islami. *Nationalities Papers, 34*(1).

Karlybaev, M. (2002). L'instruction musulmane et les ishan chez les Karakalpaks du XIXeme siecle. *Cahiers d'Asie centrale, 10*, 177-191.

Karpat, K. H. (2002). *The Politicization of Islam: Reconstructing Identity, State, Faith, and Community in the Late Ottoman State*. Oxford University Press.

Kassenova, N. (2022). China-Central Asia Relations: Re-learning to live next to a giant. In R. Isaacs & E. Marat (Eds.), *Routledge Handbook of Contemporary Central Asia*. Routledge.

Katzenstein, P. (1996). *The Culture of National Security: Norms and Identity in World Politics*. Columbia University Press.

Keller, S. (2001). *To Moscow, Not Mecca: The Soviet Campaign against Islam in Central Asia*. Praeger Publishers.

Keller, S. (2020). *Russia and Central Asia: Coexistence, Conquest, Convergence*. University of Toronto Press.

Kelly, P. (2016). *Classical Geopolitics: A New Analytical Model*. Stanford University Press.

Kennan, G. F. (1947). The Sources of Soviet Conduct. *Foreign Affairs, 25*(4).

Kennan, G. F. (2012). *American Diplomacy: Sixtieth-Anniversary Expanded Edition*. University of Chicago Press.

Keohane, R., & Martin, L. (1995). The Promise of Institutional Theory. *International*

Security, 20(1), 39-51.

Keskitalo, C. (2007). International Region-Building: Development of the Arctic as an International Region. *Cooperation and Conflict, 42*(2), 187-205.

Khalid, A. (1994). Printing, Publishing, and Reform in Tsarist Central Asia. *International Journal of Middle East Studies, 26*(2).

Khalid, A. (1999). *The Politics of Muslim Cultural Reform: Jadidism in Central Asia.* University of California Press.

Kiessling, K. L. (1998). Conference on the Aral Sea: Women, Children, Health and Environment. *Ambio, 27*(7), 560-564.

Kinross, L. (1979). *Ottoman Centuries* (10 ed.). William Morrow Paperbacks.

Kissinger, H. (1994). *Diplomacy.* Simon & Schuster.

Kissinger, H. (2001). *Does America Need a Foreign Policy? Towards a Diplomacy for the 21st Century* Simon & Schuster.

Kobori, I., & Glantz, M. H. (Eds.). (1998). *Central Eurasian Water Crisis: Caspian, Aral, and Dead Seas, Water Resources Management and Policy.* United Nations University Press.

Kochhar, G. (Ed.). (2018). *China's Foreign Relations and Security Dimensions.* Routledge.

Kolodkin, A. L., & Shinkaretskaya, G. G. (2009). O Kontinental'nom Shel'fe Rossii v Arktike [About the Russian Continental Shelf in the Arctic]. *Gosudarctvo i Pravo, 10*, 21-27.

Konyshev, V., & Sergunin, A. (2011). Arkticheskoe Napravlenie Vneshnei Politiki Rossii: Problemy i Perspektivy [Arctic Course of the Russian Foreign Policy: Problems and Outlook]. *Obozrevately, 3*, 13-20.

Kosmarskaya, N. (2005). Post Soviet Diaspora. In M. Ember, C. R. Ember, & I. Skoggard (Eds.), *Encyclopaedia of Diasporas: Immigrant and Refugee Cultures around the World.* Springer.

Kotlyakov, V. M. (1991). The Aral Sea Basin: A Critical Environmental Zone. *Environment, 33*(1).

Kovalev, S. (2017). Ministry urges easier naturalization for large-scale investors in Russian Far East. Retrieved 13 May 2020, from https://www.rt.com/russia/405381-far-east-development-urges-easier/

Kozmenko, S., Selin, V., & Shchegolkova, A. (2012). Geoekonomicheskie Vyzovy: Morskoy Politiki v Rossiyskoy Arktike. *Morskoy Sbornik, 1983*(6), 33-42.

Krasner, S. D. (1999). *Sovereignty: Organized Hypocrisy.* Princeton University Press.

Kroenig, M. (2013). Nuclear Superiority and the Balance of Resolve: Explaining Nuclear Crisis Outcomes. *International Organization,, 67*(1).

Kuhrt, N. (2012). The Russian Far East in Russia's Asia Policy: Dual Integration or Double Periphery? *Europe-Asia Studies, 64*(3), 471-493.

Lagutina, M. L. (2021). *Russia's Arctic Policy in the Twenty-First Century: National and International Dimensions.* Lexington Books.

Lane, D., & Samokhvalov, V. (Eds.). (2015). *The Eurasian Project and Europe Regional Discontinuities and Geopolitics.* Palgrave Macmillan.

Lanteign, M. (2007). China's Energy Security and Eurasian Diplomacy: The Case of Turkmenistan. *Politics, 27*(3), 147-155.

Lanteigne, M. (2010). Security, strategy and the former USSR: China and the Shanghai Cooperation Organisation. In S. Breslin (Ed.), *Handbook of China's International Relations.* Routledge.

Lanteigne, M. (2020). *Chinese Foreign Policy: An Introduction* (Fourth ed.). Routledge.

Larson, D. W. (1989). *Origins of Containment: A Psycological Explanation.* Princeton University Press.

Larson, D. W., & Shevchenko, A. (2019). *Quest for Status: Chinese and Russian Policy.* Yale University Press.

Laruelle, M. (2012). *Russian Eurasianism: An Ideology of Empire* (Reprint ed.). Johns Hopkins University Press.

Laruelle, M. (2014). *Russia's Arctic strategies and the future of the far north.* Routledge.

Lattimore, O. (1962). *Inner Asian Frontiers of China.* Beacon Press.

Laumullin, M. (2006). *The Shanghai Cooperation Organization as "Geopolitical Bluff?" A View from Astana* (Russie.Nei.Visions, Issue.

Lazzerini, E. J. (1992). Beyond Renewal: The Jadid Response to Pressure for Change in the Modern Age. In J. A. Gross (Ed.), *Muslims in Central Asia: Expressions of Identity and Change.* Duke University Press.

Lebedeva., N. M. (1995). *Novaya Russkaya Diaspora [New Russian Diaspora]* Institut Etnologii i Antropologii.

LeDonne, J. P. (1997). *The Russian Empire and the World, 1700–1917: The Geopolitics of Expansion and Containment.* Oxford University Press.

Lei, W., & Xuejun, L. (2007). China or the United States: which threatens energy security? *OPEC Review*(September), 215-234.

Levintanus, A. (1992). Saving the Aral Sea. *Environmentalist, 12*(2), 85-91.

Levy, J. S., and William R. Thompson. (2005). Hegemonic Threat and Great Power Balancing in Europe, 1495–2000. *Security Studies, 14*(1).

Lieber, K. A., & Press, D. G. (2006). The End of MAD? The Nuclear Dimension of U.S. Primacy. *International Security, 30*(4).

Lieber, K. A., & Press, D. G. (2020). *The Myth of the Nuclear Revolution: Power Politics in the Atomic Age.* Cornell University Press.

Lin, H.-T. (2008). From Rimland to Heartland: Nationalist China's Geopolitics and Ethnopolitics in Central Asia, 1937–1952. *International History Review, 30*

Lind, J. (2014). Geography and the Security Dilemma in Asia. In S. M. Pekkanen, J. Ravenhill, & R. Foot (Eds.), *The Oxford Handbook of the International Relations of Asia.* Oxford University Press.

Lo, B. (2002). *Russian Foreign Policy in the Post-Soviet Era Reality, Illusion and*

Mythmaking. Palgrave Macmillan.

Lorenz, R. (1994). Economic Bases of the Basmachi Movement in the Farghana Valley. In E. Allworth (Ed.), *Muslim Communities Reemerge*.

Lukin, A. (2006). The Russian Approach to China under Gorbachev, Yeltsin, and Putin. In G. Rozman, K. Togo, & J. P. Ferguson (Eds.), *Russian Strategic Thought toward Asia*. Palgrave Macmillan.

Lyons, G. M., & Mastanduno, M. (Eds.). (1995). *Beyond Westphalia?: State Sovereignty and International Intervention*. The Johns Hopkins University Press.

Maçães, B. (2018). Belt and Road Initiative: As Europe and Asia draw closer together, will the US become irrelevant or can it find a role as deal maker? *South China Morning Post*. Retrieved October 26, 2018, from

Mackinder, H. J. (1904). The Geographical Pivot of History. *The Geographical Journal 23*(4).

Mackinder, H. J. (1919). *Democratic ideals and reality: A Study in the Politics of Reconstruction*. Constable and Company, ltd.

Mahan, A. T. (1987). *The Influence of Sea Power on History: 1660–1783* (Revised ed.). Dover Publications.

Makari, G. (2021). *Of Fear and Strangers: A History of Xenophobia*. W. W. Norton & Company.

Mankoff, J. (2009). *Eurasian Energy Security*.

Mankoff, J. (2009). *Russian Foreign Policy The Return of Great Power Politics*. Rowman & Littlefield Publishers.

Mankoff, J. (2009). *Russian Foreign Policy: The Return of Great Power Politics* Rowman & Littlefield Publishers, Inc.

Mardin, S. (1983). *Jön Türklerin Siyasi Fikirleri 1895-1908 [Political Ideas of the Young Turks, 1895-1908]*. İletişim Yayınları.

Marketos, T. N. (2009). *China's Energy Geopolitics: The Shanghai Cooperation Organization and Central Asia*. Routledge.

Markey, D. S. (2020). *China's Western Horizon Beijing and the New Geopolitics of Eurasia*. Oxford University Press.

Martin, L. L., & Simmons, B. A. (Eds.). (2001). *International Institutions: An International Organization Reader*. The MIT Press.

Mattli, W. (1999). *The logic of regional integration : Europe and beyond*. Cambridge University Press.

Maxfield, S. (2002). International Development. In W. Carlsnaes, T. Risse, & B. A. Simmons (Eds.), *Handbook of International Relations*. SAGE Publications

Mazur, I. I. (2010). Arktika - Tochka Bifurkatsii v Razvitii Global'nogo Mira [The Arctic is the Bifurcation Point in the Global Development]. *Vek Globalizatsii, 2*, 93-104.

Mead, W. R. (2014). The Return of Geopolitics: The Revenge of the Revisionist

Powers. *Foreign Affairs*(May/June).
Mearsheimer, J. J. (1990). Back to the Future: Instability in Europe after the Cold War. *International Security 15*(1), 5-56International Security
Mearsheimer, J. J. (2001). *The Tragedy of Great Power Politics*. W.W. Norton.
Mearsheimer, J. J. (2006a). China's unpeaceful rise. *Current History, 105*(April).
Mearsheimer, J. J. (2006b). China's Unpeaceful Rise. *Current History, 105*(690).
Mearsheimer, J. J. (2010). The gathering storm: China's challenge to US power in Asia. *The Chinese Journal of International Politics, 3*(4).
Micklin, P. P. (1988). Desiccation of the Aral Sea: a water management disaster in the Soviet Union. *Science, 241*(4870), 1170-1177.
Micklin, P. P. (1991). *The Water Management Crisis in Soviet Central Asia*. University of Pittsburgh Center for Russian and East European Studies.
Micklin, P. P. (2000). Managing Water in Central Asia. In E. Herzig (Ed.), *Central Asian and Caucasian Prospects*. The Royal Institute of International Affairs.
Millward, J. A. (2021). *Eurasian Crossroads: A History of Xinjiang* (Revised ed.). Hurst & Company.
Ming, H. H. (2016). *From the Mongols to the Ming Dynasty: How a Begging Monk Became Emperor of China, Zhu Yuan Zhang*. Algora Publishing.
Mitchell, R. B. (2002). International Environment. In W. Carlsnaes, T. Risse, & B. A. Simmons (Eds.), *Handbook of International Relations*. SAGE Publications.
Mitrany, D. (1946). *A working peace system; an argument for the functional developmental of international organization* (4th ed.). National Peace Council.
Mitrany, D. (1966). *A working peace system*. Quadrangle Books.
Mitrany, D. (1976). *The functional theory of politics*. St. Martin's Press.
Mittelman, J. H. (1996). *Globalization: Critical Reflections*. Lynne Rienner Publishers.
Mittelman, J. H. (2000). *The Globalization Syndrome: Transformation and Resistance*. Princeton University Press.
Modelski, G. (1963). *The new emerging forces; documents on the ideology of Indonesian foreign policy*. Dept. of International Relations, Research School of Pacific Studies, Institute of Advanced Studies, Australian National University.
Monteiro, N. P., & Debs, A. (2014). The Strategic Logic of Nuclear Proliferation. *International Security, 39*(2).
Moran, D., & Russell, J. A. (Eds.). (2009). *Energy Security and Global Politics: The Militarization of Resource Management*. Routledge.
Moravcsik, A. (1998). Integration Theory. In D. Dinan (Ed.), Encyclopedia of the European Union. Lynne Rienner
Moravcsik, A. (1999). Is Something Rotten in the State of Denmark? Constructivism and European Integration. *Journal of European Public Policy, 6*(4).
Morgenthau, H. J. (1948). *Politics among Nations: The Struggle for Power and Peace*. McGraw-Hill, Inc.

Morrison, A. S. (2008). *Russian Rule in Samarkand 1868–1910: A Comparison with British India.* Oxford University Press.

Movkebaeva, G. A. (2013). Energy Cooperation Among Kazakhstan, Russia, and China Within the Shanghai Cooperation Organization. *Russian Politics & Law, 51*(1), 80-87.

Mueller, J. (2010). Think Again: Nuclear Weapons. *Foreign Policy, 177*

Murphy, A. B. (2015). Coping With a Fast-Changing World: Why Geography Still Matters.

Naumov, I. V. (2006). *The History of Siberia.* Routledge.

Nemchaninova, M. A., & Buldygerova, L. N. (2012). Concession as a Form of Attraction of Foreign Capital (on the Example of the Concession Policy in the Russian Far East in the 20ths of the XX century). (English). *Bulletin of PNU, 26*(3), 203-210.

Ngoei, W.-Q. (2019). *Arc of Containment: Britain, the United States, and Anticommunism in Southeast Asia.* Cornell University Press.

Nikishenkov, O. (2011). Digging to America. *The Moscow News.*

Nishimura, D. (2013). Russian Far East railway project may extend to Hokkaido. *Asahi Shimbun*

Northrop, D. (2004). *Veiled Empire: Gender and Power in Stalinist Central Asia.* Cornell University Press.

Nuttall, M., Christensen, T. R., & Siegert, M. (Eds.). (2020). *The Routledge Handbook of the Polar Regions.* Routledge.

O'Hara, S. L. (2005). Great Game or Grubby Game?: The Struggle for Control of the Caspian. In P. L. Billon (Ed.), *The Geopolitics of Resource Wars: Resource Dependence, Governance and Violence* (pp. 138-161). Routledge.

Ocelík, P., & Osička, J. (2014). The framing of unconventional natural gas resources in the foreign energy policy discourse of the Russian Federation. *Energy Policy, 72*, 97-109.

Odum, H. (1936). *Southern regions of the United States.* The University of North Carolina Press.

Odum, H., & Moore, H. E. (1938). *American Regionalism: A Cultural-Historical Approach to National Integration.* Holt.

Organski, A. F. K., & Kugler, J. (1980). *The War Ledger.* University of Chicago Press.

Ortaylı, l. (1968). *Çarlık Rusyasında Türkçülük hareketleri ve Gaspirali Ismail Bey [Pan-Turkism movements in Tsarist Russia and Gaspirali Ismail Bey].* Anadolu Matbaası.

Özdemir, E. (2009). Kazak Kültürel Hayatında Tatarların Etkisi ve Kazak Ceditçiliği'nin Gelişimi [The Influence of Tatars in Kazakh Cultural Life and the Development of Kazakh Jadidism]. *Bilig, 48*, 157-176.

Pan, C., & Kavalski, E. (Eds.). (2022). *The Rise of China and Its Challenges to*

International Relations Theory. Bristol University Press.

Panin, A. (2013). Trans-Siberian Railroad Getting New Lease on Life. *The Moscow Times*.

Pelliot, P. (1933). Les Grands Voyages Maritimes Chinois au Début XVe Siècle *T'oung Pao 30*.

Perdue, P. C. (2005). *China marches west : the Qing conquest of Central Eurasia* Harvard University Press.

Perovic, J., Orttung, R. W., & Wenger, A. (2009). *Russian Energy Power and Foreign Relations: Implications for Conflict and Cooperation*. Taylor & Francis.

Petersen, A. (2011). *The World Island: Eurasian Geopolitics and the Fate of the West*. Praeger.

Peyrouse, S. (2018). Central Asia's paradoxical role in Chinese foreign policy. *East Asia Forum*. Retrieved November 2, 2018, from

Pieper, M. (2022). *The Making of Eurasia: Competition and Cooperation between China's Belt and Road Initiative and Russia*. I.B. Tauris.

Pierce, R. A. (1960). *Russian Central Asia, 1867-1917: A Study in Colonial Rule*. University of California Press.

Pierson, P. (1995). Fragmented Welfare States: Federal Institutions and the Development of Social Policy. *Governance, 8*(4), 449-478.

Posen, B. R. (1984). *The Sources of Military Doctrine: France, Britain, and Germany between the World Wars*. Cornell University Press.

Poussenkova, N. (2009). Russia's future customers. Asia and beyond In J. Perovic (Ed.), *Russian Energy Power and Foreign Relations. Implications for conflict and cooperation* (pp. 132-154). Routledge.

Poussenkova, N. (2010). The Global Expension of Russia's Energy Giants. *Journal of International Affairs, 63*(2).

Powell, R. C., & Dodds, K. (Eds.). (2014). *Polar Geopolitics?: Knowledges, Resources and Legal Regimes*. Edward Elgar Publishing.

Pyzh, V. V., & Kononvich, I. A. (2007). Voennaya Politika Stran NATO v Arktike [Military Policy of the NATO countries in the Arctic]. *Sever i rinok: formirovanie ekonomicheskogo poryadka, 2*(18), 44-52.

Qosimov, B. (1996). Sources littérarires et principaux traits distinctifs du djadidisme turkestanais (début du XXe siècle). *Cahiers du monde russe, 37*(1-2), 107-132.

Ratzel, F. (1987). *La Géographie politique: Les concepts fondamentaux [Political Geography: Fundamental Concepts]*. Fayard.

Raustiala, K., & Slaughter, A.-M. (2002). International Law, International Relations and Compliance. In W. Carlsnaes, T. Risse, & B. A. Simmons (Eds.), *Handbook of International Relations*. SAGE Publications.

Reagan, T. (2018). *Non-Western Educational Traditions: Local Approaches to Thought and Practice* (4 ed.). Routledge.

Rieber, A. J. (2007). Colonizing Eurasia. In N. B. Breyfogle, A. Schrader, & W. Sunderland (Eds.), *Peopling the Russian Periphery Borderland colonization in Eurasian history*. Routledge.

Risse, T. (2002). Transnational Actors and World Politics. In W. Carlsnaes, T. Risse, & B. A. Simmons (Eds.), *Handbook of International Relations* SAGE Publications.

Ro'i, Y. (2000). *Islam and the Soviet Union*. Columbia University Press.

Rogan, E. (2016). *The Fall of the Ottomans: The Great War in the Middle East* Basic Books

Rosamond, A. B. (2011). *Perspectives on Security in the Arctic Area*.

Ross, M. L. (2004). How Do Natural Resources Influence Civil War? Evidence from Thirteen Cases. *International Organization, 58*(01).

Ross, R. S. (2009). China's Naval Nationalism: Sources, Prospects, and the U.S. Response. *International Security, 34*(2).

Rotar, I. (1998, 23.12.1998). Okolo Dicietka "Spornih Territorii" v Srednei Azii [Nearly Dozen of "Disputed Territories" in the Middle Asia] *Nizavisimaya Gazieta*.

Rotberg, R. I. (Ed.). (2008). *China into Africa: Trade, Aid, and Influence*. Brookings Institution Press.

Rousset, P. (2018). Chinese geopolitics: continuities, inflections, uncertainties. *International Viewpoint*. Retrieved October 29, 2018, from http://www.internationalviewpoint.org/spip.php?article5755

Rowe, E. W. (2018). *Arctic governance: Power in cross-border cooperation*. Manchester University Press.

Rozman, G. (2008). Strategic Thinking About the Russian Far East: A Resurgent Russia Eyes Its Future in Northeast Asia. *Problems of Post-Communism, 55*(1), 36-48.

Rozman, G., Hyun, I.-T., & Lee, S.-w. (Eds.). (2008). *South Korean Strategic Thought toward Asia*. Palgrave Macmillan.

Rozman, G., Togo, K., & Ferguson, J. P. (Eds.). (2006). *Russian Strategic Thought toward Asia*. Palgrave Macmillan.

Rumer, B. (1989). *Soviet Central Asia: A Tragic Experiment*. Unwin Hyman.

Russett, B. (1979). World Energy demand and World Security. *Policy Sciences, 11*(2), 187-202.

Russett, B. M. (1967). *International regions and the international system; a study in political ecology*. Rand McNally.

Rutland, P. (2008). Russia as an Energy Superpower. *New Political Economy, 13*(2), 203-210.

Sabol, S. (1995). The Creation of Soviet Central Asia: The 1924 National Delimitation. *Central Asian Survey, 14*(2).

Sabol, S. (2003). Kazak Resistance to Russian Colonization: Interpreting the Kenesary Kasymov Revolt. *Central Asian Survey, 22*(2/3).

Sagadeev, A. (1993). Russia and the Great Power Ideology. *Central Asian Survey, 12.*

Sagan, S. D. (1996/97). Why Do States Build Nuclear Weapons? Three Models in Search of a Bomb. *International Security, 21*(3).

Sahadeo, J. (2007). Progress or peril Migrants and locals in Russian Tashkent, 1906–14. In N. B. Breyfogle, A. Schrader, & W. Sunderland (Eds.), *Peopling the Russian Periphery Borderland colonization in Eurasian history*. Routledge.

Sahadeo, J. (2010). *Russian Colonial Society in Tashkent, 1865-1923* Indiana University Press.

Sale, R., & Potapov, E. (2010). *The Scramble for the Arctic: Ownership, Exploitation and Conflict in the Far North*. Frances Lincoln.

Sauvy, A. (1952). Trois mondes, une planète. *L'Observateur, 118.*

Sawhill, S. G. (2000). Cleaning-up the Arctic's Cold War Legacy: Nuclear Waste and Arctic Military Environmental Cooperation. *Cooperation and Conflict, 35*(1), 5-36.

Schmitter, P. C., & Haas, E. B. (1964). *Mexico and Latin American economic integration.* Institute of International Studies, University of California.

Schmitz, H. P., & Sikkink, K. (2002). International Human Rights. In W. Carlsnaes, T. Risse, & B. A. Simmons (Eds.), *Handbook of International Relations*. SAGE Publications.

Schweller, R. L. (1997). New Realist Research on Alliances: Refining, Not Refuting. *American Political Science Review, 91*(4).

Schweller, R. L., & Pu, X. (2011). After Unipolarity: China's Visions of InternationalOrder in an Era of U.S. Decline. International Security, 36(1).

Sechser, T. S. (2013). Crisis Bargaining and Nuclear Blackmail. *International Organization, 67*(1).

Selin, V., & Nikolaeva, A. (2010). Problemy i Vozmozhnosti Razvitiya Morskih Portov v Rossiskoy Zapadnoy Arktike [Problems and Opportunities of Development of the Seaports in the Russian Western Arctic] *Morskoy Sbornik, 1956*(3), 39-49.

Selin, V., & Tsukertan, V. A. (2008). Rossiya i Mir v XXI Veke: Geopoliticheskie i ekonomicheskie faktory Obespechniya Suvereniteta Rossii v Arktike [Russia and the World in XXI century: Geopolitical and Economic Factors of Russian Independence Security in the Arctic]. *Rossia i sovremenniy mir, 2*, 76-84.

Shahrani, N. (1993). Central Asia and the Challenge of the Soviet Legacy *Central Asian Survey 12*(2), 123-136.

Sheng, L., & Nascimento, D. F. d. (2021). *The Belt and Road Initiative in South–South Cooperation: The Impact on World Trade and Geopolitics*. Palgrave Macmillan.

Sicherman, H. (2002). The Revival of Geopolitics. *The Intercollegiate Review, Spring*

Simmons, B. A., & Martin, L. L. (2002). International Organizations and Institutions. In W. Carlsnaes, T. Risse, & B. A. Simmons (Eds.), *Handbook of International Relations*. SAGE Publications

Skrine, F. H., & Ross, E. D. (2005). *The Heart of Asia: A History of Russian Turkestan and the Central Asian Khanates from the Earliest Times* Taylor & Francis.

Smith, K. C. (2006). *Security Implications of Russian Energy Policies* (CEPS Policy Briefs, Issue.

Snyder, G. (1984). The Security Dilemma in Alliance Politics. *World Politics, 36*(4).

Sokol, E. D. (1954). *The Revolt of 1916 in Russian Central Asia*. Johns Hopkins University Press.

Song, W. (2014). Interests, Power and China's Difficult Game in the Shanghai Cooperation Organization (SCO). *Journal of Contemporary China 23*(85).

Sorensen, C. T. N., & Klimenko, E. (2017). *Emerging Chinese-Russian Cooperation in the Arctic* (46). (SIPRI Policy Paper Issue.

Specher, M., & Specher, D. (2009). *Is Russia winning in Central Asia?* (PFH Forschungspapiere, Issue.

Spechler, D. R. (2010). Russian Foreign Policy During the Putin Presidency. *Problems of Post-Communism, 57*(5), 35-50.

Spohr, K. (2018). The race to conquer the Arctic – the world's final frontier. *The New Statesman*(March 7).

Spohr, K., Hamilton, D. S., & Moyer, J. C. (Eds.). (2020). *The Arctic and World Order*. Foreign Policy Institute.

Spoor, M. (1998). The Aral Sea Basin Crisis: Transition and Environment in Former Soviet Union. *Development and Change, 29*, 409-435.

Spykman, N. (1942). *America's Strategy in World Politics: The United States and the Balance of Power*. Brace and Co.

Spykman, N. (1944). *The Geography of the Peace*. Brace and Co.

Staun, J. (2020). A Two-Faced Russia? Civilian Interests and Great Power Politics in the High North. In J. Weber (Ed.), *Handbook on Geopolitics and Security in the Arctic. The High North Between Cooperation and Confrontation*. Springer.

Stein, J. G. (2002). Psychological Explanations of International Conflict. In W. Carlsnaes, T. Risse, & B. A. Simmons (Eds.), *Handbook of International Relations*.

Stevens, C. (2018). Along the New Silk Road – Khorgos: Where East meets West. Geographical. Retrieved October 29, 2018, from http://geographical.co.uk/people/development/item/2979-along-the-new-silk-road-khorgos-where-east-meets-west

Stulberg, A. N. (2007). *Well-Oiled Diplomacy: Strategic manipulation and Russia's Energy Statecraft in Eurasia*. State University of New York Press.

Sullivan, J., & Renz, B. (2010). Chinese migration: still the major focus of Russian Far East/Chinese North East relations? *Pacific Review, 23*(2), 261-285.

Sun, J. (2021). *Red Chamber, World Dream: Actors, Audience, and Agendas in Chinese Foreign Policy and Beyond.* University of Michigan Press.

Suokas, J. (2018). China runs 11,000 'Silk Road' trains to Europe. GB Times. Retrieved May 13 2020, from https://gbtimes.com/china-runs-11000-silk-road-trains-to-europe?cat=business

Sussex, M., & Kanet, R. E. (Eds.). (2015). *Russia, Eurasia and the New Geopolitics of Energy Confrontation and Consolidation.* Palgrave Macmillan.

Sutter, R. G. (2021). *Chinese Foreign Relations: Power and Policy of an Emerging Global Force* (Fifth ed.). Rowman & Littlefield.

Tamitskiy, A. (2012). Gosudarstvennaya Politika Sovremennoy Rossiy v Arktike: Etap, Prioritety i Nekotorye Itogi [State Policy of Modern Russia in Arctic: State, Priorities and Some Results]. *Arktika i Sever, 6.*

Tamnes, R., & Offerdal, K. (Eds.). (2016). *Geopolitics and Security in the Arctic: Regional dynamics in a global world.* Routledge.

Tan, A. T. H. (Ed.). (2016). *Handbook of US–China Relations.* Edward Elgar Publishing.

Tan, C.-B. (Ed.). (2012). *Handbook of the Chinese Diaspora.* Routledge

Tan, D., & Grillot, C. (2014). *L'Asie du Sud-Est dans le Siècle Chinois (Cambodge, Laos et Viêt Nam) [Southeast Asia in the Chinese Century (Cambodia, Laos and Vietnam)].* Institut de Recherche sur l'Asie du Sud-Est Contemporaine

Tannenwald, N. (2005). Stigmatizing the Bomb: Origins of the Nuclear Taboo. *International Security, 29*(4).

Tanton, T. W., & Heaven, S. (1999). Worsening of the Aral Basin Crisis: Can There Be A Solution? *Journal of Water Resources Planning and Management*(November/December), 363-368.

Taylor, I. (2006). *China and Africa Engagement and compromise.* Routledge.

Thorun, C. (2009). *Explaining Change in Russian Foreign Policy The Role of Ideas in Post-Soviet Russia's Conduct towards the West.* Palgrave Macmillan.

Tickner, J. A. (2002). Feminist Perspectives on International Relations. In W. Carlsnaes, T. Risse, & B. A. Simmons (Eds.), *Handbook of International Relations.* Sage Publications

Titley, D. W. (2010). Arctic Security Considerations and the U.S. Navy's Roadmap for the Arctic *Naval War College Review, 63*(2), 35-48.

Toksoz, I. (2017). In Search of Peace on the Silk Road: From Theory to Practice. *Acta Via Serica, 2*(1), 7-30.

Tolstoy, L. (2005). *A Prisoner In The Caucasus.* Kessinger Publishing.

Tonami, A. (2016). *Asian Foreign Policy in a Changing Arctic: The Diplomacy of Economy and Science at New Frontiers.* Palgrave Macmillan.

Toops, S. (2004). *Demographics and Development in Xinjiang after 1949.*
Trapsh, N. (2007). The North Caucasus and the Multilevel International Subsystem. *Problems of Post-Communism, 54*(2).
Trenin, D. (2009). Russia in the Caucasus: Reversing the Tide. *Brown Journal of World Affairs, XV*(II).
Troyakova, T. (2007). The Russian Far East: Isolation or Integration? *Problems of Post-Communism, 54*(2), 61-71.
Tsai, S.-s. H. (1996). *The Eunuchs in the Ming Dynasty*. State University of New York Press.
Tselichtchev, I. (2017). Chinese in the Russian far East: A Geopolitical Time Bomb? (July 8th). Retrieved May 13 2020, from http://www.scmp.com/week-asia/geopolitics/article/2100228/chinese-russian-far-east-geopolitical-time-bomb
Tsygankov, A. P. (2019). *Russia's Foreign Policy: Change and Continuity in National Identity* (Fifth ed.). Rowman & Littlefield Publishers.
Tuathail, G. O., Dalby, S., & Routledge, P. (Eds.). (2016). *The Geopolitical Reader* (Second ed.). Routledge.
Turcsa´nyi, R. Q. (2018). *Chinese Assertiveness in the South China Sea Power Sources, Domestic Politics, and Reactive Foreign Policy*. Springer International Publishing.
Twitchett, D., & Mote, F. W. (Eds.). (2008). *The Cambridge History of China: The Ming Dynasty, 1368-1644, Part 2* (Vol. 8). Cambridge University Press.
Uitto, J. I., & Schneider, J. (Eds.). (1997). *Freshwater Resources in Arid Lands*. United Nations University Press.
Vahn, G. P. (2017). Rosneft sees Asian refiners turning more to Russian crudes to diversify. (September 26).
Vance, R. B. (1951). The Regional Concept as a Tool for Social Research. In M. Jensen (Ed.), *Regionalism in America* (pp. 119–140). Univ. of Wisconsin Press.
Vasilev, V., Selin, V., & Tereshchenko, E. B. (2009). Sotsial'no-Ekonomicheskie Posledstviya Ozhidaemogo İzmeneniya Klimata v Arktike [Socio-economic Consequences of the Expected Climate Change in Arctic] *Ekonomika i Sotsiologiya, 2*, 125-136.
Vasquez, J. A., & Elman, C. (Eds.). (2003). *Realism and the Balance of Power: A New Debate.* Prentice Hall.
Veeck, G., Pannell, C. W., Smith, C. J., & Huang, Y. (2011). *China's Geography Globalization and the Dynamics of Political, Economic, and Social Change.* Rowman & Littlefield Publishers.
Velanskaya, I. (2017). Move Moscow to Far East Russia? (August 29th).
Victor, D. G., & Victor, N. M. (2003). Axis of Oil! *Foreign Affairs, 82*(2), 47-61.
Vinogradov, S. (1996). Transboundary Water Resources in the former Soviet Union: Between Conflict and Cooperation. *Natural Resources Journal 36*(Spring).

Vinogradov, S. (2001). Managing Transboundary Water Resources in the Aral Sea: In Search of a Solution. *International Journal of Global Environmental Issues, 1*, 345-362.

Vishinevskii, D. C., & Demyanenko, A. N. (2010). Makroekonomicheskoi Zonirovanie kak metod strategicheskovo analiza: Dalnii Vostok Rossii [Macroeconomic Zoning as a Method of Strategic Analysis: the Russian Far East] *Prostranstvennaya Ekonomika, 4*, 6-31.

Walsh, J. R. (1993). China and the New Geopolitics of Central Asia. *Asian Survey, 23*

Walt, S. M. (1985). Alliance Formation and the Balance of World Power. *International Security, 9*(4).

Walt, S. M. (1987). *The Origins of Alliances.* Cornell University Press.

Walt, S. M. (2002). The Enduring Relevance of the Realist Tradition. In I. Katznelson & H. V. Milner (Eds.), *Political Science: State of the Discipline.* W. W. Norton.

Waltz, K. N. (1979). *Theory of International Politics.* Addison-Wesley.

Waltz, K. N. (1990). Nuclear Myths and Political Realities. *American Political Science Review, 84*(3).

Wang, H. (2017). The misunderstood side of China-Russia ties. *Global Times.* Retrieved November 7, 2018, from

Weber, J. (Ed.). (2020). *Handbook on Geopolitics and Security in the Arctic The High North Between Cooperation and Confrontation.* Springer.

Weinthal, E. S. (1998). *Making or Breaking the State? Building Institutions for Regional Cooperation in the Aral Sea Basin* Columbia University]. New York.

Weiss, J. C. (2013). Authoritarian Signaling, Mass Audiences, and Nationalist Protest in China. *International Organization 67*(1).

Widdis, E. (2004). Russia as space. In S. Franklin & E. Widdis (Eds.), *National Identity on Russian Culture: An Introduction.* Cambridge University Press

Wilder, M. P. (2010). Who gets the Oil Arctic Energy Exploration in Uncertain Waters and the Need for Universal Ratification of the United Nations Convention on the Law of the Sea *Houston Journal of International Law, 32*(2), 505-544.

Winchester, R. F. European Energy Security: Wrestling the Russian Bear for Caspian Natural Gas.

Winrow, G. (2007). Geopolitics and Energy Security in the Wider Black Sea Region. *Southeast European and Black Sea Studies, 7*(2), 217-235.

Woehrel, S. (2009). *Russian Energy Policy Toward Neighboring Countries.*

Wood, A. (2011). *Russia's Frozen Frontier: A History of Siberia and the Russian Far East 1581 - 1991.* Bloomsbury Academic.

Woody, C. (2020). As US tries to close 'icebreaker gap' with Russia, its only working icebreaker is making a rare trip north. *Business Insider.* Retrieved 13 May, from https://www.businessinsider.com/us-worried-about-icebreaker-gap-with-russia-in-arctic-2020-11

Wu, Z. (2018). Classical geopolitics, realism, and the balance of power theory. *Journal of Strategic Studies, 41*(6).

Yeoh, B. (2013). Chinese Migration to Singapore: Discourses and Discontents in a Globalizing Nation-State. *Asian and Pacific Migration Journal, 22*(1).

Yergin, D. (1988). Energy Security in the 1990s. *Foreign Affairs, 67*(1).

Yergin, D. (2006). Ensuring Energy Security. *Foreign Affairs, 85*(2).

Yi-chong, X. (2006). China's energy security. *Australian Journal of International Affairs, 60*(2), 265-286.

Young, O. R. (1992). *Arctic politics. Conflict and cooperation in the circumpolar North.* Dartmouth College.

Young, O. R. (2011). The Future of the Arctic: cauldron of conflict or zone of peace? *International Affairs, 87*(1), 185-193.

Young, O. R., & Osherenko, G. (Eds.). (1993). *Polar Politics: Creating International Environmental Regimes.* Cornell University Press.

Yu, S. (2019). The Belt and Road Initiative: Modernity, Geopolitics, and the Developing Global Order. *Asian Affairs, 50*(2).

Yuan, J.-D. (2010). China's Role in Establishing and Building the Shanghai Cooperation Organization (SCO). *Journal of Contemporary China, 19*(67), 855-869.

Zaletaev, V. S., & Novikova, N. M. (1995). Changes in Biota of the Aral Region as a Result of Anthropogenic Impacts between 1950 and 1990. *GeoJournal, 35*(1), 23-29.

Zartman, I. W. (1973). *Man, state, and society in the contemporary Maghrib.* Praeger Publishers.

Zausaev, V. K. (2012). General Goal of the Strategy for Socioeconomic Development of the Far East and the Baikal Region up to 2025. *Problems of Economic Transition, 55*(4), 45-51.

Zeihan, P. (2017). Analysis: Russia's Far East Turning Chinese. (July 14th).

Zellen, B. S. (2009). *Arctic Doom, Arctic Boom: The Geopolitics of Climate Change in the Arctic* ABC CLIO Publishing.

Zeng, J. (2020). S*logan Politics: Understanding Chinese Foreign Policy Concepts.* Palgrave Macmillan.

Zhang, X., Wasserman, H., & Mano, W. (Eds.). (2016). *China's Media and Soft Power in Africa: Promotion and Perceptions* Palgrave Macmillan.

Zhang, Y., & Austin, G. (Eds.). (2013). *Power and Responsibility in Chinese Foreign Policy* Australian National University Press.

Zhang, Y., Meng, Q., & Ng, S. H. (2016). Shipping efficiency comparison between Northern Sea Route and the conventional Asia-Europe shipping route via

Suez Canal. *Journal of Transport Geography, 57.*

Zhao, S. (2008). China's Global Search for Energy Security: cooperation and competition in Asia–Pacific. *Journal of Contemporary China, 17*(55), 207-227.

Zhuangzhi, S. (2004). New and Old Regionalism: The Shanghai Cooperation Organization and Sino-Central Asian Relations. *Review of International Affairs, 3*(4), 600-612.

Znamenski, A. A. (2007). The "ethic of empire" on the Siberian borderland: The peculiar case of the "rock people," 1791–1878. In N. B. Breyfogle, A. Schrader, & W. Sunderland (Eds.), *Peopling the Russian Periphery: Borderland colonization in Eurasian history*. Routledge.

Zweig, D., & Jianhai, B. (2005). China's Global Hunt for Energy. *Foreign Affairs, 84*(5), 25-38.

Index

D

E

F

L

M

S

T

About the Author

Cagri Erdem is a teacher,author, and lecturer in the fields of international relations/security andpolitical geography. He received his *Licencedegree* in *Administration Economique et Sociale* (AES) from Université deMontpellier-Ⅲ, France. Erdem continued his education in California, obtaining his BA and MA in International Relations at San Francisco State University. Next, he received his Ph.D. in political science from Syracuse University of New York.

In his university career, he has been a professor/visiting lecturer of international relations at various universities across Eastern Europe, the Middle East, and Northeast Asia with a lifelong commitment to education improvement. In addition, he participated in various specific certificate programs, such as Russian culture and language training at Moscow Lomonosov State University (2002) and Afghan culture and language at the University of Nebraska-Omaha (2008).

Before moving to the Republic of Korea in 2015, Erdem worked at British Aerospace Engineering (BAE) Systems as asocial scientist focusing on Iraq and Afghanistan (2008-09) and in Istanbul, Turkey as an assistant professor (2010-15). Currently, he is teaching courses on international security and geopolitics at Keimyung University. He lives in Daegu, South Korea.